The Experiential Ontology of Hannah Arendt

The Experiential Ontology of Hannah Arendt

Kimberly Maslin

LEXINGTON BOOKS
Lanham • Boulder • New York • London

Published by Lexington Books
An imprint of The Rowman & Littlefield Publishing Group, Inc.
4501 Forbes Boulevard, Suite 200, Lanham, Maryland 20706
www.rowman.com

6 Tinworth Street, London SE11 5AL, United Kingdom

Copyright © 2020 by The Rowman & Littlefield Publishing Group, Inc.

All rights reserved. No part of this book may be reproduced in any form or by any electronic or mechanical means, including information storage and retrieval systems, without written permission from the publisher, except by a reviewer who may quote passages in a review.

British Library Cataloguing in Publication Information Available

Library of Congress Control Number: 2020933364

Library of Congress Cataloging-in-Publication Data Is Available

ISBN 978-1-7936-1244-1 (cloth)
ISBN 978-1-7936-1246-5 (pbk)
ISBN 978-1-7936-1245-8 (electronic)

Contents

Introduction   1

1   Heidegger the Fox: Revealing the Trap   5
2   Rootlessness in Heidegger and Arendt   17
3   Concretizing Thrownness and Projection: Rahel Varnhagen   39
4   *MitDasein* I: *Understanding* Antisemitism   59
5   *Mitdasein* II: *Understanding* Imperialism   75
6   *Vorspringen* (Leaping Ahead): *Understanding* Totalitarianism   93
7   On the Political Importance of a Normative Ontology: Eichmann in Jerusalem   115
8   The Politics of Existential Loneliness   131
9   Experiential Ontology: Implications for Identity Politics   145
10   Theorizing #MeToo   167

Conclusion   185
Bibliography   191
Index   201
About the Author   211

Introduction

The recent publication of Martin Heidegger's *Black Notebooks* has led to a resurgence of interest in his affiliation with National Socialism. Most of the first wave of scholarship following the publication of these notebooks focused on the question(s) of whether or not Heidegger's antisemitism had a philosophical grounding and the implications for philosophy of answering this question in the affirmative.[1] Although these efforts produced a fascinating body of scholarship, the latter question strikes me as off the mark, which is to say it takes us down a dead end path and, in the process, it misses a productive line of inquiry. The question of Heidegger's moral standing in philosophy misses the mark and the risk we run, in dismissing Heidegger as morally bankrupt, is that despite his shortcomings, he has important things to teach us about identity. Not in spite of, but because of, his disastrous foray into the political sphere, his students struggled with a particular set of questions. Despite her intense disappointment, Hannah Arendt was unable to abandon either existential philosophy or Heidegger's basic precepts. These precepts help us understand Heidegger's own failure, by suggesting that even the great philosopher existed in the world in a state of thrownness, simultaneously transcending and falling prey to his own throw. Given that falling prey and projectivity represent the quintessential human struggle, ever present in our daily lives, why would we expect Martin Heidegger to be exempt from this most human of all challenges?

Hannah Arendt shifts to political philosophy, less to escape her own personal disappointment than to reveal (and ultimately remedy) the flaws of fundamental ontology. She not only grew beyond the role of naïve and beguiled student: she became one of Heidegger's most astute critics. Well acquainted with and deeply respectful of his contributions to existential philosophy, Arendt viewed Heidegger's work both as profoundly insightful and extraordinarily myopic. Moreover, not contented to simply offer a critique of her mentor's work, Arendt engaged in a lifelong struggle to come to terms with the political implications of fundamental ontology. In short, Arendt's goals are more distinctly Heideggerian than previous scholarship would have us believe. Moreover, I suggest that Arendt's work, far from rejecting fundamental ontology, may be to offer a politically responsive, hence responsible, modification of Heidegger's fundamental ontology. In other words, she suggests that Heidegger's descriptive and non-normative insight into the nature of being is necessarily incomplete, and potentially irresponsible, unless it is undertaken in a manner which is mindful of the collective implications, as such she constructs an *experiential ontology*. Drawing on Heidegger's fundamental ontology, she turns our attention to the ways in which concrete structures and experiences in the world shape our manner of being. In so doing, she illustrates the importance of political ontology.

Many have noted the Heideggerian impulse in *The Human Condition* and the philosophical preoccupation of *The Life of the Mind*. In this vein, *The Human Condition* is sometimes described as Arendt's return to philosophy. It is my contention that Arendt never returns to philosophy because she never leaves it. Rather, her entire *oeuvre* can be understood as an attempt to modify Heidegger's descriptive framework for use in the political sphere, because philosophy and politics, perhaps particularly existential philosophy and democratic theory, are utterly inseparable. Her Heideggerian roots are not something Arendt returns to, rather she uses Heidegger's insight into the nature of *Being* to help us understand the plight of the nineteenth-century Jewess, the development of antisemitism, as well as, imperialism. My claim is that all of Arendt's work can be read as existential philosophy; my aim is to reveal the Heideggerian impulse in her early work, in particular. In what follows, I argue, first, that our reading of Arendt is informed by an examination of the Heideggerian concepts underlying it. Second, Arendt's project, far from rejecting fundamental ontology, may be to offer a politically responsive, hence responsible, modification of Heidegger's fundamental ontology, by grounding it in lived experiences, hence her work should be read as *experiential ontology*.

In the first chapter I examine Arendt's "Heidegger the Fox" essay, suggesting that Arendt uses the metaphor of a physical trap to both conceal and reveal her critique of Heidegger.[2] She opines that Heidegger's approach to fundamental ontology leaves him unable to extricate himself from his own conceptual framework. Heidegger's project is to develop fundamental ontology and to reveal the limitations of philosophy as a mode of inquiry under conditions of modernity. Ironically he becomes so thoroughly subsumed by ontological questions that he fails to recognize that he has fallen victim to several of his own concerns about modernity. In the second chapter, I examine the role of rootlessness in the thought of both Heidegger and Arendt.

Though their politics differ, both assert that a lack of grounding in a particular place lies at the core of the Jewish problem. Moreover, their notions of rootlessness are strikingly similar as both derive from a deficient connectedness and lead to an inauthentic manner of being-in-the-world. The third chapter takes up the often overlooked, *Rahel Varnhagen*, arguing it should be read as a case study of three of Heidegger's most political concepts: thrownness, fallenness and projectivity. In short, Arendt undertakes an examination of Varnhagen's life in order to "thickly constitute" thrownness, fallenness, and projectivity, to reveal the ontological core of rootlessness, as well as the political implications of taking oneself up as a project. *The Human Condition* is often touted as Arendt's return to philosophy; whereas *Origins of Totalitarianism* is usually described as either a piece of political sociology or a historical text and vehemently criticized, as such. In chapters four, five and six, I examine *Origins*, not as a traditional historical work, but rather as a public performance of Heideggerian historicity which has two predominant impulses. First, it comprises part of the constitutive structure of *Dasein*, as such it plays a critical role in the search for transcendence. Second, it serves as a critique of the dominant interpretation of historical events. Thus, in her quest to take herself up as a project, Arendt challenges the dominant interpretations of Jewish and European history, by highlighting the interaction between ontic structures, existential choice and ontological conditioning.

The trial of Adolph Eichmann has often been described as a point of transition in the work, as well as the life, of Hannah Arendt. In the seventh chapter I argue, alternatively, that it represents a point of continuity in the development of Arendt's normative experiential ontology, both with and against Heidegger. Though Arendt never does get around to laying out a systematic theory of evil, she begins from a more or less Kantian perspective, uses the lived experiences of Adolph Eichmann to concretize abstract Heideggerian concepts in an attempt to understand both the ontological conditions, as well as the political implications of evildoing.

Chapters eight, nine and ten consider the implications of Arendt's *experiential ontology* for the political philosophy. Loneliness draws on the Heideggerian notion of the inauthentic and applies it to the public sphere. The eighth chapter examines the use of isolation and loneliness in Arendt's work and suggests that a richer understanding of both concepts, as well as their political importance, can be attained by examining them through a Heideggerian lens. Building on the notion that Arendt's work can be understood as an attempt to take seriously Heidegger's claim that the ontological can only be approached through the ontic, chapters nine and ten turn our attention to identity politics. Both Heidegger and Arendt are often read as either indifferent to or hostile to identity politics. Since Arendt's project is to first ground herself ontically, a re-reading of Arendt, suggests that both thinkers are productive resources for contemporary identity politics. Chapter nine demonstrates that Arendt ends up anticipating someone like Judith Butler, by pointing us toward a phenomenological approach to identity.[3] Moreover like Adriana Cavarero, she understands that taking seriously concrete political identities requires listening to historical narratives.[4] In ways that will be picked up and expanded by thinkers such as Jean-Luc Nancy, they both attend to the ontological stakes of such identity.[5] Finally, chapter ten turns our attention to what these efforts might have to say about a moment in identity politics, such as #MeToo and its potential to rethink democratic theory, particularly the concrete ways that we construct our *Being-with*.

In the end, Arendt carves out her own path, an experiential ontology, by drawing on Heideggerian concepts, grounding them in lived experiences, demonstrating their political value and transforming the purely descriptive concepts into prescriptive ones. Any notion of a political ontology must draw on individual lives set in socio-historical context and only as such can they illuminate political events. Thus far from rejecting philosophy, she simply admonishes that as a matter of political prescription, philosophical categories can be used only with the utmost circumspection. Arendt's *experiential ontology* transforms fundamental ontology from its, at best, apolitical and, at worst, anti-political orientation and allows the ontological to assume its rightful place at the cornerstone of democratic theory. Since as she makes clear in *The Human Condition*, one's manner of being in the world is of the utmost importance in public life.

NOTES

1. Andrew J. Mitchell and Peter Trawny, eds. *Heidegger's Black Notebooks: Responses to Anti-Semitism* (New York: Columbia University Press, 2017).

2. Hannah Arendt, "Heidegger the Fox," in *The Portable Hannah Arendt*, ed. Peter Baehr (New York: Penguin Putnam, 2000[1964]), 543–44.

3. Judith Butler, *Undoing Gender* (New York: Routledge, 2004); Judith Butler, *Giving an Account of Oneself* (New York: Fordham University Press, 2005).

4. Adriana Cavarero, *Relating Narratives: Storytelling and Selfhood*, trans. Paul A. Kottman (New York: Routledge, 2000).

5. Jean-Luc Nancy, *Being Singular Plural*, trans. Robert D. Richardson and Anne E. O'Byrne (Stanford, CA: Stanford University Press, 2000).

Chapter One

Heidegger the Fox

Revealing the Trap

In "Heidegger the Fox" Hannah Arendt accuses Heidegger of sitting in a trap of his own making; a trap, moreover, that he constructed for the purpose of outsmarting all the other foxes. Arendt's fox spends his early life getting caught in the traps of other people. This fox differs from other foxes in two ways. First, he lacks the "natural protection" of the fox since he spent so much time getting stuck in other peoples' traps, all his fur has been lost.[1] Second, he utterly fails to recognize traps for what they are. He cannot recognize the traps of others nor even the trap that he builds for himself; thus, he is a fox "lacking in slyness." He eventually tires of getting caught in the traps of others, builds his own and sits in it. Since he is sitting in the trap, no one else can enter. Disgruntled that no one else has gotten stuck in the trap he so carefully set, he decorates it and advertises it to the world—as a trap. Many choose to visit the fox in his trap and, recognizing it as a trap, they are able to easily remove themselves. Arendt's fox could not, however, remove himself since he had built the trap "literally, to his own measurements."[2] He was so pleased that others came to visit him in his trap that he proclaimed himself "the best of all foxes."[3] Though Hannah Arendt's tumultuous relationship with Martin Heidegger is by now well-documented, her critique of, as well as her debt to, Heidegger remain perplexing. In what follows I illustrate the critical nature of Arendt's essay by contrasting it with Isiah Berlin's original essay with the ultimate aim of answering the critical question—for what is the trap a metaphor?

Isaiah Berlin's essay "The Hedgehog and the Fox" was published by Simon and Schuster in 1953, the same year that Arendt wrote her polemical "Heidegger the Fox." Drawing on the Greek proverb, "the fox knows many things but the hedgehog knows one big thing," Berlin crafts a picture of Tolstoy in which he argues that Tolstoy "was by nature a fox, but believed in being a hedgehog." The hedgehog "relate[s] everything to a single central vision, one system more or less coherent," focuses on big questions and "a single universal, organizing principle." The fox, on the other hand, "pursue[s] many ends, often unrelated and even contradictory, connected, if at all, only in some de facto way . . . related by no moral or aesthetic principal . . . seizing upon the essence of a vast variety of experiences and objects for what they are in themselves, without . . . seeking to fit them into . . . any one unchanging, all-embracing . . . unitary inner vision."[4] Thus, Tolstoy is both difficult to classify and vulnerable to misinterpretation. Furthermore, he created a novel of unparalleled complexity out of his own natural inclination to seek causal explanations, coupled with his belief that history did not "reveal causes; it present[ed] only a blank succession of unexplained events."[5] In so doing, he juxtaposed several *great* men, who were vain and arrogant enough to believe themselves responsible for events, with "a thick, opaque, inextricably complex web of events, objects, characteristics, connected and divided by literally innumerable unidentifiable links."[6] Thus those who view Tolstoy as a literary genius and lament the historical or philosophical musings of the text fail to understand that Tolstoy was a "sharp-eyed fox . . . utterly incapable of being deceived by the many subtle devices, the unifying systems and faiths and sciences, by which the superficial or the desperate sought to control the chaos from themselves and from one another."[7] In short, Berlin's fox is a self-aware creature, compelled by his own inclination to develop a nearly impenetrably complex series of characters, yet mindful of and curious about the big questions as well. Hence it is self-awareness which allows Tolstoy to produce his masterpiece by emulating the most desirable characteristics of both the fox and hedgehog. Juxtaposed with Berlin's eulogistic essay of Tolstoy, Arendt's sardonic essay appears all the more cutting.

It might be counterintuitive for a philosopher to be classified as a fox; as a philosopher interested in the nature of Being, Heidegger certainly fancied himself as asking the big questions. Arendt adds insult to injury, however, as Heidegger is also a fox "lacking in slyness." Not only does Heidegger lack the virtues of the hedgehog, in that he is ill-suited to asking the big questions. He is also lacking the greatest virtues of a fox: he is not sly, perceptive, clever, nor is he self-aware. Hence the *Existenz* philosopher is apparently not only ill-suited to asking the big questions, neither is he clever in "seizing up a vast variety of experiences for what they are."[8] Arendt's less than sharp eyed fox is deceived by, in Berlin's words, "the many subtle devices, the unifying systems and faiths and sciences."[9] Moreover, he may be foolish enough to view great men as capable of controlling events and perhaps arrogant enough to view himself as capable of controlling great men.[10] Though he regards himself as clever, it is his lack of skill in this area, which is ultimately his undoing; the fox builds himself a trap as his burrow, proclaims to the world that his burrow is a trap and yet fails to recognize his own plight. Thus, Arendt's fox took up his own trap as his abode, leaving him to negotiate the world without the virtues of either the hedgehog or the fox. The question becomes: for what precisely is the trap a metaphor?[11] In what follows, I will consider three different, and by no means mutually exclusive, answers to this question.

HEIDEGGER THE FOX

In Arendt's essay, the young fox kept falling into the traps of others, just as the young Heidegger experimented with theology and mysticism. Moreover, these early experiences left the fox with no fur and convinced of his own expertise. It bears noting that there are two other possible translations of *verfallen*, which is usually translated as *falling prey*. They are ensnarement or entanglement. Moreover, *verfallen* conveys a kind of motion that is unable to actually progress.[12] Additionally, for Heidegger, falling prey "belongs to the constitution of the being of *Dasein* . . . [b]ecause it essentially falls prey to the world, *Dasein* is in 'untruth' in accordance with its constitution of being." In other words, Heidegger, himself, asserts that it is in the nature of Being for humans to be deceived by idle talk, appearances and distortions, in short, "untruths." These distractions impede *Dasein*'s efforts to take him or herself up as a project. Arendt uses the metaphor of a physical trap for the purpose of suggesting, not only that Heidegger, himself, was deceived by "untruths" or systems of thought but that fundamental ontology subsequently became one of these entanglements, from which he was unable to free himself. Finally, she suggests that Heidegger's fundamental ontology itself leaves one perennially ensnared in an activity in which forward motion is nearly impossible. In short, Heidegger's fundamental ontology illuminates certain aspects of the nature of Being, though it provides no meaningful guidance for living life with others. As such, at its best, fundamental ontology leaves each of us ensnared in our own isolated quest. Thus, Arendt's project, far from rejecting fundamental ontology, may be to offer a modification of Heidegger's fundamental ontology. She grounds the political, ontologically, and demonstrates that one's manner of being-in-the-world is necessarily political. In other words, she advocates an approach to the study of Being that not only remains mindful of the collective but grounds the ontological in the world, particularly in the *Being-with* others.

THE TRAP OF WORLDLESSNESS

The simplest interpretation of Arendt's account posits that the trap is a more or less physical one—Heidegger's withdrawal to the Black Forest. The trap becomes, in a sense, the hut and, in a sense, the act of withdrawal. Literally speaking, anyone wishing to visit Heidegger at home had to go to the Black Forest and obviously many did. Figuratively, though, he also withdrew into the recesses of fundamental ontology and anyone wishing to engage Heidegger had to do so on *his* terms within the confines of phenomenological terminology and the conceptual constraints of fundamental ontology. For example, someone wishing to engage Heidegger had to do so by accepting that proposition that the ontological is more fundamental than the ontic. Thus all questions of a worldly nature were easily pushed aside as further evidence that modern man had forgotten the nature of Being. The, not so sly, fox thus understands the withdrawal better than anyone and does not recognize that his own disconnection from the world fits him perfectly because he constructed it to his own specifications. He, alone, defined the boundary between the ontic and the ontological. He, alone, created the terminology of fundamental ontology. Meanwhile, he refused to engage issues he described as ontic using anything other than *his* ontological framework, which necessarily relegated them to secondary status and allowed him to summarily dismiss his critics, with an air of superiority. The questions—for what should I be resolute or for what was Hitler resolute—were relegated to ontic status. He ceased to be able to engage with others utilizing any other conceptual framework. His withdrawal or worldlessness became such an important element of how he viewed himself that he ceased to be able to rejoin the world. Moreover, he failed to recognize that many of his *existentials* were implicitly normative and seemed to dismiss questions of their collective implications. In so doing, he failed to recognize that the deficiency of his *Being-with* had intellectual as well as political costs. In other words, Heidegger failed to recognize the implications of *mitdasein* "as a constitutive structure of *Dasein*."[13] As such his withdrawal or worldlessness was physical, intellectual and conceptual; and in all three respects, it was of his own making.

THE TRAP OF STILLNESS

Among the many complimentary things that Arendt says about Heidegger in the "Martin Heidegger at Eighty" tribute, the most effusive is that he brought thinking to life. Yet, as Dana Villa notes, the essay is also littered with caveats[14] and it bears noting that Heidegger and Arendt employ very different conceptual notions of thinking. Heidegger argued that thinking involves an iterative process of burrowing deeply into and then stepping back from the object of one's thinking. In the *Discourse on Thinking*, he refers to thinking as a process which involves "coming-into-the-nearness of distance."[15] Moreover whatever role *being-with* (*mitdasein*) may play in Heidegger's philosophy, its role in transcendence and authenticity appears to be limited. One might reasonably expect that the centrality of *mitsein* in Heidegger's account would yield consequences for his own conception of thinking. Yet, far too often, it seems that thinking is something understood by Heidegger in solitary terms and the role of others appears to be that of a distraction or an impediment.

For Arendt, alternatively, thinking is a dialectical and critical process, an ongoing, soundless dialogue with oneself, a "habit of examining whatever happens to come to pass or to attract attention," that reveals the inherent duality in human nature.[16] Thinking reveals the disconnect or disharmony between our appearance, or what we reveal of who we are in the public realm, and our consciousness, our true selves, which we may or may not reveal in the public realm. Thinking requires solitary time and space. "To be in solitude means to be with one's self, and thinking, therefore, though it may be the most solitary of all activities, is never altogether without a partner and without company."[17] Thinking is an activity that can only be engaged in by oneself and with oneself as the only partner, the process of going home to face the "partner who comes to life when you are alert and alone."[18] The role of the partner in this activity is to take and represent the role of other in soundless, self-reflective dialogue. Thus, contra Heidegger, Arendt's thinking requires *being-with*. Consciousness is a state of self-awareness, which is both a prerequisite for thinking to occur and is enhanced or facilitated by the thinking process. Consciousness is facilitated by solitude since in Arendt's words, "as long as I am together with others, barely conscious of myself, I am as I appear to others" largely unaware of any disharmony that may exist with my inner partner.[19] It neither requires nor produces a specific body of knowledge nor any tangible results. To the degree that there is any outcome at all, it is limited to the ambiguous Arendtian notion of being *at home in the world*, which may involve the ability to move between self-reflection and an awareness of or concern for collective implications. In other words, thinking provides an opportunity to reconcile one's actions with the "who," to reconcile one's public self with one's inner partner.

In other words, thinking for both Arendt and Heidegger is a solitary endeavor. As Arendt notes, "when I am thinking I move outside the world of appearances, even if my thought deals with ordinary sense-given objects and not with such invisibles as concepts or ideas."[20] As such thinking requires an artificial and self-imposed isolation that has been known to "exact a price—the price of blinding the thinker . . . to the visible world."[21] In "Martin Heidegger at Eighty," Arendt both applauds Heidegger for his originality and notes his reputation as a thinker. "The rumor about Heidegger put it quite simply: Thinking has come to life again; the cultural treasures of the past, believed to be dead, are being made to speak, in the course of which it turns out that they propose things altogether different from the familiar, worn-out trivialities they had been presumed to say. There exists a teacher; one can perhaps learn to think."[22] Moreover, she goes on to distinguish between different types of thinking. She mentions "wondering at the simple," of which all are capable and taking up thinking as one's abode, which few attempt, and is perhaps the condition of the professional thinker.[23] The distinction between wondering at the simple and taking up thinking as one's abode is a pervasive stillness, so pervasive in fact that it protects the thinker "against all sounds, even the sound of his own voice."[24] Moreover, this "stillness" is, for Heidegger, an "indispensable condition" for thinking.[25] Thus, in taking up thinking as one's residence, the absence of sound, even the sound of one's own voice or, moving "outside the world of appearances," must necessarily become a persistent condition.

Given that for Arendt, thinking is primarily characterized by a two-in-one dialogue, the type of thinking for which she compliments Heidegger is antithetical to the type of thinking necessary in order to render judgment. Hence, one is tempted to read irony into the telling clause of the following line— "one could well imagine that—though this hardly the case with Heidegger— the passion of thinking might suddenly beset the most gregarious man and, in consequence of the solitude it requires, ruin him."[26] Heidegger certainly was not the most gregarious of men. Thus, the aforementioned clause (though this is hardly the case with Heidegger) could have applied sincerely to that particular phrase and ironically to the remainder of the sentence since it might well be said from an Arendtian perspective that the absence of the other in his thinking, or his inability to understand the significance of events transpiring in the world of appearances, allowed him to embrace National Socialism. Heidegger might well have known "passionate thinking" or "taking up thinking as one's abode" better than any other fox and, in Arendt's view, it was his passionate thinking that distinguished him. Yet given his own understanding of thinking as an iterative process of distancing and de-distancing, of "coming into-the-nearness of distance," he might have been utterly unable, while sitting in the trap, to recognize the absence of another perspective as problematic. Heidegger, himself, argued that thinking involves an iterative process of burrowing into and stepping back from the object of one's thinking.[27] He might have been utterly unable, while burrowing in to the nature of Being to recognize that the silence excluded the voice of the Other. If the solitude required by passionate thinking could "even beset the most gregarious" of men and Heidegger's thinking was notable in so far as he descended "to the depths [and] . . . persistently remain[ed] there," it could be said that passionate thinking and solitude became for Heidegger a trap, of his own making, and the absence of the sound did, indeed, ruin him.

THE TRAP OF UNIVERSAL GUILT

For Heidegger, *Dasein* exists in the world with the potential to understand his or her own uniqueness, which derives in part from his or her individual place in the world. In her 1946 article on *Existenz* philosophy in which she tried to explain German philosophy to an American audience, Arendt entitled the Heidegger section—"The Self as All and Nothing." In this section she criticizes Heidegger's substitution of the Self or *Dasein* for Man as the focal point of *Existenz*. In so doing, she argues, Heidegger isolates the Self in its own nothingness and vilifies the "they." Ironically, Heidegger succumbs to both of his own unique contributions to *Existenz* philosophy, as we shall soon see. One of Heidegger's most insightful contributions to German philosophy was his description of the "they." Heidegger refers to the public realm that lures *Dasein* away from transcendence and authentic selfhood as the "they": it is an amorphous, collectivity characterized by preoccupation with mundane trivialities. It is not an event or "accident which can befall *Dasein*," but rather it is a mode of being in the world, which is to say it is an omnipresent, fundamental condition or characteristic of being human.[28] Our manner of being-with is conditioned by the constant possibility even high probability of being seduced by the everyday, by the pressing need to take care of things, complete tasks, by the appeal of idle chatter and material objects. In other words, we are constantly tempted by trivialities and lured away from self-fulfillment, away from self-understanding and transcendence. In his formulation, "everything that is real or authentic is assaulted by the overwhelming power of 'mere talk' that irresistibly arises out of the public realm."[29] Thus, the irony of Heidegger's predicament is that in having identified the dangers inherent in the public realm, he, himself, fell prey to the "highly efficient talk and double talk" of the Third Reich. Hence in Arendt's interpretation Heidegger's brilliance lies in identifying the power of the "they" and the irresistible nature of "idle talk" or "double talk."

Despite his prescient contribution to our understanding of the dangers of the public sphere, Heidegger is still seduced by the mere talk of the Third Reich and by the "master stroke" and misleading nature of Hitler's Peace Speech, in particular. Otto Pöggeler argues that for Heidegger, the Peace Speech is the moment when Heidegger was persuaded by Hitler's "program of self-determination for peoples."[30] Despite numerous misleading claims in the Speech, one can imagine several themes resonating with Heidegger. First, Hitler criticized the League of Nations and the Treaty of Versailles, not only as flawed economic policy but harmful to all European peoples. "The degradation of a great people to a second-rate nation was proclaimed in the same breath with which a League of Nations was called into being. This treatment of Germany could not lead to a pacification of the world . . . until now the League of Nations has been incapable of providing appreciable assistance to the weak and unarmed." Second, Hitler took up a topic closely linked to Heidegger's notion of rootlessness, as he pledges to respect the national identities of other peoples. "In that we are devoted to our identity as a Volk in boundless love and faith, we also respect the national rights of other peoples. . . . Thus, the process of Germanization is alien to us. The mentality of the past century, on basis of which it was believed possible to make Germans of Poles and Frenchmen, is foreign to us. . . . We view the European nations as a given fact."[31] Hitler gets close, in this line, to an endorsement of the idea that a people can have an essence that ought to be respected and valued.

As Jesús Adrián Escudero points out, Heidegger offers us two definitions of "idle talk" (*gerede*).[32] The initial description is that idle talk "is the possibility of understanding everything without any previous appropriation of the matter."[33] This view seems to suggest a superficial level of comprehension that requires only a basic understanding of the words that have been spoken, without an understanding of the implications or the events lying behind the words. While in the second, Heidegger describes the passing along of "something groundless" in a "further retelling."[34] The first approach is essentially a passive one though the second suggests an active role akin to gossip.[35] Both lead to a closing off, rather than any further disclosure. Both hold "any new questioning and discussion at a distance."[36] In short, the superficially appealing nature of Hitler's critique of the Treaty of Versailles, as well as, his apparent commitment to the notion of a people, perhaps having an essence, discouraged Heidegger from engaging in any further examination or inquiry as he embraced the Third Reich and the possibility that Hitler was offering an authentic revolution.

We cannot fault Heidegger for being seduced by the "overwhelming power" of mere talk and the alluring promise of greater prosperity; these are, after all, characteristics of being human. Moreover, it is worth noting that since the only escape from the power of the everyday, the assault of mundane trivialities, is withdrawal, the "most essential characteristic of the Self is its absolute egoism, its radical separation from all its fellows."[37] For Heidegger, *Dasein*'s inherent nullity means that all who respond to the call of conscience are necessarily guilty (*schuld*). Arendt notes that *schuld* can be translated as guilty of, responsible for or indebted to.[38] This responsibility or indebtedness, which for Heidegger arises when *Dasein* responds to an internal, possibly mystical, call to conscience is universal and is transformed, in Arendt's view, into one of the quintessential challenges of modernity: nihilism. Since Heidegger's notion of existential guilt is not grounded in "omissions or commissions" in the world, it does not have political or experiential value.[39] Thus, Arendt observed, "[i]t apparently never occurred to Heidegger that by making all men who listen to the 'call of conscience' equally guilty, he was actually proclaiming universal innocence: where everybody is guilty, nobody is."[40] Hence in proclaiming the nullity of *Dasein*, in acknowledging the relative inconsequentiality of individual human responsibility, Heidegger inadvertently lays the conceptual groundwork for universal guilt. Thus, the philosopher who cautions us to beware of the role of technology in redefining history also ends up sanctioning the most horrific use of technology of the twentieth century. In defining the Self essentially as a nullity and linking that nothingness to guilt or responsibility, Heidegger inadvertently sanctions the notion of universal guilt which will become one of the defining features of genocide. As such, an astute observation regarding the limitations of individual culpability translates into a philosophical or rhetorical justification for a collective catastrophe.

ON THE IMPORTANCE OF AN EXPERIENTIAL ONTOLOGY

In a 1953 lecture entitled "The Great Tradition and the Nature of Totalitarianism," Arendt lays out the political importance of loneliness—which can be understood as a variation on Heideggerian inauthenticity—though with an emphasis on its collective importance, as we shall see. The political value of loneliness lies principally in the lack of judgment. According to Arendt, judgment requires rules or standards by which to assess individual cases,[41] and "other people to control (*validate*) my senses." In a state of loneliness both the standard of judgment and external validation are lost.

> If I can't realize the dialogue of solitude I have lost the world and myself, that is capacity for thought and for experience . . . I am One but without anybody to confirm my identity. I do no longer trust my sense[s] because they are no longer confirmed by common sense. I can't have any judgment. . . . In loneliness, I lose both self and world, the faculties of thought and experience and making things, creativity in the largest sense.[42]

Arendt mentions the dialogue of solitude as an important component of loneliness in this passage and explores the components of judgment. Communication as a validation of the self remains key and that communication can occur, literally, with another person or, figuratively, through an internal dialogue, provided that an *other* is represented in that dialogue in the form of the two-in-one. In short, Arendt concurs with Heidegger that the loss of traditional moral and ethical standards of judgment constitutes one of the most profound challenges of modernity. In their stead, she substitutes a definition of thinking in which the Other is necessarily represented and proposes the sense common to us all as the standard for rendering judgment.[43] Thus, Arendt not only criticizes Heidegger as having profoundly isolated the Self and proclaimed its nullity, but also for leaving *Dasein* with utterly no standards by which to render judgment in the public sphere. The absence of a standard of judgment becomes particularly problematic when the brilliant philosopher decides to enter the public realm. Hence, Heidegger lends his support to Hitler and the Third Reich, since "action and authenticity were what mattered."[44] Arendt concurs with Heidegger in so far as action and authenticity belong in public life; moreover, she attempts to remedy the deficiencies of his *Being-with* for use in the public realm by reserving crucial places in thinking and judgment for the Other.

Simply put, whatever her personal feelings about Heidegger, Arendt was unable to dismiss his intellectual contributions to philosophy and perhaps more importantly she engaged in a lifelong struggle to come to terms with the implications of fundamental ontology for the political realm. She remained steadfast in her assessment that his contributions to philosophy were virtually unparalleled, and that a myopic approach, while brilliant in its exceedingly narrow focus nonetheless presents catastrophic risks if we fail to consider the collective and political implications since myopic analysis rarely translates into a simple formula for political action. Arendt's playful essay, which draws on Isaiah Berlin's famous examination of Tolstoy, sheds a much needed light on her intellectual assessment of her excoriated mentor and in so doing reveals that Arendt's own project, far from leaving philosophy behind, sought to remedy the crucial deficiencies of fundamental ontology.[45] In its stead, Arendt proffers an *experiential ontology* since, in her view, the question(s) of *being-with* can only be understood and judged with lived experiences as guideposts. Heidegger's fundamental ontology, replete with non-normative *existentials*, offers abstract categories which may illuminate the nature of being as a descriptive matter, but offers little insight into the challenge of living together as a prescriptive matter. Moreover, he does not seem to recognize, either personally or professionally, the collective implications of his solitary quest. Arendt not only resuscitates *Being-with* but elevates living together to a position of primary importance, in so doing she concretizes Heidegger's *existentials*, which is to say, she grounds them in socio-historical context.[46] In the process the ontological stakes in democratic theory are revealed as are the political implications of one's ontological condition.

NOTES

1. Hannah Arendt, "Heidegger the Fox," in *The Portable Hannah Arendt*, ed. Peter Baehr (New York: Penguin Putnam, 2000[1964]), 543.
2. Ibid., 544.
3. Ibid.
4. Isaiah Berlin, *The Hedgehog and the Fox: An Essay on Tolstoy's View of History* (New York: Simon & Schuster, 1953), 1–2. Berlin went on classify a number of literary figures. Dante, Plato, Hegel, Nietzsche and Dostoevsky are among the hedgehogs; Shakespeare, Aristotle, Goethe, Pushkin and Joyce are viewed by Berlin as foxes.

5. Ibid., 13.
6. Ibid., 63.
7. Ibid., 80.
8. Ibid., 1.
9. Ibid., 80.
10. Fred Dallmayr, "Heidegger and Politics: Some Lessons," in *The Heidegger Case: On Philosophy and Politics*, eds. Tom Rockmore and Joseph Margolis (Philadelphia: Temple University Press, 1992), 289.
11. In her interview with Günter Gaus, Arendt says of intellectuals during Hitler's rise to power, "they made up ideas about Hitler, in part terrifically interesting things! Completely fantastic and interesting and complicated things. . . . Today I would say that they were trapped by their own ideas" (Hannah Arendt, "'What Remains? The Language Remains': A Conversation with Günter Gaus" in *The Portable Hannah Arendt*, ed. Peter Baehr (New York: Penguin Putnam, 2000[1964]), 12).
12. Joan Stambaugh, "Translator's Preface," in *Being and Time*, trans. Joan Stambaugh (Albany, NY: SUNY Press, 1997), xv.
13. Dana Villa, *Arendt and Heidegger: The Fate of the Political* (Princeton, NJ: Princeton University Press, 1996), 216.
14. Dana Villa, *Politics, Philosophy and Terror: Essays on the Thought of Hannah Arendt* (Princeton, NJ: Princeton University Press, 1999), 61–86.
15. Martin Heidegger, "Conversations on a Country Path About Thinking," in *Discourse on Thinking*, trans. John M. Anderson and E. Hans Freud (New York: Harper and Row, 1966), 68.
16. Hannah Arendt, *Life of the Mind: Thinking* (New York: Harcourt Brace, 1978), 5–6.
17. Hannah Arendt, *The Human Condition*, 2nd ed. (Chicago: University of Chicago Press, 1998[1958]), 76.
18. Arendt, *Life of the Mind: Thinking*, 188.
19. Ibid., 183.
20. Hannah Arendt, "Thinking and Moral Considerations," in *Responsibility and Judgment*, ed. Jerome Kohn (New York: Schocken Books, 2003), 165.
21. Ibid., 167.
22. Hannah Arendt, "Martin Heidegger at Eighty," *The New York Review*, October, 21, 1971, 51.
23. Ibid., 53.
24. Ibid., 52.
25. Ibid.
26. Arendt, "Martin Heidegger at Eighty," 52.
27. Heidegger, "Conversations on a Country Path," 68.
28. Magda King, *A Guide to Heidegger's Being and Time*, ed. John Llewelyn (Albany: State University of New York Press, 2001), 88.
29. Hannah Arendt, *Men in Dark Times* (New York: Harcourt Brace, 1968), ix.
30. Otto Pöggeler, *The Paths of Heidegger's Life and Thought*, trans. John Bailiff (Atlantic Highlands, NJ: Humanities Press, 1997), 167.
31. Adolph Hitler, Speech of May 17, 1933, Berlin Reichstag, http://der-fuehrer.org/reden/english/33-05-17.htm.
32. Jesús Adrián Escudero, "Heidegger on Discourse and Idle Talk: The Role of Aristotelian Rhetoric," *Gatherings* 3 (2013): 10.
33. Heidegger, *Being and Time*, 158.
34. Ibid.
35. Escudero, "Heidegger on Discourse and Idle Talk," 10.
36. Ibid.
37. Hannah Arendt, "What Is *Existenz* Philosophy?," *Partisan Review* 13 (1946): 50.
38. Hannah Arendt, *Life of the Mind: Willing* (New York: Harcourt Brace, 1978), 184.
39. Ibid.
40. Ibid.
41. Arendt labels the source of these standards—common sense or "the sense common to us all."

42. Hannah Arendt, "The Great Tradition and the Nature of Totalitarianism" (Hannah Arendt Manuscripts Collection, container #74, Library of Congress, 1953), 11.

43. Common sense relies on "the intersubjectivity or 'presence of others'" allows us to trust in our own "sense experience" as a reliable and valid source of information about the world (Marieke Borren, "'A Sense of the World': Hannah Arendt's Hermeneutic Phenomenology of Common Sense," *International Journal of Philosophical Studies* 21 (2013): 225–55).

44. Richard Wolin, "An Affair to Remember: Hannah and the Magician," *The New Republic*, October 9, 1995, 36.

45. Arendt, "What Remains? The Language Remains," 3–21.

46. I think of and refer to Heidegger as an existentialist knowing full well that he rejected the label, as Arendt rejected the label—philosopher—and there are, of course, risks in imposing an undesired label on anyone. Though Heidegger certainly viewed himself as explicating something more fundamental about the nature of Being or the ontological, he also acknowledges the importance of the ontic in allowing that the place we go to work through ontological questions is necessarily to the ontic. In other words, the Being, by whom questions of Being can be taken up, is necessarily ontically situated in the world.

Chapter Two

Rootlessness in Heidegger and Arendt

The recent publication of a few of Martin Heidegger's *Black Notebooks* has led to a resurgence of interest in the degree to which and the ways in which antisemitism is central to his philosophy. His use of the wandering Jew trope in the *Black Notebooks* has by now been well documented.[1] Interestingly, the *Black Notebooks* also reveal that there is more than a passing similarity in the way that Heidegger and Arendt conceptualize the problem of rootlessness. Both of their understandings of Jewish existence are based on the metaphysical notion of being uprooted. This rootlessness leads to a particular manner of *being-in-the-world*, which is to say, an ontic trait leads to a particular ontological condition. Heidegger finds in Jewishness a particularly threatening form of inauthenticity; in fact, Jewishness becomes virtually synonymous with an inauthentic existence. Arendt accepts that an ontic characteristic can be constitutive of one's manner of being; yet she does not view the trait as deterministic. Instead, she draws our attention to the social and political power (or lack thereof) associated with the ontic trait. Thus, for Heidegger, an ontic characteristic becomes constitutive of one's manner of *being-in-the-world*. Whereas for Arendt, it is the need to seek social acceptance under persistent conditions of powerlessness that leads to an inauthentic manner of *being-in-the-world*. In other words, Arendt casts a light on the social and political structures that press upon our existential choices, leading to a particular manner of *being-in-the-world*.

In this chapter, I examine Heidegger and Arendt's use of rootlessness. They both view rootlessness as lying at the core of the challenges of modern life; as such, they both explore remedies to the problem of rootlessness. Heidegger imagines a people, rooted in a place, in which questions of being can call them to being. Failing that, he holds out hope that we can learn to use technology and calculative thinking without succumbing to either. Arendt alludes to the possibility that a state or homeland could provide a group, not only with representation and protection, but also facilitate the development of culture, language and a sense of belonging. This undertaking, not only sheds light on the roles Heidegger imagines for *Mitdasein* in transcendence, it also reveals that while Arendt utilized rootlessness in ways that are very similar to Heidegger's, she also subtly transformed the concept to neutralize its most troubling facets. Yet her transformation of roots is even more consequential. For Arendt, the aim of philosophy must become to grapple with our collective project of sharing the earth. It is therefore imperative, though not sufficient, for *mitdasein* to be constitutive of *Being* in some meaningful way. Thus in her transformation of rootlessness, Arendt aspires to a reconfiguration philosophy itself.

That Heidegger bought into anti-Semitic stereotypes has long been suspected: that he lent them "philosophical height, weight and sophistication" is, since the publication of his *Black Notebooks*, no longer contestable.[2] He repeatedly refers to Jews as groundless or uprooted. Moreover, this groundlessness is no benign state; rather it threatens the very project of Being. "[G]roundlessness in the most varied and opposed forms—without recognizing themselves as of the same distorted essence—falls into an extreme hostility and a mania for destruction."[3] Less well established is how this stereotype translates into a threat and what precisely is threatened by rootlessness. Groundlessness is certainly not a term applied to Jews alone; the English, the Americans, as well as, the Bolsheviks are all described at some point as rootless, calculating and engaged in machination. Yet in the Jews, this rootlessness seems to take on a particularly ominous quality. Even though others are also engaged in machination and calculative thinking, it is the Jews who have undertaken this "task," who have made "the uprooting of all beings from being" their project.[4] Moreover, they have done so in an *utterly unrestrained*, seemingly purposeful way. In short, it is assimilated Jews, living among Germans, that threaten the German national project of returning to their national essence. Given that the recently published *Black Notebooks* reveal rootlessness at the core of Heidegger's philosophical antisemitism, and Arendt shares at least some of Heidegger's concern with metaphysical roots, this examination of their respective understandings of roots reveals Arendt's project to be, in part, a response to "being historical anti-Semitism."[5]

HEIDEGGERIAN ROOTS AND TRANSCENDENCE

For Heidegger, roots play a critical role in an authentic existence, by linking *Being* to its past, to its core essence. Heidegger's notion of historicity has two predominant impulses. First, it is part of the constitutive structure of *Dasein*, as such it plays a crucial role in the search for transcendence. One can only take oneself up as a project with an understanding of one's origins. Thus, transcendence is an historically conditioned endeavor. It not only occurs in a particular time and place, but one's project is conditioned by an understanding of the inescapable historicity of one's own existence. Second, the Heideggerian notion of historicity serves as a critique of the study of history. Historical inquiry should not be understood as an attempt to construct an orderly sequence of facts. Rather the study of history requires challenging the dominant interpretation of the meaning of these facts. Heidegger does not suggest that an awareness of the factual events contributing to one's condition of thrownness is a precondition of taking up one's own existence as a project. Awareness has never been a prerequisite for the authentic life.[6] In fact, Heidegger says, "[t]his elemental historicity of *Dasein* can remain concealed from it."[7] Though he would likely also caution that "[a]s having been, *Dasein* is delivered over to its own thrownness."[8] In other words, since we are all thrown beings, historically situated, the possibility of remaining trapped in our thrownness is ever present, with or without an awareness of the historicity of one's own existence. Since the pursuit of authenticity is a continuous struggle, awareness of one's thrownness can increase the likelihood of taking oneself up in a resolute manner.

Heidegger identifies a critical perspective as one of the fundamental components of historicity.[9] In other words in order to constitute an authentic project, historical inquiry must have as its aim—unconcealment, challenging the dominant interpretation of events for the purpose of recovering possibilities. In this sense the historian's aim is not separable from the philosopher's and is ontological in nature. In other words, "the historian's task is most essentially not the reconstruction of facts but of possibilities, that is, of the existential choices underlying the historical fate of individuals and the destiny of peoples."[10] The historian who approaches inquiry in this manner pursues his or her own project in a mode of *being-with* that hands down to others their "inherited possibility" as such, historicity is an act in which the historian not only challenges a dominant interpretation of past events but in so doing "leap[s] ahead . . . not in order to take 'care' away . . . but . . . to give it back."[11] Historicity retrieves possibilities and thus serves as a precursor to both transcendence and to an authentic existence. Simply put, the past plays an integral role in taking up the future. It is thus not surprising to find that Heidegger's roots are historical.

In a selection from the *Black Notebooks*, labeled—History—Heidegger offers a description of the historical nature of roots. He writes "if a clearing track of being shoots through beings and if this track in its obliteration remains there imperceptibly, so as always to offer beings an errancy and a wide space to feel at home."[12] In other words, faint traces of the truth of being remain even as we go through daily life, preoccupied with idle chatter and trivial, worldly distractions. The "track of being" remains, allowing the perennial possibility of returning to that track up again. It is, thus, roots that keep alive the potential of taking up the question of being in the midst of the everyday and roots that allow one to "feel at home." Rootedness allows the call of being to find Being even without an active, ongoing, purposeful engagement with philosophical questions. Heidegger goes on to assert that "[h]istoriology and all remembrance move in the obliterated tracks of being, without ever recognizing them as such."[13] In this passage, roots, for Heidegger, appear to be primarily historical and the role of the collective in taking up questions of being remains ambiguous. While the questions at stake in rootedness are ontological, Heidegger's notion of roots is also notable for its literal, if ambiguous, connection to the earth and the soil. In working the soil or engaging in a form of work that "remains embedded"[14] in the earth, "we labor authentically."[15] By authentic work, he refers not only to manual labor but to a labor that discloses. He certainly has in mind his own philosophical work, as well as, certain forms of art, including Van Gogh's painting of a well-worn pair of shoes.[16] When we labor authentically, the soil, the landscape ceases "to be either raw material for industrial production or a beautiful sight for excursioners from the city."[17] In other words, we cease to view the earth simply as ready-to-hand; through authentic labor, the earth shapes us. It prepares us to take up questions of being; it shields us from a form of thinking that views the earth merely as a set of natural resources to be exploited. It connects us to the past, to our history and to a traditional way of life: it also serves as a buffer between us and the Other, as we shall soon see.

ARENDT'S ROOTS: STORYTELLING

Arendt's notion of roots, conversely, does not utilize soil, landscape or the earth. Rather, her roots connect people to each other and to events. Roots, for her, can be historical and the methodology of connection is storytelling. The importance of storytelling as a methodology in the work of Hannah Arendt has been well documented. Though its importance is a matter of consensus, its precise functioning and purpose is not. Elisabeth Young-Bruehl suggests that storytelling is a particularly crucial form of action during "dark times." Dark times are those moments when prior explanations for contemporary events fail us. During these moments when familiar concepts and modes of thinking prove unable to explain events "the result was that whenever they thought in general or theoretical terms . . . their thought would remain shallow and the depth of their experiences would remain inarticulate.[18] Accordingly, Arendt "viewed this rupture as a sign that the threads, the thought fragments, were to be gathered, freely and in such a way as to protect freedom, and made into something new, dynamic and illuminating."[19] Since in moments of dramatic rupture, fragments may be all that remain: the act of gathering and offering up these thought fragments in the public realm constitutes a political act for Arendt. Young-Bruehl notes that Arendt told stories "with a charming disregard for mere facts . . . and an unfailing regard for the life of the story."[20] Since as a phenomenological matter the story, once told, becomes a presence in the public space, subject to interpretation and reinterpretation in light of different perspectives and subsequent events. As Arendt herself said, "what interests us is not the truthfulness of a person but the truth of the story."[21] The meaning revealed in or the understanding derived from a story depends on the context in which it is told and retold and the diverse perspectives from which it is told.

Benhabib identifies two forms of storytelling in Arendt's work: one public, one private. In the public version, "the theorist as storyteller . . . converts the memory of the dead" into something meaningful and in so doing interprets the past in light of the present.[22] In the private version, "we discover who we are and come to know ourselves through the words and deeds we engage in, in the company of others."[23] Thus, like historicity, Arendtian storytelling facilitates both the individual's search for authenticity, as well as the collective pursuit of meaning. Arendt's notion of storytelling replaces objectivity with impartiality. Lisa Disch uses the terms "situated impartiality" and "visiting" which requires telling a story or recounting an event from "the plurality of perspectives that constitute it as a public phenomena."[24] The challenge becomes to take up the position of numerous others in the recounting of an event. Meaning or truth derives from the diverse perspectives that are brought to bear on a story. For Disch the critical point is that Arendtian storytelling invites "contestation from rival perspectives" and in so doing provokes rather than forecloses dialogue.[25] Thus, the role of storytelling for Arendt, like Heideggerian historicity, is necessarily critical. In light of these observations, Arendt's penchant for storytelling can be understood as both a request for a plurality of perspectives, as well as a substantive space of appearances in which to contest the events themselves, their meaning and also a space in which people can connect. The stories relayed provide individuals with a sense of connection to the past and to a people. As such storytelling draws on the past, re-invents itself in the present and looks toward the future.

The similarity in the way Heidegger and Arendt approach rootedness lies in the importance of a shared history and memory, both of which are crucial for thinking. Their notions of rootedness also reveal their respective critiques of the study of history and social science. The "tracks" of which Heidegger writes, bear a striking resemblance not only to his paths in the woods, but also to Arendt's monuments or guideposts. For Arendt, the goal of historically based inquiry is to erect monuments in the space of appearances. Particularly if bound to incident, these monuments offer either examples to emulate or cautionary tales. Since they are bound to isolated incidents and *if* their interpretation is contested, they rarely stake a claim to represent an absolute and enduring truth, hence the resulting narrative is less coercive than a Darwinian or Marxist interpretation of history. Narratives bound to incident are less likely to either claim to explain all of human history or to claim a rigidly predictive quality. In that sense both Heidegger and Arendt view rootedness as facilitating a type of thinking: both envision one's roots as providing a bulwark against a particular kind of thinking, a thinking that lacks depth.

HEIDEGGER'S DEEP THINKING: MEDITATIVE

Given the importance Heidegger attaches to remembrance, its appearance in a discussion of roots is hardly surprising. For both Arendt and Heidegger remembering plays an integral part in thinking, particularly Heidegger's meditative thinking. Heidegger notes that one's innermost essence, "the heart's core . . . the gathering of all that concerns us, all that we care for" can only "unfold in memory."[26] In other words, since care or concern is one of the constitutive structures of *Dasein* and our care or concern emerges only through memory, remembrance constitutes a necessary but not sufficient condition for engaging others in a mode of care that is proficient. Thus, the act of remembering becomes a precondition for transcendence. He suggests that meditative thinking need not occupy itself with or focus on specialized themes or processes. It "need by no means be 'high flown.' It is enough if we dwell on what lies close."[27] We can and should allow ourselves to contemplate the questions that present themselves. Meditative thinking is characterized by two qualities. First, it is iterative by its very nature: he refers to it as a process that involves "coming into the nearness of distance" an examination and a release.[28] Second, the thinker is more of a passive than active agent in meditative thinking. She waits "for the arrival of the nature of thinking."[29] The wait is an important step that must be learned and practiced "because waiting moves into openness."[30] Thinking presents itself; the thinker resists calculative or specialized thinking while waiting "for the opening of openness."[31] It is in the quietness of waiting that questions present themselves—"Is there still a life-giving homeland in whose ground man may stand rooted, that is be autochthonic?" and "what is really happening in our age?"[32] Questions like these cannot present themselves in the midst of calculative thinking because "[c]alculative thinking computes . . . races from one prospect to the next . . . never stops, never collects itself."[33] Deep thinking for Heidegger is contemplative, reflective and it is a solitary endeavor; whatever role being-with (*mitdasein*) may play in Heidegger's philosophy, its role in transcendence and authenticity appears to be limited and the meditative thinking of which Heidegger is so fond, bears no trace of *being-with*. Thinking is an activity that takes place in solitude and the role of others appears to be exclusively that of a distraction or an impediment.

In "The Origin of the Work of Art" Heidegger asserts that the rootlessness of thinking originates in the translation of Greek into Latin, "what is concealed within the apparently literal, and hence faithful, translation is a translation of Greek experience into a different mode of thinking."[34] In other words, a common language, for Heidegger, is one of the crucial components of "roots," as it serves as a requisite for a common mode of thinking. That language denotes a particular way of thinking for Heidegger is not surprising, yet, the relationship between shared language and authenticity warrants attention. If a shared language is a prerequisite for authenticity, then the collectivity's importance has been elevated considerably beyond that of a distraction. Actualization may even be an inherently collective process. Moreover, the notion that the mode of thinking derives from or is shaped by a shared language signals a shift toward an authenticity in which *Mitdasein* is, in fact, constitutive of one's *Being-in-the-world*. The suggestion that *Mitdasein* assumes greater importance finds further support in Heidegger's description of the clearing as a presencing that happens

> [i]n the midst of beings as a whole an open place comes to presence. . . . The being can only be, as a being, if it stands within, and stands out within, what is illuminated in this clearing. Only this clearing, grants us human beings access to those beings that we ourselves are not and admittance to the being that we ourselves are.[35]

In other words, the appearance of a clearing, in which being reveals itself, is by its very nature a collective phenomenon, since it occurs "in the midst of beings as a whole." In order to gain "access" to others and "admittance" to Being, there is a simultaneous standing "within, and stand[ing] out within, what is illuminated." In other words, with respect to the presencing or in the moment when the nature of Being (i.e., truth) reveals itself, in order to connect with others and reveal the Being that I already am, I must accept both my own uniqueness and my place in the collective. It is only in connection with others that each of us begins to understand her own Self. Only in the presence of others can we begin to understand what "we ourselves are" as well as, what "we ourselves are not."

With his version of thinking, Heidegger aspires to contemplate the wonders of life (the heaviness of stone, the vibrancy of color),[36] as well as, seriously engage philosophical questions. What is the essence of the German *volk*? Is life in the mountains more authentic or virtuous than city life?[37] How has modernity changed what it means to be human? In order to undertake these questions, we must prepare ourselves to receive this wisdom, as it presents itself. Calculation, on the other hand, aspires to assign a number to the heaviness of the stone. That number may well leave us with a "precise determination" of the weight, though the sense of awe we experience at the "heaviness of the weight escapes us."[38] This sense of wonder or awe "shows itself only when it remains undisclosed" since wonder itself resists "every attempt to penetrate it." Calculation, calculative thinking and the various attempts at mastery constitute for Heidegger "act[s] of destruction."[39] The attempt to count, to explain (in technical terms), to compute and to master the natural world destroys our wonder at the beauty and undisclosed mysteries of life. Heidegger holds out the possibility that "a new ground and foundation [may] be granted again to man"[40] that we can develop a new relationship with technology (and presumably) calculative thinking in which we allow both to play a role in our lives and at the same time "leave them outside."[41]

In other words, although the traditional ways of being rooted may no longer be possible under conditions of modernity, the negative effects of rootlessness could still be mitigated if we adopt a comportment (or an approach) which Heidegger terms "releasement towards things and openness to the mystery."[42] We can use technology without succumbing to it, as the driving force in our lives. The risk for Heidegger in failing to remain open to meditative thinking is that "man would have denied and thrown away his own special nature—that he is a meditative being"[43] capable of wondering at the heaviness of the stone or the German essence. Thus, the relationship between calculative and meditative thinking shifts somewhat across Heidegger's work. In the *Black Notebooks*, he portrays the Jews as purveyors of calculative thinking and attributes to them the status of an enemy of *Dasein*.[44] Whereas, in the *Memorial Address*, which he delivers in 1955, he seems to allow for the possibility that calculative and meditative thinking could coexist. The question is—can calculative thinking and meditative thinking, which require different training and different mindsets, both flourish? Calculative thinking moves from one task to the next, aspires to mastery, and is, at least to some degree, necessary to daily life. Meditative thinking cultivates patience and receptivity; it aspires to receive the world's wisdom. The danger, according to Heidegger, is that calculative thinking may spread, and to the degree that we engage in it exclusively, we deny our "own special nature."

ARENDT'S DEEP THINKING: IN THE WORLD

Like Heidegger, Arendt believes that rootlessness is characterized by a type of thinking that lacks depth; in other words, it is disconnected from the world. Contra Heidegger, what she means by a lack of depth is a disconnection from the realities of a human world. Adolph Eichmann serves as the quintessential case; the type of thinking he exemplifies bears a strong resemblance to Heidegger's calculative thinking. The banality of evildoers, of which Arendt offers Eichmann as a prime example, rests with the inability to think, which in turn leads to a lack of understanding and judgment. For Arendt, thinking is a dialectical and critical process, an ongoing, soundless dialogue with oneself, a "habit of examining whatever happens to come to pass or to attract attention," that reveals the inherent duality in human nature.[45] Like Arendt's storytelling, thinking serves two purposes: one individual and one collective. Individually, thinking reveals any disconnect or disharmony between our appearance, or what we reveal of who we are in the public realm, and our consciousness or our true selves. It allows us to "discover who we are and come to know ourselves."[46] As such, thinking requires solitary time and space. "To be in solitude means to be with one's self, and thinking, therefore, though it may be the most solitary of all activities, is never altogether without a partner and without company."[47] Thinking is an activity that can only be engaged in by oneself and with oneself as the only partner, the process of going home to face the "partner who comes to life when you are alert and alone."[48] Collectively, thinking allows us to derive meaning from events. Without the inner dialogue to force him to reconcile his actions with his inner critic, or the ability to derive meaning from events, the rootless individual is vulnerable to what Arendt refers to as deductive reasoning or logical thinking: the cornerstone of ideology.

> The tyranny of logicality begins with the mind's submission to logic as a never-ending process, on which man relies in order to engender his thoughts. By this submission, he surrenders his inner freedom as he surrenders his freedom of movement when he bows down to an outward tyranny.[49]

Moreover, logical thinking occurs when "[t]he idea [of class or race] becomes a premise in the logical sense from which a process is being deduced . . . [According to this approach, thinking involves] conclusions instead of judgment, [and becomes subsumed] under certain rules."[50]

Without the benefits of self-reflection or the ability to interpret meaning, rootless individuals find "comfort and consolation" in rules, logical and deductive reasoning.[51] In short, Adolph Eichmann illustrates a type of thinking that lacked depth. He lacked the ability to divide into the two-in-one, to self-reflect, to assign meaning to events around him and instead sought validation in the rules, logic, clichés and euphemisms.[52] As Arendt noted, "[t]he longer one listened to him, the more obvious it became that his inability to speak was closely connected with an inability to think, namely to think from the standpoint of somebody else."[53] Without the ability to connect to his own inner partner, the rootless individual seeks acceptance and connection without discernment. He seeks solace in the feeling of belonging afforded by any social movement.

> [A] thinking being, rooted in his thoughts and remembrances, and hence knowing that he has to live with himself, there will be limits to what he can permit himself to do, and these limits will not be imposed on him from the outside, but will be self-set. These limits can change considerably . . . but limitless, extreme evil is possible only where these self-grown roots, which automatically limit the possibilities are absent. They are absent where men skid only over the surface of events, where they permit themselves to be carried away without ever penetrating into whatever depth they may be capable of.[54]

This lack of depth or rootedness may not create an obvious problem *until* uncertainty and fear become politicized, as we shall soon see. In other words, evildoing does not require a malicious intent or a malevolent character. A simple failure to think, "namely, to think from the standpoint of someone else" and "remember what they did" creates an ontological condition which can be exploited under certain circumstances.[55]

Thinking, either meditative or self-reflective, requires roots for both Hannah Arendt and Martin Heidegger, which is to say the most valuable kinds of thinking must necessarily be tethered to something. For Heidegger, the most valuable kind of thinking gets beyond the everyday and examines the fundamental essence of being (meditative); whereas dangerous forms of thinking are those that merely float along the surface, never acquiring any depth (calculative), attempting to understand the brilliance of color, merely by assigning a numerical value to wave length, for example. Arendt concurs that thinking merely along the surface is a troubling phenomenon, though she also worries about a thinking that acquires depth but does not remain mindful of the world (abstract thinking). For Heidegger, a people has a core essence and one's roots link back to that essence, connecting back to that which one already was. Thus, roots are primarily historical or linguistic and are closely tied to the soil, landscapes and iconic works of art. The notion of circling back to an original essence also leaves Heidegger's notion of authenticity dependent on the traditional, hence tethered to stereotypes. For Arendt, the two-in-one dialogue requires two things: it requires us to think from "the standpoint of someone else" and to "remember what [we] did." Arendt's thinking thus invokes the Other and connects to both an empirical reality and her own inner critic.

ACTUALIZATION: THE ROLE OF ART

Both Heidegger and Arendt are also mindful of the way authentic thinking acquires meaning. As such they both explore the possibility that the collective could play a role in actualization. For Heidegger, in particular, art is the vehicle through which the authentic, individual experience can shape others.

Actualization, for Heidegger, seems to require three things: a decision (an overturning or rejection of metaphysics) or a creative act, drawn from communal *[volklich]* roots that reveals a "previously unknown ... essence."[56] He anticipates a creative impulse that reaffirms or recasts something essential while simultaneously breaking decisively with something familiar.

> all creativity from the very first shatters what is historiologically familiar since precisely as a creating it ventures out into something indeterminate and other. This venture, however, arises so strictly from the genuine communal *[volklich]* rootedness and there is neither talk of it nor any sort of reference to it, because indeed the venture transforms the communal *[volklich]* for the first time into its previously unknown ... and unusual essence.[57]

For Heidegger the ability to reveal something essential derives from one's rootedness in a particular place. The essence of being reveals itself through roots. If authenticity contains two simultaneous impulses: an affirmation, as well as, a rupture, Heidegger recognizes only a rupture with metaphysics and an affirmation of the core essence.

The nature of the revelation itself is also collective, insofar as, it tells us something about who we are and who we are not. Charles Bambach suggests that Heidegger's notion of rootedness has its origins in the German Youth Movement of the early twentieth century, in which the term *[Bodenständigkeit]* referred to a "rootedness in the soil and in the earth but it c[ould] also denote rootedness in tradition or community."[58] These youth groups took excursions to the countryside to develop a connection with and an appreciation for the German landscape, nature and rural life. They "hiked, sang songs, communed with nature, and formed their own unique *Gemeinschaft* (community) modeled on the erotic spirit of Plato's *Symposium*."[59] Heidegger both participated in, as well as led, excursions like this in which German youth rejected the cosmopolitan, bourgeoisie ideal of Weimar Germany and sought instead a return to their authentic, Alemannic roots and the spirit of comradery with other, like minded, young people. Heidegger may well have had one of these excursions in mind when he wrote, "[i]n the midst of beings as a whole an open place comes to presence." Karsten Harries asserts that the appearance of the terms *Holzweg* (path) and *Lichtung* (clearing) are significant. *Holzweg* "suggests a path cut by foresters to allow some trees that have been cut down to be brought out of the forest. A *Holzweg* therefore often ends in a *Lichtung*."[60] This *Lichtung* is often a circular space; it allows light to enter an otherwise dense and dark forest. "In a sense such a path is a dead end. For a hiker to be on a *Holzweg* means he has lost his way. But is such a loss of way—what the Greeks called *aporia*—not the beginning of authentic thinking."[61] With this in mind, one way of understanding Heidegger's rootedness and its relationship to *Being* is by imagining a cadre of young people engaged in a spiritual and philosophical trek through the Black

Forest in search of both a return to their German essence and a renewed role for Germany in the world. For this experience as well as those aspirations, connection to others is critical. The others who are represented in this experience, however, are like-minded, similar in age and background. Thus, Heidegger acknowledges *being-with* as a constitutive feature of transcendence but since this *being-with* includes other who look and think like he does, Heidegger has made room for the Other without making room for diversity.

Artistic or creative works can also serve as "the beginning of authentic thinking." Both Heidegger and Arendt view works of art as having the potential to facilitate transcendence. In "The Origin of the Work of Art" Heidegger describes the "circular character of *Dasein*, as a being existing for its own sake and becoming what it already was."[62] The roots which prove so important for Heidegger serve as the only means by which this circle can be completed, as they provide the only link to that which *Dasein* "already was." Thus without roots, the circle cannot be complete. *Being* cannot become fully self-aware because it has no way to get back to its origin. For Heidegger, the return to an origin is a crucial aspect of transcendence. The future is, thus, grounded in the past; projection grows out of tradition.

Arendt also values the creative impulse and the products of creativity, as authentic representations of the human experience, which can facilitate transcendence. Yet she seems to suggest that the rootless may be in a unique position to create works of art with social importance. She suggests, for example, that assimilated Jews could be in an ideal position to initiate this creative overturning. They were connected in many ways to German communal life and also existed as outsiders; they embody the simultaneous impulses of destruction and affirmation. For Arendt, the experience of outsider might reveal something essential, albeit perhaps critical, rather than affirming. Rahel Varnhagen illustrates the potential for creative works to reveal something essential. Rahel, as we shall soon see, is clearly and repeatedly seduced by the inauthentic. In fact, she spends most of her time engaged in idle chatter, gossip and seeking to escape her Jewishness through marriage. Yet as an outsider, Rahel also offers a poignant description of life as a Jewess in the nineteenth century. Herein lies the unique opportunity of the outsider—to serve as social critic, rejected, yet still self-revealing. This self-revealing facilitates transcendence for the artist, as well as those who subsequently grapple with the meaning of the work.

Art, thus, illustrates the difference between Heidegger and Arendt on the notion of *essence*. For Heidegger art affirms the essence of a people. It reveals something about a collective past and "gives to men their outlook on themselves."[63] In other words, if the defining authentic moment, the uncon-cealing, involves both an affirming and shattering impulse, Heidegger's notion of the role of art is primarily an affirming one, in the sense of affirming a traditional way of life. For Arendt, on the other hand, the power of art lies in the its ability to facilitate an unconcealment, but what makes art "original" is the shattering impulse. The examples that each invokes illustrate this point. Heidegger is fascinated by Van Gogh's painting of shoes, which he mistakenly describes as the shoes of a peasant woman.[64] Moreover, the value of the painting, and thus art, for Heidegger is that it has revealed to us the actual nature of the shoes, in this case, their reliability.[65] In short, art reveals an actual or essential nature, but it is a nature that is stable, established. Its unconcealment creates continuity with the past. The work of art reveals something that already was, as such Heidegger's authentic moment involves a reverence for the past and a celebration of a traditional way of life.

Conversely, Arendt does not believe that a people has an essence in any ontological sense.[66] Rather, a people's essence is, in her view, socially constructed. Any traits or characteristics associated with a group may reveal something about the ontic conditions in which they live, but they do not reveal anything essential or ontological. Thus, roots for Arendt are ontic in nature, as roots can only be established in the world. Moreover, those roots necessarily connect to *other* people, as such they reflect economic, philosophical, historical and religious structures in the world. These are the structures that shape one's thinking, that keep one tethered to the world.[67] In terms of art, it is the originality of Rahel's prose that she finds most valuable, her ability to convey the poignancy of her own experience. She provides a striking description of the inauthenticity of modern life and her relationship to it. She depicts the moment, not in abstract or analytical terms but rather, simply as it struck her, as her personal experience. She conveys a very personal experience, yet an experience with which many would be familiar, the feeling of being a part and yet not a part of some collective experience, present, yet oddly disconnected. Thus, the power of art, for Arendt, lies in its potential to facilitate understanding, to create "something new, dynamic and illuminating."[68] If Heidegger values art as an opportunity to create continuity with the past, Arendt values the potential for art to facilitate a rupture.

ARENDT'S ROOTLESSNESS: TERRITORIAL AND METAPHYSICAL

Heidegger's notion of rootlessness is ontological in nature. For Heidegger uprootedness is the philosophical concept that allows Jewishness, the ethnicity, to become virtually synonymous with an inauthentic existence. Moreover, uprootedness is not a benign characteristic; rather it takes on a menacing quality since the type of thinking that results has a contagious quality. It is the contagion factor that renders a form of ethnicity threatening to the dominant culture. Arendt's transformation of rootlessness is, first and foremost, notable for its shift to and focus on the ontic. In keeping with Heidegger, Arendt accepts that an ontic trait can be constitutive of Being; yet she does not view the ontic trait as deterministic. Nor does she view one's manner of being-in-the-world as deriving from the ontic trait itself; instead, she directs our attention to the social or political power associated with ontic traits. In Arendt's view, it is the social construction of this ontic trait that merits attention, as one's manner of being in the world derives, not from a core essence, but rather from the persistent condition of powerlessness that renders social acceptance paramount. She not only alerts us to the ontic antecedents but also to the potential political consequences of rootlessness, as well shall soon see. Along the way, she distinguishes between two varieties of rootlessness: territorial uprootedness and metaphysical rootlessness. Territorial uprootedness may occur for a variety of reasons; her two main examples are the Boers and the Jews, yet it is a condition that also affects refugees and has an application in the context of urbanization. In short, territorial uprootedness can affect individuals as individuals; it can also affect a group of people, as a group. An individual can leave his or her ancestral home for urban life or "a people" can find itself separated from its homeland.

While she periodically mentions rootlessness in conjunction with Jews, rootlessness is not for Arendt a quintessentially Jewish trait. In order to highlight rootlessness as a general condition, and perhaps to separate her usage of the term from Heidegger, the first rootless group Arendt discusses are the Boers. The Boers are rootless, in the sense of, living under conditions of *territorial uprootedness*; having chosen to forgo their claim to the land as an act of resistance to British rule.

> It is characteristic of the Boers that these reactions followed the same, repeated pattern throughout the nineteenth century: Boer farmers escaped British law by treks into the interior wilderness of the country, abandoning without regret their homes and their farms. Rather than accept limitations upon their possessions, they left them altogether.[69]

In this case, *roots* consist of a claim to property and the act of becoming rootless was a deliberate choice. Though the Boers may have been lacking in territorial roots, they were, according to Arendt, metaphysically rooted. In other words, they did not require either a legal claim to property or location in a particular geographic area of origin to experience a sense of belonging to a people. In Arendt's words, they managed to feel at home in the world "wherever the horde happened to be."[70] Metaphysical roots, thus, allow one to feel at home in the world, to experience a sense of connection, of *mitdasein*. In her discussion of Disraeli, an exception Jew caught between the role of Court Jew and modern antisemitism, Arendt offers a concrete description of some of the different experiences that allowed one to be rooted in the Jewish community.

Judaism, and belonging to the Jewish people, degenerated into a simple fact of birth only among assimilated Jewry. Originally it had meant a specific religion, a specific nationality, the sharing of specific memories and specific hopes, and, even among the privileged Jews, it meant at least still sharing specific economic advantages. Secularization and assimilation had changed self-consciousness and self-interpretation in such a way that nothing was left of the old memories and hopes but the awareness of belonging to a chosen people.[71]

For Arendt, *roots* can include religion, history, class or status. In other words, roots include many of the things that might, in Heideggerian terms, comprise one's throw or, in Arendt's terminology, *facts* of birth, though she also includes memories and hopes. As forms of connectedness, these shared experiences create a metaphysical rootedness, a "self-interpretation" or a sense of belonging. While Heidegger tries to forge a link between or the soil and the national soul, Arendt severs any connection between the soil and the soul. In fact, she dismisses the very idea of a national essence. Her *roots* connect people to events and experiences.

The value of territory is, thus, not ontological; rather, it is one tangible sign of belonging to *a people*. Its importance is social in that it is one possible indicator of social status. Moreover, she simultaneously points toward other possible signs of belonging which could be constructed: a country or a state. Yet even in the absence of a territory or a state, the potential to create tangible signs of *a people* exist; she mentions, for example, historic achievements. Moreover, the appearance of language raises the possibility that cultural achievements which are literary, philosophical, sporting or artistic may also qualify as sources of metaphysical rootedness. All of these experiences or achievements derive from, as well as constitute, one's *Being-with*. Familiarity with particular sculptures, literary works, or the rules of a sport, are concrete indications of having come from somewhere, as Arendt claims to have come from the tradition of German philosophy.[72] In short, for Arendt, territorial roots are useful insofar as they create a physical space in which people can connect and remember. In other words, territorial roots create a physical space in which a people can draw on the past to create a shared history and individuals can take an understanding of the past to construct a self-interpretation. Metaphysical roots are useful insofar as they create a set of experiences in which people can connect and hope; in other words, they facilitate the process of constructing an identity by using the past to project toward the future.

These two forms of uprootedness do not necessarily occur simultaneously, as she illustrates with the Boers; but when they do, the situation is ripe for exploitation. It is this opportunity that was "well suited to the needs of the shifting masses of modern cities and was therefore grasped at once by totalitarianism."[73] Rootlessness is the metaphysical condition or "preliminary condition"[74] underlying the economic or political condition that Arendt describes as superfluousness, which totalitarian movements learned to exploit. For Arendt, the exploitation of rootless or superfluous people is the link that connects the Bolshevik and Nazi movements: "their factories of annihilation . . . [are] the swiftest solution to the problem of overpopulation, of economically superfluous and socially rootless human masses."[75] The originality of totalitarian movements is that they exploit superfluous persons in order to annihilate an uprooted people. The Nazi regime utilized Adolph Eichmann (and others like him) to annihilate the Jewish people. With this in mind, one way of reading Arendt is as redirecting Heidegger's notion of uprootedness in a decidedly ontic way. In focusing our attention on the ontic "causes" of rootlessness, Arendt robs the Heideggerian concept of its two most troublesome facets—ontological determinism and ethnic bias. Moreover, she subsequently turns her attention to two related issues. In *Origins of Totalitarianism*, she explores how rootlessness has been exploited, politically. Whereas in her Jewish writings, she examines the possibilities of ameliorating rootlessness.

As much as Hannah Arendt claimed not to be a Zionist, she also viewed the development of a Jewish homeland as an important piece in the recognition and "integration of the Jewish people into the future community of European peoples."[76] She consistently refers to the Jews as a "people like all others" by which she means "a people [that] . . . have special interests and demands that we must represent one way or another."[77] In particular, she firmly roots her political agenda in a phenomenological understanding of Jewish history, challenging the dominant narrative and inviting contestation. Moreover, she attempts to construct historical roots for the Jewish people by telling the stories of resistance. She tells, for example, the story of the Warsaw ghetto uprising.[78] But Arendt does not simply tell the story, she transforms the meaning of the story from one that illustrates the futility of resistance to one that demonstrates the value of a heroic death. She casts it as a new beginning, in which the resistance fighters decided, "if they themselves could not be saved . . . to salvage 'the honor and glory of the Jewish people.'"[79] She re-interprets Jewish history and hands back to her fellow Jews an alternative to the victim role. She draws on the past to create the possibility of a new self-interpretation. At the same time, she offers an alternative narrative to the dominant anti-Semitic narrative of a calculating people aspiring to world domination, suggesting instead a people seeking acceptance, survival, and in some cases, even honor, in other words, "a people like all others."[80]

Arendt's roots are not only historical; they may also be philosophical or literary. In "Creating a Cultural Atmosphere" Arendt offers some suggestions for reclaiming "a remarkably great number of authentic Jewish writers, artists and thinkers."[81] These efforts should in her view focus on two crucial pieces. The first is a question, perhaps philosophical, of how a traditional way of life makes room for or adapts itself to the new. She hopes that Jewish scholarship could offer "the first models for that new amalgamation of older traditions with new impulses and awareness."[82] Second, she aspires to "rescue . . . the Yiddish writers of Eastern Europe."[83] The reason for her optimism regarding a new Jewish culture is political and Palestine lies at the heart of it. Palestine can provide Jewish writers and artists with an audience but it also allows artists the opportunity to practice their craft—as Jews. In other words, the emergence of a Jewish culture would provide Jews the opportunity to learn and grow from the experiences of others; it also provides Jewish artists with the opportunity to achieve transcendence. In this way Arendt illustrates that historical, linguistic and even philosophical rootedness can be constructed in a human built world. She focuses on the political realities and while political solutions certainly cannot cure the modern problem of rootlessness, she holds out hope that political remedies might be able to facilitate a sense of being at home in the world.

CONCLUSION

Both Heidegger and Arendt are critics of modernity. They worry that philosophy may prove inadequate to the tasks of human existence in the contemporary world and they view rootlessness as one of the fundamental challenges of modern life. Heidegger's reliance on abstract categories, coupled with the shift in focus from the individual to a people leaves us with an uncritical acceptance of, and even a philosophical endorsement of, stereotypes.[84] Thus, Heidegger leaves us with two unsatisfactory possibilities for the role of *Mitdasein*. In the first, the notion of community plays very little role in *Dasein*'s search for authenticity. Instead, it draws *Dasein* away, toward its inauthentic self. In the second, the track to Being is laid down in the roots of one's homeland. In other words, *Dasein* finds her authentic self only by returning to her German or feminine essence.[85] The first approach renders us atomized individuals with no communal bonds to tether us. In terms of transcendence, it leaves each of us ensnared in our own isolated quest. While the second option leaves us with very limited agency in determining what constitutes an authentic project. Owing to the importance of language, the options tend to be nationalistic and tend to be limited to fulfilling stereotypical notions of destiny. With these two inadequate alternatives to define the roles available to the collective in our search for authenticity, Heidegger finds himself "trapped" in his own framework, trapped in the very notion of an essence.[86] His reliance on tradition and soil may well leave individuals unable to progress beyond stereotypical roles or nationalistic projects.

In grappling with both Heidegger's brilliance and his "banality"[87] Arendt offers two crucial correctives, both of which shift us in the direction of concrete rather than abstract categories. First, she locates the origin of a people squarely in the world, in "interests" which must be "represented."[88] Second, these interests derive from a phenomenological account of history, which should not only be contested but must be interpreted in light of the present, from multiple perspectives. Arendt views rootlessness as the metaphysical condition of not feeling connected in the world. Ultimately, Arendt turns to the political as a remedy and locates in the public sphere the possibility that a state could provide a group, not only with representation and protection, but also facilitate the development of culture, language and a sense of belonging. Arendt turns to the political because a human built world can facilitate an authentic existence. Arendt transforms Heidegger's anti-Semitic trope by suggesting that the aspiration of politics should be to ameliorate rootlessness and facilitate a sense of being at home in the world.

NOTES

1. Sander L. Gilman, "Cosmopolitan Jews v. Jewish Nomads: Sources of a Trope in Heidegger's *Black Notebooks*," in *Heidegger's Black Notebooks: Responses to Anti-Semitism*, eds. Andrew J. Mitchell and Peter Trawny (New York: Columbia University Press, 2017); Donatella Di Cesare, "Heidegger's Metaphysical Anti-Semitism," in *Reading Heidegger's Black Notebooks, 1931–1941*, eds. Ingo Farin and Jeff Malpas (Cambridge, MA: MIT Press, 2016).

2. Eduardo Mendieta, "Metaphysical Anti-Semitism and Worldlessness: On World Poorness, World Forming, and World Destroying," in *Heidegger's Black Notebooks: Responses to Anti-Semitism*, eds. Andrew J. Mitchell and Peter Trawny (New York: Columbia University Press, 2017), 41.

3. Martin Heidegger, *Ponderings VII–XI: Black Notebooks 1938–1939*, trans. Richard Rojcewicz (Bloomington: Indiana University Press, 2017), 75

4. Martin Heidegger, *Ponderings XII–XV: Black Notebooks 1938–1939*, trans. Richard Rojcewicz (Bloomington: Indiana University Press, 2017), 191

5. Peter Trawny, "The Universal and Annihilation: Heidegger's Being Historical Anti-Semitism," in *Heidegger's Black Notebooks: Responses to Anti-Semitism*, eds. Andrew J. Mitchell and Peter Trawny (New York: Columbia University Press, 2017); Peter Trawny, *Heidegger and the Myth of a Jewish World Conspiracy*, trans. Andrew J. Mitchell (Chicago: University of Chicago Press, 2016); Peter Trawny, "Heidegger, World Judaism, and Modernity," trans. Christopher Merwin, *Gatherings: The Heidegger Circle Annual* 5 (2015): 1–20.

6. Paul Farwell, "Can Heidegger's Craftsman be Authentic?" *International Philosophical Quarterly* 29 (1989): 77–90.

7. Martin Heidegger, *Being and Time*, trans. Joan Stambaugh (Albany, NY: SUNY Press, 1997), 18.

8. Ibid., 362.

9. Ibid., 368.

10. David Couzens Hoy, "History, Historicity and Historiography in *Being and Time*," in *Heidegger and Modern Philosophy*, ed. Michael Murray (New Haven, CT: Yale University Press, 1978), 347.

11. Heidegger, *Being and Time*, 115.

12. Heidegger, *Ponderings VII–XI*, 35.

13. Ibid.

14. Martin Heidegger, "Why Do I Stay in the Provinces?," in *Martin Heidegger: Philosophical and Political Writings*, ed. Manfred Stassen (New York: Continuum, 2003), 16.

15. Christopher Rickey, *Revolutionary Saints: Heidegger, National Socialism, and Antinomian Politics* (University Park, PA: Penn State University Press, 2001), 207.

16. Martin Heidegger, "The Origin of the Work of Art," in *Off the Beaten Path*, ed. and trans. Julian Young and Kenneth Haynes (Cambridge: Cambridge University Press, 2002).
17. Rickey, *Revolutionary Saints*, 207.
18. Hannah Arendt, "Action and the Pursuit of Happiness" (Hannah Arendt Manuscripts Collection, Library of Congress, 1960), 12.
19. Elisabeth Young-Bruehl, "Hannah Arendt's Storytelling," *Social Research* 44 (1977): 183.
20. Ibid.
21. Arendt, "Action and the Pursuit of Happiness," 6.
22. Seyla Benhabib, *The Reluctant Modernism of Hannah Arendt* (New York: Rowman & Littlefield, 2000), 93.
23. Ibid., 126.
24. Lisa J. Disch, "More Truth than Fact: Storytelling as Critical Understanding in the Writings of Hannah Arendt," *Political Theory* 21 (1993): 666; Lisa J. Disch, "Please Sit Down but Don't Make Yourself at Home: 'Visiting' and the Prefigurative Politics of Consciousness-Raising," in *Hannah Arendt and the Meaning of Politics*, eds. Craig Calhoun and John McGowan (Minneapolis: University of Minnesota Press, 1997), 132–65.
25. Disch, "More Truth than Fact," 667.
26. Martin Heidegger, "What Is Called, What Calls for, Thinking," in *Martin Heidegger: Philosophical and Political Writings*, ed. Manfred Stassen (New York: Continuum, 2003), 83.
27. Martin Heidegger, "Memorial Address," in *Discourse on Thinking*, trans. John M. Anderson and E. Hans Freud (New York: Harper and Row, 1966), 47.
28. Martin Heidegger, "Conversations on a Country Path About Thinking," in *Discourse on Thinking*, trans. John M. Anderson and E. Hans Freud (New York: Harper and Row, 1966), 68.
29. Ibid., 69.
30. Ibid.
31. Ibid.
32. Heidegger, "Memorial Address," 48–49.
33. Ibid., 46.
34. Heidegger, "The Origin of the Work of Art," 6.
35. Ibid., 30.
36. Ibid.
37. Heidegger, "Why Do I Stay in the Provinces?"
38. Heidegger, "Memorial Address," 53.
39. Ibid.
40. Ibid.
41. Ibid., 54.
42. Ibid., 55.
43. Ibid., 56.
44. Martin Heidegger, *Ponderings XII–XV: Black Notebooks 1939–1941*, trans. Richard Rojcewicz (Bloomington: Indiana University Press, 2017), 191; Di Cesare, "Heidegger's Metaphysical Anti-Semitism," 184–85; Gregory Fried finds the most troubling articulation in a lecture from 1933 ("The King is Dead: Martin Heidegger after the Black Notebooks," in *Reading Heidegger's Black Notebooks, 1931–1941*, eds. Ingo Farin and Jeff Malpas (Cambridge, MA: MIT Press, 2016), 53–54).
45. Hannah Arendt, *Life of the Mind: Thinking* (New York: Harcourt Brace, 1978), 5–6.
46. Benhabib, *The Reluctant Modernism of Hannah Arendt*, 93.
47. Hannah Arendt, *The Human Condition* (New York: Harcourt Brace, 1958), 76.
48. Arendt, *Life of the Mind: Thinking*, 188.
49. Hannah Arendt, "The Great Tradition and the Nature of Totalitarianism" (Hannah Arendt Manuscripts Collection, container #74, Library of Congress, 1953), 8.
50. Hannah Arendt, "Ideology and Terror: A Novel Form of Government," *Review of Politics* 15 (1953): 320.
51. Jeffrey C. Isaac, *Arendt, Camus and Modern Rebellion* (New Haven, CT: Yale University Press, 1992).
52. Ibid., 56.

53. Arendt, *Eichmann in Jerusalem*, 49.
54. Hannah Arendt, "Some Questions of Moral Philosophy," in *Responsibility and Judgment*, ed. Jerome Kohn (New York: Schocken Books, 2003), 101.
55. Arendt, *Eichmann in Jerusalem*, 49; Arendt, "Some Questions of Moral Philosophy," 112.
56. Heidegger, *Ponderings VII–XI*, 88.
57. Ibid.
58. Charles Bambach, *Heidegger's Roots: Nietzsche, National Socialism and the Greeks* (Ithaca, NY: Cornell University Press, 2005), 42.
59. Ibid.
60. Karsten Harries, "Nostalgia, Spite, and the Truth of Being," in *Reading Heidegger's Black Notebooks, 1931–1941*, eds. Ingo Farin and Jeff Malpas (Cambridge, MA: MIT Press, 2016), 208–9.
61. Ibid.
62. Jacques Taminiaux, *Poetics, Speculation and Judgment: The Shadow of the Work of Art from Kant to Phenomenology*, trans. and ed. Michael Gendre (Albany: State University of New York Press, 1993), 167.
63. Heidegger, "The Origin of the Work of Art," 21.
64. Ibid., 14; Meyer Shapiro, "The Still Life as a Personal Object—A Note on Heidegger and Van Gogh," *Theory and Philosophy of Art: Style, Artist and Society* (New York: George Braziller, 1994), 135–49.
65. Heidegger, "The Origin of the Work of Art," 14.
66. Hannah Arendt to Karl Jaspers, September 7, 1952, in *Hannah Arendt to Karl Jaspers Correspondence, 1926–1969*, eds. Lotte Kohler and Hans Saner, trans. Robert and Rita Kimber (New York: Harcourt Brace Jovanovich, 1992), 196–201.
67. In her letter to Gershom Scholem, regarding *Eichmann in Jerusalem*, Arendt clarifies her own roots—"I am not one of the 'intellectuals who come from the German Left' . . . I came late to an understanding of Marx's importance because I was interested neither in history nor politics when I was young. If I can be said to 'have come from anywhere,' it is from the tradition of German philosophy" (Hannah Arendt, "The Eichmann Controversy: A Letter to Gershom Scholem," in *The Jewish Writings*, eds. Jerome Kohn and Ron H. Feldman (New York: Schocken Books, 2007), 466).
68. Young-Bruehl, "Hannah Arendt's Storytelling," 183.
69. Hannah Arendt, *Origins of Totalitarianism* (New York: Harcourt Brace, 1951), 196.
70. Ibid.
71. Ibid., 73.
72. Arendt, "The Eichmann Controversy: A Letter to Gershom Scholem," 466.
73. Arendt, *Origins of Totalitarianism*, 236.
74. Ibid., 475.
75. Ibid., 459.
76. Hannah Arendt, "For the Honor and Glory of the Jewish People," in *The Jewish Writings*, eds. Jerome Kohn and Ron H. Feldman (New York: Schocken Books, 2007), 201.
77. Hannah Arendt, "Zionism Reconsidered," in *The Jewish Writings*, eds. Jerome Kohn and Ron H. Feldman (New York: Schocken Books, 2007), 357; Hannah Arendt, "Jewish Chances: Sparse Prospects, Divided Representation," in *The Jewish Writings*, eds. Jerome Kohn and Ron H. Feldman (New York: Schocken Books, 2007), 238.
78. Arendt, "For the Honor and Glory of the Jewish People."
79. Ibid., 201.
80. Arendt, "Zionism Reconsidered," 357.
81. Hannah Arendt, "Creating a Cultural Atmosphere," in *The Jewish Writings*, eds. Jerome Kohn and Ron H. Feldman (New York: Schocken Books, 2007), 300.
82. Ibid., 301.
83. Ibid.
84. This move, in and of itself, would have given philosophy much with which to contend, but Heidegger took it one step further by declaring a metaphysical people to be a political enemy.

85. Heidegger points Arendt toward her "innermost purest feminine essence" as a solution to her "disquiet" (Iain Thompson, "Thinking Love: Heidegger and Arendt," *Continental Philosophy Review* 50 (2017): 463; Martin Heidegger to Hannah Arendt, February 10, 1925, in *Hannah Arendt and Martin Heidegger: Letters, 1925–1975*, ed. Ursula Ludz, trans. Andrew Shields (New York: Harcourt, 2004), 3).

86. Hannah Arendt, "Heidegger the Fox," in *The Portable Hannah Arendt*, ed. Peter Baehr (New York: Penguin Books, 2000), 543–44.

87. Heidegger's use of euphemisms and philosophical jargon is part of the banalization and intellectual normalization of antisemitism (Jean Luc Nancy, *The Banality of Heidegger* (Minneapolis: University of Minnesota Press, 1991), 2–3).

88. Arendt, "Jewish Chances: Sparse Prospects, Divided Representation," 238.

Chapter Three

Concretizing Thrownness and Projection

Rahel Varnhagen

Hannah Arendt's work has often been noted for its methodological innovations, as well as, for challenging disciplinary boundaries. Moreover, applying labels or categories to Arendt has always been challenging. Though she was born a German-Jew and raised in a non-religious, leftist milieu, she denied that she was an assimilated Jew. She studied philosophy with some of the greatest German philosophers of the twentieth century, yet refused to claim for herself the label: philosopher. She told the stories of Rahel Varnhagen, Rosa Luxembourg and Isak Dinesen, smoked cigars with the boys and suggested that certain occupations were not very becoming to women. She strove to be an innovative thinker and in so doing published numerous, fascinating, insightful works, which are also difficult to categorize. Her biography of Rahel Varnhagen is one such text. There is a tendency in Arendtian scholarship to draw a line of demarcation between *Rahel Varnhagen* and *Origins of Totalitarianism* and to either ignore the earlier work or treat it as deeply perplexing and perhaps unsuccessful, at any rate divorced from her subsequent work.[1] This interpretation is particularly disappointing given that the importance of storytelling or visiting for Arendt has been well documented.[2] Moreover, this "peculiar biography"[3] is certainly not the only time Arendt uses vignettes to illustrate an abstract point. She weaves historically situated experiences, including those of Varnhagen, Benjamin Disraeli and Georges Clemenceau into *Origins of Totalitarianism*; in *Eichmann in Jerusalem*, she tells the stories of Werner Best, Zindel Grynszpan and Anton Schmidt.[4] Additionally, *Men in Dark Times* sets out to reveal the experiences of the few men and women whose lives offer insight and clarity despite the prevalence of double talk and "mere talk."[5] Finally, the central role played by duality in thinking, understanding and judgment is also well documented.[6] Arendt argues that modernity has obliterated any and all of the previous guideposts by which to understand and to judge our collective project of learning to share the earth. Moreover, some of our recent experiences, most notably totalitarianism and genocide, represent a fundamentally new and different experience in the political sphere, to which previously existing analytical categories do not apply.

In light of these two developments, standards by which to judge our collective experiences no longer exist and the absence of judgment has proven catastrophic, Arendt proffers an *experiential ontology*. In her view the question(s) of *being-with* can only be understood and judged with lived experiences as guideposts. Rahel's lived experiences illustrate both the danger of assimilation and the process by which an ontological struggle becomes political. Heidegger's fundamental ontology, replete with non-normative *existentials*, offers abstract categories which may illuminate the nature of being (i.e., provide paths in the woods), but his work does not contain standards by which to render judgment (pillars or guideposts, as Arendt calls them). Arendt draws on Heidegger's *existentials*, occasionally transforming them, adding to them or normatizing them, in order to facilitate judgment. The marginalization of *Varnhagen* in the Arendt corpus obscures her Heideggerian roots and ultimately renders the overarching purpose of and value of her work less readily discernible.

EXPLODING CATEGORIES[7]

The Varnhagen text purports to be a biography yet in many ways it deviates dramatically from the genre. Biographies tend to define "the individual and claim his or her importance,"[8] Arendt's biography is thoroughly enigmatic. The chronology is nebulous; numerous factual matters remain unclear. Tone is difficult to discern. If most biographers write admiringly of their subjects, Arendt's feelings about Varnhagen appear ambivalent. For these reasons among others, the overall message of the text remains obscure. Moreover, the secondary literature, far from clarifying, adds to the uncertainty. One thing, however, seems apparent: Arendt wrote this text in order to challenge certain assumptions about existing literary, philosophic and political categories. A precise understanding of the implicit criticisms and the resulting modifications to existing categories is more difficult to discern. Given that Arendt weaves together a multitude of criticisms, the task of this chapter is to disentangle those threads. In the process the Heideggerian nature of Arendt's undertaking will become evident.

One widespread point of agreement in the secondary literature regarding the Varnhagen text is that Arendt's sojourn into the biographical genre is undertaken not only in an effort to "narrate the story of Rahel's life" as she suggests in the preface,[9] but also to contest the genre itself. To contest the genre for what purpose and with what modifications, however, remains a point of considerable contention. Deborah Hertz argues that Arendt takes existentialism with her as she migrates from philosophy to history. In this text, according to Hertz, Arendt sides with the Romantics in a debate between romanticism and enlightenment regarding otherness because she finds in romanticism a precursor to existentialism. Hertz is correct that in many ways Arendt considered romanticism a precursor to existentialism and she certainly maintained many ties to existentialism throughout her career; however, that Arendt narrates the story of Varnhagen's life in order to celebrate "the Romantics' enthusiasm for the individual, for feelings, for friends, and for the irrational" is an untenable position in light of her subsequent comments regarding romanticism and introspection.[10]

Joanne Cutting-Gray, alternatively, suggests that Arendt offers a critique of both introspection and biography. First, she argues that Arendt views Varnhagen's introspection as an impediment to political action for her as an individual. Focusing on her own interiority "prevents her from becoming an identifiable agent who acts in the public world"; it does so in part because "[h]er interiority nihilates others, turns them into nonbeings in a kind of negative ontology."[11] Moreover, biographies which focus on "boundless interiority" are detrimental to the public sphere.[12] They "illuminate only the singular personality removed from a public world."[13] Alternatively, Arendt attempts to carve out a niche for biography in the public realm. The value of biography lies in utilizing an individual life to illuminate an historical moment. Biographies can reveal "the historical period in question" better than "all but the most outstanding history books."[14] Similarly, Julia Kristeva and Martine Leibovici find a larger and enduring purpose behind Arendt's flirtation with biography. They argue that Arendt uses Varnhagen, following Kant's notion of exemplary validity, to make the pariah/parvenu distinction sensible. In other words, Arendt ventures into the biographical genre in order that Varnhagen's experiences may provide a standard by which Jewish *existence* can be understood and judged.[15]

In an attempt to uncover the intent behind or the overarching message of Arendt's biography, many have sought to reveal Arendt's feelings about Varnhagen, an attitude not easily discernible from the text itself. Several critics, including Karl Jaspers, commented on the ambivalent tone in Arendt's text. Jaspers described the treatment of Varnhagen as "loveless" whereas Sybille Bedford uses the phrase "curiously oppressive."[16] Subsequent attempts at analysis have offered similarly contradictory portraits. Deborah Hertz finds in Arendt's text an "empathetic portrait" while Julia

Kristeva argues that Arendt seems to approach Varnhagen with contempt, mocking her frequently, almost as if she were "settling a score with . . . an alter ego."[17] Seyla Benhabib describes Arendt's role as "bearing testimony to a political and spiritual transformation" while Martine Leibovici offers the possibility that Arendt is taking up "the other's point of view," which will later become the cornerstone of political engagement.[18]

It is reasonably clear that Arendt attempts to flesh out Lazare's conceptual distinction between a pariah and a parvenu. However, there is no consensus in the secondary literature regarding the category into which she places Rahel. Hertz believes that Arendt holds Varnhagen up as an example of a conscious pariah, though Hertz finds conscious parvenu to be a more apt description. Kristeva suggests that Varnhagen ventures through life first as a pariah, then as a parvenu before finally adopting the role of conscious pariah; whereas Judith Shklar views Varnhagen as living virtually her entire life as a parvenu.[19] This ambivalence is easily explicable, however, once we recognize that Lazare's conceptual scheme is not the only one working in the background of Arendt's text. Heidegger looms larger since in many respects Lazare's notions of the pariah/parvenu stretch existential concerns with authenticity into the political realm. Thus, in order to unravel the threads of this particular story, we must first recognize that Arendt's understanding of how one orients oneself in the world owes much to the Heideggerian notion of the self as *being-in-the-world*. But first, who was Rahel Varnhagen and why did Hannah Arendt tell her story?

RAHEL VARNHAGEN

Rahel Varnhagen, virtually unknown in the United States, was born, Rahel Levin, in Berlin in 1771, to a Jewish diamond merchant. Her father was a wealthy man who did not educate his daughters and left all his money to his sons. After her mother died, Levin was entirely dependent upon her brothers. She grew up in Berlin in the 1790s a time when the spirit of the French Revolution drew together the ideals of the Enlightenment and Romanticism held out the brief, if fleeting, hope "that one could—out of the materials of one's own particular mind and soul—literally create one's own life."[20] Traditional constraints of class, wealth and education ostensibly gave way to originality and personality. In this atmosphere, intellectuals (Hegel, Goethe, Schlegel, and Humboldt) and noblemen flocked to Jewish salons. Levin was bright but uneducated, insightful yet not predictable, she "never had a memorized formula ready. . . . She lived in no particular order of the world . . . her wit could unite the most incongruous things, in the most intimately unified things it could discern incongruities."[21] Therein lies the source of her originality and, for Arendt, the allure of her salon. Moreover, this lack of formal education allowed her to reveal her journey from parvenu to pariah, from rootless Jewess to political actor.

Levin fell in love with and became engaged to Count von Finckenstein. Though the engagement lasted several years, it ended around 1800. By 1806, the Napoleonic wars were in full swing; antisemitism had resurfaced. Salons ceased, almost overnight, to provide a social opportunity for Jews and Gentiles to interact. Levin's salon was finished, as was her second engagement to a Gentile. From the mistress of the most notable salon in Berlin, she became persona non grata. "The aristocratic men who had fallen in love with her bold and striking manner in *Jagerstrasse* now disavowed her in public, the women who had made a confidant of her crossed the street when they saw her coming."[22] Levin endured several failed love affairs before converting, marrying Karl August Varnhagen and changing her name in 1814. Karl Varnhagen achieved a certain amount of success during the war. Hence in some respects Rahel's attempts at assimilation were ultimately successful, for her individually. In assuming Prussian citizenship, she was able to eliminate any trace of her "infamous birth."[23] The Varnhagens returned to Berlin after the war and she resumed her place amidst the literati at the center of the Goethe cult. However, the point of undertaking a biography of Varnhagen, for Arendt, is not to ask whether assimilation succeeded in general. "In light of its risks and necessity" Arendt characterizes such questions as "idle." Nor is the point to judge Rahel's individual success. Rather the "course of her life" is described by Arendt as exemplary (perhaps in the Kantian sense) precisely because the situation, her plight was not "hers alone."[24] Hence Arendt sought to narrate Varnhagen's story "as she herself might have told it."[25] Rahel's extraordinary penchant for relaying her experiences to others opens a window into the life of a first generation assimilated Jewess. Though Varnhagen assimilates in many conventional ways, she also maintains the perspective of outsider. Thus, she beautifully illustrates the challenges of thrownness and falling prey while simultaneously projecting herself toward her ownmost-potentiality-of-being.

HEIDEGGER AND *EXISTENZ* IN UNDERSTANDING *RAHEL VARNHAGEN*

Existenz philosophy attempts to identify a series of traits or characteristics (existentials) that distinguish human beings from animals or inanimate objects. In other words, Heidegger sets out to identify the elements of a uniquely human existence. For Heidegger, *Dasein* exists in the world with the potential to understand his or her own uniqueness, which derives in part from his or her individual place in the world. The primary way that we can understand Dasein's situation in the world is that *Dasein*'s mode of being is one of care (*Sorge*).[26] Its primary orientation in the world must be understood as comprising three integral parts: *thrownness, falling prey* and *projectivity*.[27] *Thrownness* refers to the fact that we find ourselves as beings in the world in ways that are not of our own making or choosing and which may restrict not only our ability to choose[28] but also our ability to really "live" which is to say, our prospects of achieving transcendence.[29] Thrownness is characterized by a profound lack of agency and in many cases reveals the socio-political limitations of agency in a particular historical context.[30] Thrownness refers to individual characteristics—physical, social or intellectual capacities which condition our manner of being-with others in the world. *Thrownness* intrudes upon the present from the past. Moreover, one's individuality is constituted in the present from the thrownness of the past, if not necessarily Dasein's own individual past.[31] There is vulnerability inherent in and revealed by *thrownness*, which is the only component of Dasein's mode of being which is almost entirely past in its temporal orientation. *Falling prey* or *fallenness* is the present experience which arises out of the "throw of thrownness."[32]

Falling prey or *fallenness* involves a move away from authenticity or transcendence toward an everyday mode of taking care of things. Heidegger refers to the collective or public realm that lures Dasein away from transcendence and the search for an authentic selfhood as the "they": an amorphous, collective blob characterized by preoccupation with mundane trivialities. It is not an event which can "befall Dasein like an accident,"[33] but rather it is a mode of *being in the world*, which is to say it is an omnipresent, fundamental characteristic of the way we engage with others. Our manner of *being-with* is conditioned by the constant possibility and high probability of being seduced by the everyday, by the pressing need to take care of things, complete tasks, by the appeal of idle chatter and material objects. In Heideggerian terminology, we are constantly at risk of succumbing to the "they" (*das Man*). It is a movement away from our "ownmost potentiality-of-being," away from self-understanding and transcendence. Heidegger describes this movement as both seductive and tranquilizing, which suggests that this form of self-estrangement is accompanied by a sensation of exhilaration or calm reassurance.[34] Falling prey is the present experience which impedes Dasein's future prospects of genuine self-disclosure and self-understanding. *Project* or *existence* is the component of care which is futural in its orientation. Projectivity occurs when *Dasein*, from its state of fallenness, undertakes a forward motion toward "its ownmost potentiality-of-being."[35] Authentic *Dasein* acts with agency, if not necessarily planning or forethought, in an effort to transcend its own thrownness and overcome fallenness. The futurally oriented motion associated with projection comprises "the very essence of freedom," authenticity and transcendence for Heidegger.[36]

One way of reading Arendt is as attempting to humanize Heidegger, which is to say, as grounding Heideggerian concepts in a historically located body. Though rootlessness clearly is not limited to the twentieth century, nor is it uniquely Jewish. Rootlessness, for Heidegger, represents the collective manifestation of fallenness. Understood in this way, Arendt's "peculiar biography" of Rahel Varnhagen becomes far more than an idiosyncratic or self-revelatory work.[37] Rather, it can be understood as an ontological examination of rootlessness in which Arendt humanizes fundamental ontology by illustrating thrownness, fallenness and projectivity, as well as the political implications of each, at work in the life of Rahel Varnhagen. Moreover, we begin to see Arendt's own approach to roots, as Varnhagen ultimately tethers herself not to a place, but to people and becomes a political actor. While Arendt herself is, obviously, at home in the world of philosophical abstraction, she also recognizes the elitism inherent in fundamental ontology, and the pedagogical value of storytelling.[38] In what follows I argue that *Rahel Varnhagen* should be read as an examination of three of Heidegger's most political concepts: *thrownness*, *fallenness* and *projectivity*. In undertaking an examination of Varnhagen's life, Arendt "thickly constitutes" *thrownness*, *fallenness* and *projectivity*; reveals the ontological core of rootlessness, as well as, the political implications of fallenness and projectivity. Moreover, since Heidegger would reject the very notion of a case study, favoring instead the examination of the mode of being of a being, *Rahel Varnhagen* also serves a critique of fundamental ontology, in which Arendt both draws on Heideggerian concepts and reveals the limitations of his approach. In so doing, she draws attention to the value of lived experiences and charts for herself a new course, an *experiential ontology*.

THROWNNESS (*GEWORFENHEIT*)

The experience of thrownness in the world occurs when one's unique set of physical, intellectual and socio-historical (i.e., ontic) characteristics intrudes upon present experiences and, in so doing, limits future prospects of achieving transcendence. Thrownness reveals that the human being "is always already in a definite world and together with . . . definite innerworldly beings."[39] Thrownness refers to immutable traits. According to Heidegger, "Dasein, as long as it is what it is, remains in the throw and is sucked into the eddy of the they's inauthenticity."[40] In other words, the challenge presented by the social value associated with these immutable traits draws us away from our own authentic selves toward the inauthentic temptations of everyday life. Thrownness can consist of all facets of existence which limit one's ability to choose and act in a particular socio-historical context. In Varnhagen's case her throw consisted primarily of her Jewishness, gender and her financial dependence on her brothers. Her letters beautifully illustrate the intrusion of thrownness into her choices. As Heidegger says, as long as

Dasein exists, she "remains in the throw." Her gender and Jewishness are utterly inescapable elements of her existence and they condition her relations with other beings-in-the-world. Moreover, the rather severe restrictions imposed by the throw presented her with the constant temptation of many different types of fallenness, as we shall soon see.[41]

Varnhagen, herself, offers an insightful description of thrownness in a letter to David Veit, a friend and medical student.

> I have a strange fantasy: it is as if some supramundane being, just as I was thrust into this world, plunged these words, with a dagger into my heart: 'Yes, have sensibility, see the world as few see it, be great and noble, nor can I take from you the faculty of eternal thinking. But I add one more thing: be a Jewess!' And now my life is a slow bleeding to death.[42]

Among the things that fascinate Arendt about Varnhagen are her extraordinary insight and her ability to relay her insights through prose. In reflecting upon her own despair, she beautifully captures the Heideggerian notion of thrownness, which encompasses ethnicity, gender and also intellectual capacities. Moreover, the image of a slow, painful death not only forces the reader to empathize with her plight but also anticipates the source of angst. This quotation is a classic illustration of romanticism and illustrates Hertz's contention that romanticism serves as a precursor to existentialism. It is clearly Varnhagen's introspection and preoccupation with her own emotions that enables her to make such an astute observation. At the same time, the exclusively self-referential nature of her reflections is certainly an approach that Arendt would find troubling, thus rendering Hertz's conclusion that Arendt sides with the Romantics and celebrates "feelings . . . friends, and . . . the irrational" dubious at best.[43]

Arendt's Heideggerian roots are so transparent that at several points in the text the term—throw—is used to describe the intrusion of Varnhagen's Jewishness into her present circumstances. In discussing her penchant for self-thinking, Arendt writes, "[n]o human being can isolate himself completely; he will always be thrown back upon the world again if he has any hopes at all for the things that only the world can give."[44] In this case the throw is clearly something that befalls the unfortunate shlemihl. Additionally, her criticism of Varnhagen's introspection becomes glaringly apparent. While there are undoubtedly benefits to self-thinking and Varnhagen's self-awareness and uncanny ability to communicate in a genuine, self-revealing manner is certainly among those benefits, introspection is not a solution. The creation of a fantasy life does not allow her to escape her Jewishness because as Arendt notes, she "will always be *thrown* back upon the world again."[45] Denial or avoidance, whether self-delusion or erasure of outward signs, never allows an individual to escape his or her *thrownness*, hence part of Arendt's critique of assimilation is simply that it can only fail and that failure exacerbates the already unavoidable tendency toward *fallenness*.

Finckenstein is also caught in the throw. In his case, the throw consists of the nobility of his birth and the class based expectations that accompany his status. Just as Varnhagen finds herself in the world as a Jewess; Finckenstein, similarly, was thrust into the world, as a Count. His status affected, not only the way he encountered himself, but also the way he engaged with others in the world. Arendt portrays Varnhagen as possessing a remarkable insight into the existential nature of Finckenstein's dilemma. The class structure in which he took comfort "evaporated like a phantasm" in the context of Varnhagen's salon and he stood revealed in "all his nullity."[46] Disturbed by this experience, he returned to his family and to the comfort of the noble rank that insulated him against genuine self-disclosure. From the perspective of Romanticism, Varnhagen viewed class as constraining Finckenstein in much the same way her Jewishness constrained her. As Arendt puts it, "[c]onsiderations of class seemed to her merely fetters from which she must free him, from which he ought to free himself."[47] In other words, the emphasis which Romanticism placed on individuality and self-thinking allowed her to anticipate the subsequent emergence of existentialism, if Heidegger was the last Romantic, perhaps Rahel Varnhagen was the first existentialist.[48]

FALLING PREY (*VERFALLENHEIT*)

Since one of the definitive characteristics of human beings, for Heidegger, is that human beings always exist in the world with others, *being-in-the-world* is always *being-with*, in Heideggerian phraseology. Existence is characterized by the constant temptation to succumb to idle chatter, worldly objects and the tranquilizing effect of the everyday. Far from a definitive event or single occurrence, falling prey or fallenness constitute a consistent temptation for humans in the world. As such we can see multiple illustrations of the seduction of the everyday and Varnhagen succumbed to many of them. Yet despite repeatedly falling prey, she managed to maintain a self-revealing mode which ultimately enables her to transcend her own fallenness. Given that, for existentialists, falling prey and projectivity represent the quintessential human struggle, Varnhagen's route to her authentic self and finally to political action is of considerable interest to Arendt.

Varnhagen's propensity to engage in gossip and idle chatter was well documented and constituted a classic example of fallenness. Everyday life provides a multitude of opportunities to engage in a less than authentic or self-disclosive mode of idle chit chat. Gustav von Brinckmann, the Swedish ambassador, once said of Rahel, "[s]he came, she talked and conquered."[49] Moreover, the salon exemplified the inherent duality in Dasein between fallenness and projectivity. Her gender and Jewishness imposed limits on her "ability to choose" in socio-political context. The salon, to some degree, presented an opportunity to overcome that thrownness, yet even the salon, complete with its rejection of various social norms, was characterized by the "double structure" of the human experience.[50] Seeking to transcend the context in which she finds herself, uneducated, without recourse to employment or political rights, Varnhagen embraces the brief opportunity to entertain notables and make a name for herself in the salon. Yet even within this educated milieu, the seduction of the idle chatter exerts a powerful force. The salons, in part because they flaunted the rejection of social mores, were also noted for the gossip, intrigue and sexual promiscuity. Her many love affairs also represent the triumph of the everyday. Her preoccupation with romance tempted her with physical pleasure in lieu of authenticity. It was a temptation to which she routinely succumbed.

> Ever since she had met Gentz, reality had been tempting her again. Since she had seen that pleasure need not be merely a lovely parenthesis in life, pleasure had begun to exert a strong attraction upon her. Suddenly she no longer wanted to be merely a theatre for the actions of others; she wanted to have her share also, to take part. She no longer desired something extraordinary, a great love, or marriage to a nobleman, but the natural, everyday experience that was accessible to almost everyone. She wanted to take this handsome Spaniard as Gentz had taken his beautiful actress.[51]

The euphoria associated with a new romance can certainly keep angst at bay, albeit temporarily. It is often in a subsequent state of despair that Varnhagen makes her most insightful observations.

The ultimate illustration of fallenness clearly arises from her conversion, marriage to Karl August Varnhagen and her subsequent Prussian citizenship. With her newfound citizenship, Varnhagen not only achieved financial security, but she rid herself of any trace of "her 'infamous birth' . . . she was simply the wife of the Prussian *charge d'affaires*."[52] Arendt notes that "it had been necessary to run away from home in order to cast off her origins and all those who knew about these origins."[53] She is clearly and repeatedly seduced by the inauthentic. In fact, she spends most of her time engaged in idle chatter, gossip and seeking escape through marriage. In short, she exemplifies the Heideggerian notion of fallenness. At the same time, Varnhagen offers an extraordinarily vivid depiction of the "they" and the temptation of falling prey. In a letter to Alexander von Marwitz, a Prussian junker, she captured the "they." "Yesterday . . . I was swept by such a queer mood . . . the people . . . seemed all frighteningly strange . . . not one of them had a face, a physiognomy; the silliest, most superficial, most wooden, most distracted expression."[54]

She, subsequently, went on relate her own role in the strange scene and to illustrate the role of the pariah. She was both part of the doomed collective and yet she also stood apart. "I among them, still more unrelated, with full, empty heart, as if I stood before a temple of magic—for the soul still had enough life in it to make reality vanish—a temple I can already see swaying; its collapse is certain and it will inevitably come down on me and everyone else."[55] She stands "among them" yet "still more unrelated." The doom she foresees could be that of German Jewry or the temple, whose collapse she predicts, may represent the Enlightenment. Though Varnhagen predicts the impending destruction, she also realizes that it is possible neither to prevent this collapse nor to escape it. Herein lies the unique challenge of the pariah—to serve as social critic, rejected, yet still self-revealing.

According to Arendt, this vision represents the beginning of her transition to political actor. In this moment, Varnhagen became cognizant of the fact that her "despair was no longer her own private affair."[56] Rather her personal despair was predestined by social forces and precipitated by political events. Her friendship with the similarly doomed, Marwitz, prompted her to see her individual angst "as the specific misfortune of having been born in the wrong place, assigned by history to a doomed world"[57] that of German Jews of the Enlightenment. Moreover, Arendt reveals the powerful temptation exerted by fallenness exists in a desire to belong which can fend off, albeit only fleetingly, angst and despair. "If the collapse crushed her (Rahel) along with everyone else, she would achieve belonging, even though only as a part of a general ruin."[58] With this sentence, Arendt encapsulates Rahel's destiny, the fate of German Jewry and the experience of falling prey all in a single sentence. The powerful temptation of belonging to the "they" can only draw her toward the destruction of German Jews, as the profound pull of the "they" leads Dasein to greater and greater despair. Yet despite the rather pervasive nature of the inauthentic in her experience, she finally overcomes her self-estrangement, takes herself up as a project and even engages in an Arendtian form of action. It is Varnhagen's progression from an inauthentic (*parvenu*) to an authentic self (*pariah*), politically aware and captures Arendt's attention.

PROJECTIVITY (*ENTWERFEN*)

The fundamental tension of human existence for Heidegger, lies in the duality of Dasein as simultaneously fallen and projecting. As a being always in the throw, always vulnerable to and constrained by his or her own thrownness, Dasein is always both falling prey to the everyday and projecting him or herself toward his or her ownmost potentiality. Arendt's interest in narrating Varnhagen's life derives, in part, from the poignant manner in which she depicts her own thrownness, but additionally from her vivid and poetic descriptions of her own projectivity. In other words, Varnhagen conveys not only her own despair but also her, ultimately successful, efforts to move forward from a position of fallenness toward her own transcendence. She begins in the letter to Marwitz to recognize the simultaneous power, appeal and vacuity of the "they." Each of her letters can be viewed as projecting, in the Heideggerian sense. The letters themselves represent attempts to make sense of her own feelings, milieu, opportunities or lack thereof. The attempt to understand, particularly if accompanied by a genuine self-disclosure is necessarily projecting; it represents movement that is directed toward some future aim. Projectivity is closely linked to the life of the pariah, in so far as it involves a decision to step outside of social convention and embrace one's own uniqueness despite potentially unpleasant social consequences. Varnhagen engages in projecting early in her life, and though these efforts do not have any explicitly political value, they are precursors of Arendtian action.

As a young girl, she expressed discomfort when visiting her poor relatives in the East. "She was welcomed to the affair as if the Grand Sultan were entering a long neglected seraglio. And she added promptly: 'This made me ashamed.'"[59] In recognizing the double edged sword of assimilation, Varnhagen set herself apart not only from "the dark mass of the people" but also the far more necessary solidarity with the tiny group of Prussian 'exception Jews' from whom she sprang and whose destiny she shared."[60] She rejected not only the social conventions that cast her in a negative light but also those that established her exceptionalism. Moreover, in a subsequent letter, again to Veit, Varnhagen demonstrates a willingness to not only defy social conventions of the day, but also to deny the legitimacy of unacknowledged, unaccepted, uninternalized facts: "Facts mean nothing to me, for whether true or not, facts can be denied; if I have done something, I did it because I wanted to; and if someone wants to blame me or call me a liar, there's nothing for me to do but say 'No,' and I do."[61] Varnhagen's isolation in thought or reason led her to create a fantasy world for herself in which she could deny her Jewishness as an individual and deny the limitations imposed on her by society as a result of both her Jewishness and her gender. Though Arendt repeatedly expressed concern with introspection and Varnhagen's propensity for creating a fantasy world in which she could deny her Jewishness, the status of pariah also requires a bold spirit in the face of oppressive social conventions, which she certainly exhibits. This bold spirit, which Arendt celebrates, bears a striking resemblance to the Heideggerian notion of resoluteness.

Some have interpreted the fact that she does not marry Finckenstein as his rejection of her and he certainly did pull away, leaving her devastated. However, this interpretation does not square with Arendt's view.[62] In Arendt's version, it is Varnhagen who rejected Finckenstein; she told him that in order for them to find happiness together, he would have to "[b]e something and I will recognize you." She decided not to pursue him at this critical moment. According to Arendt, Finckenstein was waiting for her "to pull him to her" when *she* "suddenly gave ground, abandoned the struggle, declared that he must decide for himself."[63] Arendt argues that Varnhagen probably could have married him despite his family's objections, so strong was the influence she had over him yet she ultimately realized "the price she would have to pay" and instead, told him to make his own decision.[64] Arendt does not say explicitly what price she would have to pay. One can, however, infer that since Finckenstein probably represented her best chance to assimilate through marriage and Arendt argues that "it is possible to assimilate only by assimilating to anti-Semitism";[65] she may be suggesting that Varnhagen began to realize at this point that the marriage to Finckenstein would require an element of self-negation. Though her message is a bit ambiguous, she certainly felt that Varnhagen abandoned the fight to marry Finckenstein at a critical juncture, simultaneously abandoning social convention, respectability, wealth, status and opted to move through the world on her own talents.[66] It is certainly not clear that this choice was an entirely conscious one. Still one detects a certain amount of admiration in Arendt's ironic tone as she notes that Varnhagen's "fatal error" lay in "requir[ing] her lover to be an individual, to amount to something."[67] In short, the decision to abandon the fight for Finckenstein represents an act of courage and rejection of social conventions, if not necessarily a conscious or deliberately political one.

Varnhagen's inner conflict, the "double structure" of identity struggle is perhaps most eloquently revealed in a letter she wrote to a friend, in the later years of her life, in which she offered the friend some apparently contradictory advice. She first advised the friend as to how one could rid oneself of any trace Jewishness: change her name, be baptized, and have her children baptized. Additionally, she counseled her friend that it was important to adopt the customs and culture of the class to which she wished to belong. Immediately after offering her friend sage advice regarding assimilation, Varnhagen switched her tact and warned the friend "not to be ashamed of Jewish birth" and even if she succeeded in erasing all trace of her Jewish heritage "always to aid the wretched survivals." She both offered assimilation advice and suggested the path of a conscious pariah.[68] Moreover toward the end of her life, she began to actively encourage friends and family to forgo assimilation and work for political rights, since [f]reedom and equality were not going to be conjured into existence by individuals' capturing them by fraud as privileges for themselves."[69] Thus ultimately, Varnhagen, without money, education or political rights became a political actor. She is one of the exemplary few of whom Arendt speaks when she says "even in the darkest of times we have the right to expect some illumination, and that illumination may well come less from theories and concepts than from the uncertain, flickering and often weak light that some men and women in their lives and their work, will kindle."⁷⁰

Arendt tells the story of Rahel's life in order to reveal this "uncertain, flickering" light. Varnhagen came, in her lifetime, to understand the dangers of assimilation and the importance of action. In telling her story, Arendt concretizes Heideggerian concepts, examines the ontological core of rootlessness and attempts to ground ontology in the world, which is to say, she offers a political ontology, grounded in the lived experiences of real people. She illustrates the political and social importance of thrownness and fallenness, as well as offers a guide to how an individual in the throw, in the process of falling prey, can take herself up as a project and resolutely undertake forward motion toward an authentic existence. She ultimately projects herself forward out of her fallenness through genuine self-disclosure and by remaining open to the self-disclosure of others. Her openness when combined with the relentless pursuit of understanding allows her to kindle an uncertain and flickering light which can be used to illuminate not only the plight of the German Jews, but marginalization as a social and political phenomenon. Her experiences allow Arendt to demonstrate, following Heidegger, that thrownness and fallenness constitute the ontological core of rootlessness. Moreover, she asserts, contra Heidegger, that projection leads to action since the public realm is "the unique locus of an 'authentic' *Existenz*."⁷¹

ARENDT'S *EXPERIENTIAL ONTOLOGY*

In accepting the Lessing Prize in 1959, Arendt referenced Lessing's standards for judging art with admiration. He was "either unable or unwilling to judge a work of art 'in itself,' independent of its effect in the world."⁷² For Lessing and Broch, as well, artistic, political and scientific pursuits are neither mutually exclusive activities nor are they separable from one another, since an aspiration of truth and understanding lie at the core of all three pursuits. Broch, she argues, demanded of "literature that it possess the same compelling validity as science" and "summon into being the 'totality of the world.'"⁷³ If we are to apply the Lessing standard to philosophy, hence to Heidegger's work, Arendt's apparently contradictory assessments of Heidegger become easily explicable. According to this proposition, an assessment of Heidegger's fundamental ontology in the world (particularly if *the world* is conceptualized in Arendtian terms, which is to say, as the "irreplaceable in-between which should have formed between this individual and his fellow men") should generate some ambivalence. In this formulation, art for art's sake is utterly nonsensical. Arendt seems to have reached a similar conclusion with respect to philosophy: that philosophizing, devoid of an examination of the collective implications or its implications for the public sphere, is dangerous and irresponsible. She takes issue with the attempt to understand *Dasein* in isolation and in the abstract, since human beings exist neither in isolation, nor in the abstract.

Jacques Taminaux is most likely correct to suggest that Arendt's feelings for Martin Heidegger shift fairly dramatically over the course of their relationship and the ebb and flow of their personal relationship affected her assessment of his work.[74] Yet despite the fluctuation in tenor from the bitter "What is Existenz Philosophy?" to the mocking "Heidegger the Fox," to the laudatory "Martin Heidegger at Eighty," the fact remains that whatever the tone of her assessment, the content of her critique remains fairly consistent. Whatever her personal or professional feelings about Heidegger, her regard for his contributions to philosophy never waivered. Moreover, she shared many of his deep and abiding concerns about modern life. She found extraordinary insight in his description of the problems, be it his critique of metaphysics or his analysis of the "they." Yet she also consistently worried about his judgment. In particular, she expressed concern about the way he deployed his perspicacious concepts in the world, particularly in the context of political or social power. For example, Arendt shared Heidegger's concern with the role of rootlessness in modern life. She even concurred that rootlessness was an issue facing the Jewish community. Yet in using rootlessness to justify intellectual antisemitism, Heidegger takes an astute description of modern life and uses it, uncritically, as a prescription for political action. Abstract analysis, regardless of how insightful and illuminating, rarely translates into a simple prescription for action in the political realm. Herein lies Arendt's deep and abiding skepticism of philosophy, in general. Any philosophical insights, even when extraordinary in their descriptive value, become prescriptive only at considerable risk. Arendt prefers, on the other hand, to use lived experiences in their historical context to serve, not as a prescription for the future, but as cautionary tales.

In the context of this assessment, Arendt offers through her unique biography of Rahel Varnhagen, an experiential ontology. Her letters demonstrate both the limits of reason as a political concept, and also that neither education nor abstract thought predisposes one to *Existenz*. Since Varnhagen views herself as engaging in a rational process and indeed there is something understandable, perhaps even reasonable in much of her thought process, it also literally leads her to a disastrous outcome, namely assimilation. Thus Arendt's *experiential ontology* demonstrates, contra Kant, that reason cannot be an ideal manner of engaging in the world if it leads to results which make it impossible to be in the world. The letters also demonstrate that an individual's ability to comprehend her own *Existenz* and act in the world does not require education, abstract thinking, nor a deep understanding of philosophy. The possibility of making sense of the world and one's unique place in it lies within the grasp of individuals, if like Varnhagen, they continually seek disclosure and self-revealing. Thus, Arendt notes that Rahel's "whole effort was to expose herself to life so that it could strike her 'like a storm without an umbrella.'"[75] Moreover, she wrote to Karl Jaspers that Varnhagen's willingness to allow life to strike her made her both unique and insufferable.[76] The unfiltered revelation of one's experiences and reactions lends her correspondence a certain authenticity. This openness, rather than knowledge, status or intellect, allows her to achieve that which eludes both Heidegger and Eichmann: authentic selfhood. This openness to a self-revealing dialogue allows her to evolve from preoccupation with her own romantic exploits concerned with political plight of Jews. In short, Varnhagen's self-disclosure allows her ultimately to transcend her thrownness and to emerge as a political actor.

By drawing on the Heideggerian existentials (thrownness, fallenness and projectivity) in the Varnhagen text, Arendt locates these concepts at work in an individual life set in socio-historical context and uses them to illuminate, not only Varnhagen's personal struggle but the predicament of German Jews. Any subsequent notion of political ontology must, therefore, be grounded in lived experiences and only as such can it hope to illuminate political events. Far from rejecting philosophy, Arendt merely admonishes that as a matter of political prescription, philosophical categories can be used only with the utmost circumspection. Arendt's experiential ontology transforms fundamental ontology from its, at best, apolitical and, at worst, anti-political orientation to its rightful place as the cornerstone of the political; since as she makes clear in *The Human Condition*, one's manner of being in the world is of the utmost importance in the public sphere. By grounding her politically responsible ontology in the lived experiences of the everyday, Arendt both democratizes thought and renders both evil and heroism attainable to common folk, as we shall see.

NOTES

1. Adam Kirsch ("Beware of Pity," *The New Yorker*, January 12, 2009, 64) describes *Rahel Varnhagen* as the "orphan in the Arendt canon."

2. Liliane Weissberg, "Hannah Arendt, Rahel Varnhagen and Writing of (Auto)biography," in *Rahel Varnhagen: The Life of a Jewess*, ed. Liliane Weissberg (Baltimore, MD: Johns Hopkins University Press, 1997), 3–69; Lisa J. Disch, "More Truth than Fact: Storytelling as Critical Understanding in the Writings of Hannah Arendt," *Political Theory* 21 (1993): 665–94; Lisa J. Disch, "Please Sit Down but Don't Make Yourself at Home: 'Visiting' and the Prefigurative Politics of Consciousness-Raising," in *Hannah Arendt and the Meaning of Politics*, eds. Craig Calhoun and John McGowan (Minneapolis: University of Minnesota Press, 1997), 132–65; Ernst Vollrath, "Hannah Arendt and the Method of Political Thinking," *Social Research* 44 (1977): 160–82; David Luban, "Explaining Dark Times: Hannah Arendt's Theory of Theory," *Social Research* 50 (1983): 215–47.

3. Joanne Cutting-Gray, "Hannah Arendt's *Rahel Varnhagen*," *Philosophy and Literature* 15 (1991): 229.

4. Hannah Arendt, *Origins of Totalitarianism* (New York: Harcourt Brace, 1958), 59–61, 68–79, 105–20; Hannah Arendt, *Eichmann in Jerusalem: A Report on the Banality of Evil* (New York: Viking Press, 1963), 173–75, 228–30, 230–32.

5. Hannah Arendt, *Men in Dark Times* (New York: Harcourt Brace, 1968), vii–x.

6. Leibovici suggests that Arendt is taking up the "other's point of view" or imagining "the world as it might appear to that person" (Martine Leibovici, "Arendt's *Rahel Varnhagen*: A New Kind of Narration in the Impasses of German-Jewish Assimilation and *Existenzphilosophie*," *Social Research* 74 (2007): 907).

7. Arendt uses this phrase in a discussion of totalitarianism, she asserts that the acts associated with totalitarianism have "exploded our categories of political thought" (Hannah Arendt, "Understanding and Politics," in *Essays in Understanding, 1930–1954*, ed. Jerome Kohn (New York: Schocken Books, 1994), 310.

8. Weissberg, "Hannah Arendt, Rahel Varnhagen and Writing of (Auto)biography," 8.

9. Hannah Arendt, *Rahel Varnhagen: The Life of a Jewess*, ed. Liliane Weissberg (Baltimore, MD: Johns Hopkins University Press, 1997), 81.

10. Deborah Hertz, "Hannah Arendt's *Rahel Varnhagen*," in *German Women in the Nineteenth Century: A Social History*, ed. John C. Fout (New York: Holmes and Meier, 1984), 77. Hannah Arendt, "What is Existenz Philosophy?" *Partisan Review* 13 (1946): 34–56.

11. Cutting-Gray, "Hannah Arendt's *Rahel Varnhagen*," 231, 236.

12. Ibid., 238.

13. Ibid., 232.

14. Arendt, *Men in Dark Times*, 33, as cited in Cutting-Gray, "Hannah Arendt's *Rahel Varnhagen*," 241.

15. Julia Kristeva, *Hannah Arendt* (New York: Columbia University Press, 2001), 49–50; Leibovici, "Arendt's *Rahel Varnhagen*," 907.

16. Karl Jaspers to Hannah Arendt, August 23, 1952, in *Hannah Arendt-Karl Jaspers Correspondence, 1926–1969*, eds. Lotte Kohler and Hans Saner, trans. Robert and Rita Kimber (New York: Harcourt & Brace, 1992), 193; Sybille Bedford, "Emancipation and Destiny," *Reconstructionist*, December 12, 1958, 23.

17. Hertz, "Hannah Arendt's *Rahel Varnhagen*." Kristeva, *Hannah Arendt*, 9.

18. Seyla Benhabib, *The Reluctant Modernism of Hannah Arendt* (New York: Rowman & Littlefield), 10; Leibovici, "Arendt's *Rahel Varnhagen*," 907.

19. Kristeva, *Hannah Arendt*, 63–65; Judith N. Shklar, "Hannah Arendt as Pariah," *Partisan Review* 50 (1983): 64–65.

20. Vivian Gornick, "Outsidedness Personified," *The Village Voice*, January 6, 1975, 33.

21. Hannah Arendt, "Original Assimilation: An Epilogue to the One Hundredth Anniversary of Rahel Varnhagen's Death," in *The Jewish Writings*, eds. Jerome Kohn and Ron H. Feldman (New York: Schocken Books, 2007), 25.

22. Gornick, "Outsidedness Personified," 33.

23. Arendt, *Rahel Varnhagen*, 89.

24. Arendt, "Original Assimilation," 25.

25. Arendt, *Rahel Varnhagen*, 81.

26. For Heidegger the mode of being is one of care or concern. He uses two different words to describe this mode of being: *besorgen* and *fürsorge*. *Besorgen* usually refers to tasks which can be resolved or completed, errands. *Fürsorge*, on the other hand, refers to matters of concern related to human issues or human interaction (Joan Stambaugh, "Translator's Preface," in Martin Heidegger, *Being and Time*, trans. Joan Stambaugh (Albany, NY: SUNY Press, 1997), xv).

27. Martin Heidegger, *Being and Time*, trans. Joan Stambaugh (Albany, NY: SUNY Press, 1997).

28. Arendt describes beauty, in *Rahel Varnhagen*, as a source of power for women. It creates "a perspective from which she can judge and choose. In other words, thrownness affects an individual's power, at least in terms of Arendt's initial notion of power" (Arendt, *Rahel Varnhagen*, 87).

29. The question of whether Jewishness constitutes an *existential* seems to lie at the crux of the discussion between Arendt and Jaspers regarding *Rahel Varnhagen* (Hannah Arendt to Karl Jaspers, September 7, 1952, in *Hannah Arendt-Karl Jaspers Correspondence*, 198).

30. Reiner Schürmann, "Heidegger's *Being and Time*," in *On Heidegger's Being and Time*, ed. Steven Levine (London: Routledge, 2008), 89.

31. Hubert Dreyfus, *Being-in-the-World: A Commentary on Heidegger's Being and Time, Division I* (Cambridge, MA: MIT Press, 1991), 180

32. Magda King, *A Guide to Heidegger's Being and Time*, ed. John Llewelyn (Albany: State University of New York Press, 2001), 248.

33. Jacques Derrida, *Heidegger: The Question of Being and History*, eds. Thomas DuToit and Marguerite Derrida, trans. Geoffrey Bennington (Chicago: University of Chicago Press, 2016), 116.

34. King, *A Guide to Heidegger's Being and Time*, 88–89.

35. Heidegger, *Being and Time*, 203–4.

36. Simon Critchley, "Originary Inauthenticity—on Heidegger's *Sein und Zeit*," in *On Heidegger's Being and Time*, ed. Steven Levine (London: Routledge, 2008), 142.

37. Cutting-Gray, "Hannah Arendt's *Rahel Varnhagen*," 229; Weissberg, "Hannah Arendt, Rahel Varnhagen and Writing of (Auto)biography."

38. George Kateb, "Ideology and Storytelling," *Social Research* 69 (2002): 321–58; Elisabeth Young-Bruehl, "Hannah Arendt's Storytelling," *Social Research* 44 (1977): 183–90; Disch, "More Truth than Fact"; Disch, "Please Sit Down but Don't Make Yourself at Home."

39. Heidegger, *Being and Time*, 203

40. Heidegger, *Being and Time*, 167

41. In translation the term, throw, appears both to indicate Dasein's lack of agency in the discussion of *thrownness* (Gerworfenheit) and to suggest the assumption of agency in the case of *projectivity* (entwerfen). The term throw appears in the Varnhagen text in each of these contexts (Arendt, *Rahel Varnhagen*, 93; 220).

42. Arendt, *Rahel Varnhagen*, 88.

43. Arendt's commitment to her friends is well documented. Her husband, Heinrich Blücher, went as far as to suggest that friendship was the cornerstone of the political (Mildred Bakan, "Arendt and Heidegger: The Episodic Intertwining of Life and Work," *Philosophy & Social Criticism* 12 (1987): 95). While the value of emotion and the irrational remains ambiguous, the consistent preoccupation with emotion demonstrated by Rahel would certainly have concerned Arendt; it is as if Rahel took up self-referential emotive reflections as her abode.

44. Arendt, *Rahel Varnhagen*, 93.

45. Ibid.

46. Ibid., 112.

47. Ibid.

48. Arendt, "What Is Existenz Philosophy?"

49. Arendt, *Rahel Varnhagen*, 101.

50. Critchley, "Originary Inauthenticity," 142.

51. Arendt, *Rahel Varnhagen*, 151.

52. Ibid., 241.

53. Ibid.

54. Arendt, *Rahel Varnhagen*, 212.

55. Ibid.

56. Ibid. Arendt's admiration for Marwitz's political insight only becomes clear in *Origins*, as she describes his opposition to imperialism (Arendt, *Origins of Totalitarianism*, 170).

57. Ibid.

58. Ibid.

59. Ibid., 250.

60. Ibid., 251.

61. Ibid., 91.

62. Gornick, "Outsidedness Personified," 33; Cutting-Gray, "Hannah Arendt's *Rahel Varnhagen*," 236; Seyla Benhabib, "The Pariah and Her Shadow: Hannah Arendt's Biography of Rahel Varnhagen," *Political Theory* 23 (1995): 18.

63. Arendt, *Rahel Varnhagen*, 113.
64. Ibid.
65. Ibid., 256.
66. Arendt, "Original Assimilation," 26.
67. Arendt, *Rahel Varnhagen*, 113.
68. Ibid., 255–56.
69. Ibid., 258.
70. Arendt, *Men in Dark Times*, ix.
71. Dana Villa, "Arendt, Heidegger and the Tradition," *Social Research* 74 (2007): 991.
72. Arendt, *Men in Dark Times*, 7.
73. Ibid., 112.
74. Jacques Taminiaux, *The Thracian Maid and the Professional Thinker: Arendt and Heidegger*, ed. and trans. Michael Gendre (Albany, NY: SUNY Press, 1998).
75. Arendt, *Rahel Varnhagen*, 81.
76. Arendt to Jaspers, September 7, 1952, in *Arendt-Jaspers Correspondence*, 198.

Chapter Four

MitDasein I

Understanding Antisemitism

There has been a resurgence of interest in Hannah Arendt's work since the early 1990s. Two areas of Arendtian scholarship that have benefitted from this renewed attention are Arendt's Jewish scholarship and the literature exploring her debt to Heidegger. Scholars have often noted Arendt's Jewishness as an impetus for the emergence of several themes in her work: pariah, natality, thinking and judgment. Barnouw, Bernstein, Feldman and Kohn suggest that Arendt's work cannot be understood without granting a formative role to her Jewish identity and her experience during the German genocide. Each of these scholars finds, in Arendt's work, uniqueness attributable to her experiences as a Jewish woman. Barnouw views the originality as deriving from her dialectical notion of thinking. Bernstein argues that "her confrontation with the Jewish question was the catalytic agent for crystallizing her thinking." Feldman argues that the Jewish experience serves as a harbinger of genocide, "when political issues are dealt with on an individual, private level rather than a collective, public level." Similarly, Jerome Kohn claims the experience of living through the German genocide actualized her Jewish existence or called it into full existence and as such it informed her secular writings. In short despite the renewed interest in Arendt's Jewish writings, the question—what did Arendt make of her Jewish identity as a thinking, judging and above all, politically engaged Being, remains perplexing.[1] She both claimed her Jewishness as an "undisputable fact," denied any particular love of the Jewish people and lamented the Jewish claim to "existence per se—without any national or usually any religious content—as a thing of value."[2] She offered a devastating critique of assimilation, despite the fact that she was an assimilated Jew. In short, Barnouw, Bernstein, Feldman and Kohn suggest that Arendt's thought cannot be fully understood without granting a pivotal role to her Jewish writings.

Conversely I contend that Arendt's eclectic Jewish writings cannot be fully appreciated until her debt to Heidegger is more fully fleshed out. I suggest that in approaching her Jewish identity, Arendt was engaging in an act of Heideggerian historicity, which is to say, she took more seriously than did Heidegger himself one of the basic, even if often overlooked, precepts of his fundamental ontology. One can only approach the ontological through the ontic,[3] which is to say the nature of being can only be understood (or perhaps even taken up) through the unconcealment of some concrete aspect of one's existence as it presents itself. In other words, one's project is conditioned by an understanding of the inescapable historicity of one's own existence. With the publication of *Anti-Semitism* in 1951, Arendt offers a re-interpretation of Jewish history by calling attention to the existential choices that individuals make which lead them to a certain manner of *being-in-the-world*. These existential choices came to characterize the Jewish personality and Jewish culture. In short, she takes up her own existence and projects herself forward by offering an existential interpretation of Jewishness, one grounded in a re-interpretation of Jewish history, in which she highlights the structures that pressed upon Jews, the existential choices made by a few individuals, and the subsequent structures that, in turn, press upon others.

One of the basic, even if often overlooked, precepts of Heidegger's fundamental ontology is that one can only approach the ontological through the ontic,[4] which is to say the nature of being can only be understood (or perhaps even taken up) through the unconcealment of some concrete aspect of one's existence as it presents itself. Similarly, Heidegger's notion of historicity has two predominant impulses. First, it is part of the constitutive structure of *Dasein*, as such it plays a crucial role in the search for transcendence. One can only take oneself up as a project with an understanding of one's origins. Thus, transcendence is a historically conditioned endeavor. It not only occurs in a particular time, a specific place, and within certain cultural constraints, but one's project is conditioned by the inescapable historicity of one's own existence. Second, the Heideggerian notion of historicity serves both a condition of, and a critique of, the study of history. Historical inquiry should not be understood as an attempt to reconstruct and relay an orderly sequence of facts. Rather the study of history requires challenging the dominant interpretation of the meaning of these facts. Arendt's work can be understood as exemplifying a Heideggerian approach to transcendence. In *Anti-Semitism*, she orients herself toward her own future by grounding herself in an understanding of Jewish history. Moreover, she offers a reinterpretation of that history by calling attention to the existential choices that individuals make which lead them to a certain manner of *being-in-the-world*. This manner of *being-in-the-world*, hence, came to characterize the Jewish personality, Jewish culture and was ultimately exaggerated to form anti-Semitic stereotypes.

Arendt's early work takes up both facets of Heideggerian historicity. In her own project, she approaches the ontological through the ontic. Beginning with *Rahel Varnhagen*, she examines one woman's struggle, as German-Jewess, to take herself up as a project. Second, in *Origins of Totalitarianism*, she seeks to understand how the category Jewish became fateful (i.e., came to embody a certain kind of thrownness) and was ultimately manipulated for political purposes. In so doing, she challenges conventional interpretations of both German and Jewish history, an undertaking she continued with *Eichmann in Jerusalem*. Moreover, Heidegger names discovering as one mode of *Mitdasein* and writing as one way of not only preserving discoveredness but releasing one's discovery for further examination and critique by others. Thus, the tangible product of one's project becomes "an inner worldly thing . . . [which] can be taken up and spoken about further."[5] As such the product of Arendt's project becomes a public disclosure of her own thrownness, that others may understand and challenge her interpretation of events or facts. In what follows, I contend that in *Origins of Totalitarianism*, Arendt takes seriously Heidegger's proposition that the ontological can only be approached through the ontic. As such she set out to understand her own thrownness by, first, posing the question: why did antisemitism occur? Arendt's answer, as usual, seeks to reveal the interplay between the individual's existential choice and the political implications of such existential realities.

HISTORICITY

As we have already seen, Heidegger's appeal to historicity as distinguished from history, understood as historiography, has two basic tenets. Historicity serves both as a constitutive structure of *Dasein* and as a critique of historiography. Existentially speaking, *Dasein* is a historical being. Moreover, *Dasein* exists in its own thrownness, as a futurally oriented, *being-with-others*, in a mode of care. An understanding of one's *occurrence-with* may not necessarily be crucial to transcendence, though "only a being that, as futural, is equiprimordially having-been, can hand down to itself its inherited possibility, take over its thrownness and be in the Moment for 'its time.'"[6] In other words, a transcendent being must be simultaneously rooted in the past and direct itself toward the future. An awareness of one's thrownness can facilitate the process of handing "down to itself its inherited possibility." Heidegger does not suggest that an awareness of the factual events contributing to one's condition of thrownness is a precondition of taking up one's own existence as a project.[7] We are all thrown beings, historically situated, for whom the challenge of projecting ourselves forward despite our own thrownness remains ever present. With or without awareness of one's historicity, the pursuit of authenticity remains the quintessential struggle of human existence. Cognizance of one's throw may increase the likelihood of taking oneself up in a resolute manner, though transcendence exists in "[r]esolutely coming back to itself, it is open in retrieve for the 'monumental' possibilities of human existence."[8] In other words, awareness of or interest in historical inquiry is not necessary to transcendence yet Heidegger does presume that disclosure requires an examination of one's own throw. Moreover, as a scholarly undertaking Heidegger's critique of historiography revolves around its disclosive or unconcealing potential. History tends to be dominated by a mainstream interpretation of events. "The tradition that gains dominance makes what it 'transmits' so little accessible that initially and for the most part it covers over instead" of revealing.[9] In other words, the very existence of a historical narrative is antithetical to the disclosure of meaning. In the original "Anti-Semitism" essay Arendt laments that Jewish history suffers from precisely this problem. Jewish history has predominantly been told from two perspectives: assimilationist and nationalist. She charges that both approaches, perhaps particularly the assimilationist, lack a critical perspective, fail to pose the crucial questions and obscure rather than reveal the monumental events in the history of the Jewish people. In her view one of the pivotal yet omitted questions is—*What makes antisemitism possible?*[10]

Charles Guignon argues that Heidegger encourages us to avoid viewing life and, thus, history "as a sequentially ordered flow of occurrences through time that terminates in a final state." We should instead approach life and the study of history "as a movement or happening shaped by specific structures." In this approach being-toward-death is but one manifestation of a structure within which *Dasein* moves "toward the realization of one's identity or being as a person."[11] Arendt more or less adopts Heidegger's approach to historical inquiry, with her own modifications, as we shall soon see. *Anti-Semitism* represents her attempt to understand her own throw, to retrieve possibilities and to act as an agent of disclosure. With the publication of *Origins* she offers her disclosure as "an inner worldly thing at hand that can be taken up and spoken about further."[12] In so doing, she examines the social and political structures within which individuals make existential choices. She also explores the link between an existential choice and an ontological condition, since an individual choosing to assimilate leads to a particular manner of *being-in-the-world*. Finally, she turns her attention to the collective implications of those choices, since the individual's choice to assimilate, for example, is rarely a purely individual matter. Arendt's overarching purpose is simply that of handing back possibilities to both Jews and Germans since the fate or destiny of the German people is inextricably linked to the fate or destiny of the Jewish people. In short, she seeks to reveal the existential choices underlying an ontological orientation; ultimately demonstrating, that the subsequent group characteristics result from the social and political power structures themselves, rather than some kind of innate personality or national essence.

Heidegger identifies a critical perspective as one of the fundamental components of historicity.[13] In other words in order to constitute an authentic project, historical inquiry must have as its aim unconcealment, challenging the dominant interpretation of events for the purpose of recovering possibilities. In this sense the historian's aim is not separable from the philosopher's and is ontological in nature. As David Couzens Hoy says, "the historian's task is most essentially not the reconstruction of facts but of possibilities, that is, of the existential choices underlying the historical fate of individuals and the destiny of peoples."[14] The historian who approaches inquiry in this manner pursues his or her own project in a mode of *being-with* that hands down to others their "inherited possibility" as such, historicity is an act in which the historian not only challenges a dominant interpretation of past events but in so doing "leap[s] ahead . . . not in order to take 'care' away . . . but . . . to give it back."[15] Historicity retrieves possibilities and thus serves as a precursor to both transcendence and, perhaps, to an authentic identity politics. Arendt explains the purpose of her Jewish writings quite clearly when she says "if the present is to be understood at all, then the past must be explicitly seized anew."[16] Understanding the present requires constantly seizing the past anew. As a Jew, she aspires, to seize Jewish history anew which requires challenging the dominant interpretation in order to "retrieve the 'monumental' possibilities of human existence."[17]

ANTI-SEMITISM: REVISED

Arendt's *Anti-Semitism* underwent a major revision from the original draft, written around 1938–1939, to the version that appeared in *The Origins of Totalitarianism* (1951). Though we do not know precisely why she made certain additions to her discussion of antisemitism, we do know that Arendt was reunited with Martin Heidegger, after an 18-year estrangement, in February of 1950. While it is of course impossible to know what they discussed, two things are clear. First, they both left the meeting feeling understood.[18] Second, they did discuss at the very least Jaspers's perception of Heidegger's antisemitism.[19] We will obviously never know to what extent she questioned him or how he explained his affiliation with National Socialism, the later draft of *Anti-Semitism* contains terms and phrases that Heidegger used in the *Black Notebooks* (such as calculating and machination), that are not present in the original essay of the same title. Moreover, she also added the Disraeli vignette, as well as her narrative of the Dreyfus Affair, since the political implications of Disraeli's existential choices did not fully appear in his lifetime.

In what follows, I offer an examination of Arendt's *Anti-Semitism*, in light of Heidegger's philosophical antisemitism, as revealed in the *Black Notebooks*. I suggest, first, that in writing the 1951 version of *Anti-Semitism*, Arendt co-opts the terms: resolute, calculating and machination, for her own purposes, and uses them to describe the policies and behavior of National Socialists. Second, she adds Benjamin Disraeli to the discussion as counter evidence to the myth of a Jewish world conspiracy. In lieu of the calculating Jew aspiring to world domination, Arendt gives us naïve, self-promotion and luck. Finally, with that in mind, she examines the Dreyfus Affair in the attempt to understand how a form of religious bigotry became a political ideology. With these additions to the text, she offers an alternative existential interpretation of Jewishness, one grounded in a re-interpretation of Jewish history, in which she highlights the structures that pressed upon Jews, the existential choices made by a few individuals, and the subsequent structures that in turn press upon others.

At four different points in *Anti-Semitism*, Arendt uses terms that have come to be recognized as part of Heidegger's "being historical anti-Semitism," terms that he used to describe the Jews in the *Black Notebooks* (machination, calculating, gigantic).[20] None of these terms appear in the original "Anti-Semitism" essay. Most notably, in a discussion of Disraeli's naiveté, Arendt remarks

> [i]n his naïve certainty of the paramount importance of secret societies, Disraeli was a forerunner of those new social strata who, born outside the framework of society, could never understand its rules properly. . . . The outsider could not but conclude that a consciously established institution with definite goals achieved such remarkable results. And it is true that this whole society game needed only a resolute political will to transform its half-conscious play of interests and essentially purposeless machinations into a definite policy. This is what occurred briefly in France during the Dreyfus Affair, and again in Germany during the decade preceding Hitler's rise to power.[21]

Given that Arendt begins this paragraph with an explicit reference to Disraeli, the temptation is certainly to view Disraeli as the subject of the paragraph, and of course he is; but so is Heidegger. The terms resolute will and machination are unmistakably Heideggerian. The fact that both terms appear in a paragraph devoted to political naiveté raises the question—who precisely is this naïve outsider? Arendt's use of these terms is also intriguing since as Dana Villa aptly noted, Arendt has a penchant for taking Heideggerian concepts and transforming them for her own purposes.[22] In this case the resolute will becomes explicitly political. Instead of a metaphysical application, Arendt gives us in the resolute will a straightforward, self-interested play for power. Otherwise, the term appears more or less in keeping with Heidegger's use. Transformation requires a resolute will, conviction and determination. Yet the question with Heidegger's resolute will has always been—toward what is it directed?[23]

In the case of Disraeli, his "play of interests" was only "half conscious" in the sense that that he constructed a Jewish identity that emphasized "Jewish" traits without an understanding of the role traits play in antisemitism or the way anti-Semitic stereotypes have been used historically. Similarly, Heidegger's "play of interests" was only "half conscious" in the sense that he constructed a notion of Being without a concrete understanding of the thrownness of beings. He gave to Jewishness an ontological importance without an understanding of the ontic experience of living as a Jew in the world. Arendt concedes that transformation requires a resolute will and leaves no doubt as to her take on the inherent value of a resolute political will, when this resolute will derives from thinking that is mindful of the realities of the world. On the other hand, when the resolute will derives from thinking that is *not* cognizant of the world of appearances or is based on a lack of understanding, it can be not only misguided but disastrous, an observation that could easily be applied to either Disraeli or Heidegger.

Her use of machination in this paragraph is also intriguing, as the machination she refers to in this paragraph are machinations engaged in by Jews. She adds, however, the all-important qualifier—purposeless; thus, turning Heidegger's philosophical antisemitism on its head. The machinations Heidegger has in mind are not only purposeful; they are conspiratorial, menacing and contagious. The Jews who engage in Heideggerian machination are striving for world domination. Whereas Arendt concedes the occasional attempt to engage in machinations, the aim falls considerably short of world domination. Rather than seeking to secretly rule the world, Arendt paints a picture of a people desperately seeking social acceptance and security. Though in some cases, such as Disraeli, they may succeed; more commonly the results are mixed, such as in the case of Rahel Varnhagen. Arendt's concern is that even when these *machinations* appear successful, they are usually misguided, naïve and ultimately self-defeating. Thus, in constructing his identity, Disraeli succeeds in creating a career that was "much more exciting . . . for himself and for others" yet paradoxically, he also created several anti-Semitic caricatures.[24]

The term calculated also appears in a description of "Jews fateful journey to the storm center of events," yet it appears as a political term, rather than a metaphysical one.

> The deciding forces in the Jews' fateful journey to the storm center of events were without a doubt political; but the reactions of society to antisemitism and the psychological reflections of the Jewish question in the individual had

something to do with the specific cruelty, the organized and calculated assault upon every single individual of Jewish origin, that was already characteristic of the antisemitism of the Dreyfus affair.[25]

Calculation, for Arendt, refers not to an inauthentic form of thinking that is characteristic of a people, but rather to a concerted political strategy. As a political strategy it is far from benign, but rather a form of political strategy lacking in social conscience. It is a strategy employed by a dominant political group that targets the vulnerable and purposefully sews fear and hatred, that pits the dominant social group against an underrepresented, defenseless *adversary* for the purpose of consolidating political power.

Rather than Heidegger's conspiratorial trope, Arendt offers a portrait of Benjamin Disraeli, who "never thought seriously of anything except his career."[26] His Jewishness "was a fact of origin which he was at liberty to embellish unhindered by actual knowledge." It was his "display of exoticism, strangeness, mysteriousness, magic and power drawn from secret societies" that gained him social acceptance and "his virtuosity at the social game which made him choose the Conservative Party."[27] The imperialist policies he later pursued derive from his choice of a party and his desire to curry favor with the queen, rather than his role in a secret Jewish society aspiring to rule the world. Thus, Arendt, by adding one simple qualifier offers, in lieu of a self-serving manipulative people, a "downtrodden" people, seeking social acceptance by any means at their disposal, naïve enough, in some cases, to fantasize, albeit publicly, about playing a role in some secret society and to pursue energetically any policy that gained the approval of the Queen.[28]

The addition of the Disraeli narrative, in keeping with the multiplicitous aims of historicity, illustrates, not only the importance of challenging dominant interpretations of history, but also the value of storytelling. Arendt's vignettes often, to some degree, obscure rather than clarify the overall message of the text. Tone is difficult to discern: if most biographers write admiringly of their subjects, Arendt's feelings about Disraeli, like Varnhagen, appear ambivalent. Moreover, the secondary literature, far from clarifying, adds to the uncertainty. Jerome Kohn describes Arendt's depiction of Disraeli as a "scathing portrait"; whereas Norma Claire Moruzzi describes Arendt as "fascinated" by Disraeli's "authentic charlatanism."[29] In her own quest for understanding, *Anti-Semitism* positions Arendt as *Dasein* cognizant of her own connectedness to both past events and future possibilities. Her aim is less to judge, to offer kudos or place blame, than to examine the structures which press upon Jews, the choices they made and the subsequent structures which, in turn, press upon others. Phenomenologically, it is meaningless to blame an individual for events; whereas politically as well as philosophically, it is valuable to understand the collective implications of existential choices. In adding the Disraeli vignette to *Anti-Semitism*, Arendt sought to reveal the structures within which Disraeli set out to fulfill his potential. Moreover, she draws attention to the role he played in creating modern antisemitism.

If Rahel Varnhagen represents the successfully assimilated Jewess; Benjamin Disraeli is the prototype of the successfully assimilated male. In her narrative, Arendt calls attention to the structures which pressed upon Disraeli, the existential choices he made, as well as the resulting ontological orientation and long-term political implications (i.e., subsequent structures which would press upon others, including Arendt). Among the structures that press upon Disraeli, Arendt emphasizes secularization, or the transformation of Judaism, the religion, to Jewishness, the ethnicity. Like Varnhagen before him, Disraeli was raised a secular Jew, probably even more naïve about the role of Jewishness than either Varnhagen or Arendt, in part because of his gender and in part because he was British. The Jewish problem did not exist in Britain in the way that it did in continental Europe due to the absence of a Jewish underclass. Thus, as a baptized, educated Jew, Disraeli finds himself a curiosity, an anomaly without either exposure to or understanding of the way the Jewish problem pressed upon the Jewish underclass.

In this milieu, educated yet ignorant, Disraeli made existential choices, developed his "innate personality"[30] and articulated a secular notion of Jewishness. Like Varnhagen before him, Disraeli constructed his Self with admission to society as his primary goal and a "unique understanding of society and its rules."[31] With social acceptance as his goal and astute powers of observation, yet "unhindered by actual knowledge" of Jewish history or Judaism, he adopted the persona of an exception Jew.[32] Thus, Disraeli is awkwardly positioned as "one of the last Court Jews" as well as the "one of the first victims of anti-Semitism."[33]

The term Court Jew refers to the wealthy Jews who during the Middle Ages, provided financial banking for the State, in exchange for privileges that were usually not afforded to other Jews. While Disraeli was never particularly wealthy, he certainly did enjoy the favor of the Queen. Disraeli was also "the great man of the 'exception Jews.'"[34] Arendt uses the term exception Jew for someone who emphasized his or her exoticism, in other words, played up Jewish stereotypes for the purpose of attracting the attention and favor of the elite. Disraeli is the prime example. *Exceptionalism* is, in many ways, a modern and secular version of the Court Jew, in so far as it allowed certain Jews to escape the social repercussions of their Jewish identity while leaving anti-Semitic stereotypes intact. In a modern, secular environment, Arendt argues that Jews had two options as to how they dealt with antisemitism; they could approach their outsider status, either by embracing the role (pariah) or by seeking to assimilate (parvenu) and denying their Jewish heritage. The only alternative to these two choices is the exception Jew, "who was able to straddle both worlds."[35] Yet straddling both worlds, required to some degree assimilating to antisemitism and, thus, Arendt refers to the "elaborate self-deception of the 'exception Jews.'"[36]

In one of the more confounding sentences in *Anti-Semitism*, Arendt suggests that Disraeli's cheerful naiveté was both deliberately adopted and the self-serving byproduct of his great fortune, "[h]is innocence made him recognize how foolish it would be to feel *déclassé* and how much more exciting it would be for himself and for others, how much more useful for his career, to accentuate the fact that he was a Jew 'by dressing differently, combing his hair oddly, and by queer manners of expression and verbiage.'"[37] In an apparent contradiction, Arendt suggests that Disraeli's social astuteness derives from a lack of awareness of his own throw. Moreover, she also suggests the choice to comport oneself as an eccentric was deliberately made for the purpose of advancing his career. In other words, Disraeli chose to use his Jewishness to his advantage by exploiting a stereotype without an understanding of the ways Jewish stereotypes pressed on others.

It is hardly a coincidence that Rahel Varnhagen displayed many of these same traits; these are the traits of successfully assimilated Jews.[38] They are less indicative of an innate Jewish personality than they are of existential choices made within certain structures that, in turn, lead to a particular ontological orientation. Successfully assimilated Jews chose and feigned naiveté. They developed a keen social awareness, exploited malleable personality traits and made substantive political decisions for their own social advancement, rather than on the basis of principles derived from knowledge and self-awareness. These existential choices also at some point became an inauthentic manner of being in the world. In the case of Benjamin Disraeli, Arendt claims, "he played his part so well that he was convinced by his own make-believe."[39] In the case of the assimilated Jewess, the consequences of her inauthenticity are limited in scope, she was caught up in her own throw. In the case of the assimilated Jew as politician, the consequences are immeasurable. Without any knowledge of Judaism or Jewish history, Disraeli nonetheless projected himself toward his "ownmost" potential but without an awareness of his own *being-with-others*. In so doing, he "produced the entire set of theories about Jewish influence and organization that we usually find in the more vicious forms of anti-Semitism."[40] He developed imagery and rhetoric of the chosen people ruling the world through control of money and diplomacy. This malleable personality represents the existential choice of assimilation. Superficially speaking, the result is a pleasing, even entertaining personality which easily gains social acceptance. Ontologically speaking, this "innate personality" results from denial of one's authentic Self.[41] Politically speaking, this self-denial and the resulting stereotypes, particularly when linked with other oppressive political trends provides fertile ground for the transformation of a form of religious bigotry into a political ideology.

In adding the Disraeli vignette to the discussion of antisemitism, Arendt takes another important step in the direction of crafting her own, unique approach to understanding Jewish history. She tied abstract, existential categories to concrete, political events since as she put it, "the curve which the activity of thought describes must remain bound to incident as the circle remains bound to its focus."[42] Ignorant of both his religion and his own history and tethered to nothing but his own ambition, Disraeli projected himself forward, embraced some Jewish stereotypes and invented others, en route to an utterly inauthentic political existence. The critical point for Arendt, contra Heidegger, is that any exploration of ontological categories must be grounded in lived experiences, "if it is not to lose itself in the heights to which thinking soars."[43]

THE DREYFUS AFFAIR

The political implications of Disraeli's existential choices did not fully manifest themselves in his lifetime. The resulting cross national, antisemitism was, according to Arendt, first utilized for political purposes to prop up a failing state with the Dreyfus Affair. As such it stands as the first successful example of elite mobilization of the mob to instigate violence. Thus, Arendt terms it a "prelude to Nazism" and the event itself serves as a monument, invoking both a cautionary tale and an example of a political solution to a political problem.[44] During the Dreyfus Affair the mob served as agitators of violence and proved amenable both to manipulation and co-ordination by the political elite. It was the mob that escalated the controversy from an unfortunate political scandal to a series of violent political episodes by publicly calling for Jewish blood. For Arendt the mob is a necessary by-product of capitalism. It contains shades of a criminal underworld and is characterized by rootlessness and contempt for respectable society.[45] The mob are the "denizens of the frankly criminal milieu that thrived in the bowels of nineteenth- and early twentieth century capitalism, a motley assortment of 'armed bohemians' who share the respectable bourgeoisie's possessive individualism without the latter's inhibited propriety, and who bypass the much-vaunted ethic of work in favor of more or less organized violence."[46] Often mistaken for the people, by those who hope to organize it as well as by its victims, Arendt states clearly that this is an incorrect supposition; instead the mob is an angry, violent "caricature of the people."[47] It "hates the society from which it is excluded."[48] This antagonism toward respectable society is a predisposition shared by both the mob and the elite.

Arendt emphasizes that there is a striking resemblance between the mob and the elite. The elite are "completely absorbed by their desire to see the ruin of this whole world of fake security, fake culture, and fake life."[49] Their frustration was genuine, their pursuit of change, desperate. They had been "touched by misery . . . [and were] deadly hurt by hypocrisy."[50] They sought solace in the feeling of belonging afforded by social movements. The elite embraced totalitarianism in order to put an end to hypocrisy, while the mob wanted "access to history even at the price of destruction."[51] Thus, the only real common ground between the mob and the elite could be found in the depth of their dissatisfaction with the status quo and their sense of despair at their exclusion from respectable society, their superfluousness and their profound desire to belong to something. While this shared animosity does not provide an enduring basis for a long-term alliance, the intensity of their feelings of exclusion serve as a particularly powerful catalyst.

If the mob hated the "society from which it [was] excluded,"[52] the mass demonstrated no such potent animosity, no contempt, no self-interest. Rather the masses "yearn for anonymity, for being just a number and functioning only as a cog."[53] The main trait of the "mass man is not brutality and backwardness, but isolation and a lack of normal social relationships."[54] Rendered atomized and isolated by the virtually simultaneous "breakdowns of civic, political, [and] cultural associations,"[55] the mass man has lost "a stable space of reference, identity . . . a particular social perspective from which to view the world."[56] If the mob man's outlook is characterized by anger and resentment, the mass man's condition is one of isolation and loneliness. The masses can fulfill various supporting roles though on their own they lack the criminal element necessary to initiate violence; additionally, they lack the perspective necessary for judgment that might enable them to resist the onslaught of propaganda. The troubling thing for Arendt is that the mass man proves infinitely more amenable to manipulation, though the lack of animosity means that this manipulation will require both a catalyst and a justification. The mob man will undertake violence with only the slightest of provocations. Ultimately, however, it is the mass man who is capable of the greatest crimes, "provided that these crimes [are] well organized and assumed the appearance of routine jobs."[57] The point for Arendt is that just as there are two different groups of elite serving different functions, genocidal violence is perpetrated by two distinct groups. The mob, whose disaffection requires little in the way of provocation, initiates the violence. However, it is the masses, whose existential despair predisposes them to manipulation, who take up the work with a peculiar devotion, born of a desperate desire to belong to something, anything that might lend meaning to their existence. "Nazi propaganda . . . gave the masses of atomized, undefinable, unstable and futile individuals a means of self-definition and identification which not only restored some of the self-respect they had formerly derived from their function in society, but also created a kind of spurious stability which made them better candidates for an organization."[58] While Arendt finds in the Dreyfus Affair a dire warning of the explosive potential created by the mob-elite alliance, it is the mass man, utterly lacking in spontaneity, who proves to be more reliable over the long term, as long as he is carefully prepared. The Jews failure to see their plight as anything other than a personal misfortune led them to seek personal escape (as did both Varnhagen and Disraeli) through intermarriage, a pleasing personality or naked ambition, in other words, through assimilation. This strategy of seeking to make oneself agreeable within the confines of antisemitism, while individually expedient, may prepare victims, individually, to accept rather than resist violence, collectively.

The Dreyfus Affair is not, however, without its hero: Georges Clemenceau. Clemenceau was a politician and journalist who published many articles in support of Dreyfus and condemning the rampant antisemitism of the time. Clemenceau belongs to the small cadre of people who identified antisemitism as a political problem. Furthermore, he imagined a political solution and publicly advocated it. Clemenceau, himself, was not Jewish but his willingness to act on behalf of Jews gained him not only Arendt's admiration but the status of a friend to the Jews. The point that Arendt makes consistently throughout her life regarding antisemitism is that Jews were politically naïve. This naiveté consisted of, first, a penchant for viewing Jewishness as a personal problem rather than a political one, and second, the assumption that non-Jewish, personal friends were also allies. Thus, Arendt labels Clemenceau both a hero and a friend to the Jews and holds him up as an illustration of how one might understand friendship. In lieu of embracing personal friends, while denouncing Jews, thus implicitly, endorsing antisemitism, Georges Clemenceau advocated for the Jews, politically. As such he befriended Jews, collectively, by alerting them to the political nature of, as well as a political solution to, their plight. In adding the Dreyfus Affair to her text on antisemitism, Arendt draws attention to the political implications of Disraeli's existential choice. Beginning with the Dreyfus Affair, the elite identified in the Jews a common enemy and offered them up to the mob as a suitable target. Perhaps most importantly, the elite learned that it could mobilize the mob and in so doing, transformed an isolated ethnic group into a target for the political purpose of re-enforcing a failing state.

CONCLUSION

In a 1946 book review, Arendt wrote that the book failed "because its authors, submerged in a chaos of details, were unable to understand or make clear the nature of the facts confronting them."[59] Facts alone reveal little; meaning, and ultimately understanding, derive not from simply re-telling of an event or set of facts but rather from the relating of a series of events in the form of a narrative. In other words, history is less the compilation of a set of objective facts than it is the attempt to interpret events or occurrences in the spaces of appearances, such that the collective can reconcile itself to those events and take from them some kind of guide to the future. With the publication of *Anti-Semitism*, as a section of *Origins of Totalitarianism*, Arendt completes the initial phase of her examination of Jewish history. She firmly roots her Self in an understanding of Jewish history, challenging the dominant narrative and inviting contestation. In so doing, she illustrates a phenomenological approach to history by positing that "the history of anti-Semitism, of imperialism, of racism—belong to those subterranean streams of Western history which have but recently come into the open."[60] She offers an alternative narrative to the dominant anti-Semitic narrative of a calculating people aspiring to world domination, suggesting instead a people seeking acceptance, survival, love and in some cases, esteem and she highlights the structures that pressed upon Jews, the existential choices made by a few individuals and the subsequent structures that continued to press upon others. She explores the transition in antisemitism from a religious discrimination, based on hatred of the Jews for the role they played in the death of Christ, to modern antisemitism which involves ascribing to Jews, as a people, a whole manner of undesirable personal traits or vices. As a threat to the Jewish people, Jew hatred was somewhat limited. It was modern antisemitism that provides the more credible threat "when it can link itself with other political trends."[61] In this way, Arendt uses this historical essay, phenomenologically: she aspires to engage in an unconcealment of antisemitism, provide guideposts for the future, and hand back to her fellow Jews their possibilities.

NOTES

1. Dagmar Barnouw, *Visible Spaces: Hannah Arendt and the German-Jewish Experience* (Baltimore: Johns Hopkins University Press, 1990); Richard J. Bernstein, *Hannah Arendt and the Jewish Question* (Cambridge, MA: MIT Press, 1996), 9; Ron H. Feldman, "The Jew as Pariah: The Case of Hannah Arendt (1906–1975)," in *The Jewish Writings*, eds. Jerome Kohn and Ron H. Feldman (New York: Schocken Books, 2007), lxvii; Jerome Kohn, "A Jewish Life: 1906–1975," in *The Jewish Writings*, eds. Jerome Kohn and Ron H. Feldman (New York: Schocken Books, 2007), xiii-xiv.

2. Hannah Arendt, "A Letter to Gershom Scholem," in *The Jewish Writings*, eds. Jerome Kohn and Ron H. Feldman (New York: Schocken Books, 2007), 466; Hannah Arendt, "The Jewish War that Isn't Happening," in *The Jewish Writings*, eds. Jerome Kohn and Ron H. Feldman (New York: Schocken Books, 2007), 137.

3. Martin Heidegger, "On the Essence of Ground," in *Pathmarks*, trans. and ed. William O'Neill (Cambridge: Cambridge University Press, 1998[1928]), 97–135; Martin Heidegger, *Being and Time*, trans. Joan Stambaugh (Albany, NY: SUNY Press, 1997), 10–11.

4. Heidegger, *Being and Time*, 10–11.

5. Ibid., 205–6.

6. Ibid., 352.

7. Paul Farwell, "Can Heidegger's Craftsman be Authentic?," *International Philosophical Quarterly* 29 (1989): 77–90.

8. Heidegger, *Being and Time*, 362.

9. Ibid., 19.

10. Hannah Arendt, "Anti-Semitism," in *The Jewish Writings*, eds. Jerome Kohn and Ron H. Feldman (New York: Schocken Books, 2007), 49.

11. Charles Guignon, "The History of Being," in *A Companion to Heidegger*, eds. Hubert L. Dreyfus and Mark A Wrathall (Oxford: Blackwell Publishing, 2005), 395.

12. Heidegger, *Being and Time*, 205–6.

13. Ibid., 368.

14. David Couzens Hoy, "History, Historicity and Historiography in *Being and Time*," in *Heidegger and Modern Philosophy*, ed. Michael Murray (New Haven, CT: Yale University Press, 1978), 347.

15. Heidegger, *Being and Time*, 115.

16. Hannah Arendt, "Enlightenment and the Jewish Question," in *The Jewish Writings*, eds. Jerome Kohn and Ron H. Feldman (New York: Schocken Books, 2007), 16.

17. Heidegger, *Being and Time*, 362.

18. Arendt wrote to Blücher in a letter dated February 8th that she and Heidegger "had a real talk, I think, for the first time in our lives" (Arendt to Blücher, February 8, 1950, in *Within Four Walls: The Correspondence between Hannah Arendt and Heinrich Blücher, 1936–1968*, ed. Lotte Kohler, trans. Peter Constantine (New York: Harcourt Brace, 1992), 128). In a letter dated February 9th, she wrote to Heidegger, "[t]his evening and this morning are the confirmation of an entire life. A confirmation that, when it comes down to it, was never expected. When the waiter spoke your name . . . it was as if time suddenly stood still" (in *Hannah Arendt and Martin Heidegger: Letters, 1925–1975*, ed. Ursula Ludz, trans. Andrew Shields (New York: Harcourt Brace Jovanovich, 2004), 59).

19. In the same letter to Blücher, she wrote, "I'll be able to defuse that disgraceful business with Jaspers" though she does not elaborate until March 7th, "[t]he disgraceful business I wrote you about didn't actually happen. Phew. Enough has actually happened to be able to say "phew." The fact that [Heidegger] suddenly wasn't seeing Jaspers anymore was because he finally realized what he had done, and was ashamed. Totally taken aback, that Jaspers might have seen it differently. In other words, as a boycott because of his Jewish wife. Over the years he has faced a similar problem with many others; he had never reached the obvious conclusion" (Arendt to Blücher, March 7, 1950, in *Within Four Walls*, 142).

20. See also *Origins*, pages 87, 108, and 116.

21. Ibid., 77–78.

22. Dana Villa, *Arendt and Heidegger: The Fate of the Political* (Princeton, NJ: Princeton University Press, 1996).

23. Jürgen Habermas, *The Philosophical Discourse of Modernity: Twelve Lectures*, trans. F. Lawrence, ed. Richard Wolin (Cambridge, MA: MIT Press, 1987), 141; Karl Löwith, "The Political Implications of Heidegger's Existentialism," *New German Critique* 45 (1988): 121.

24. Arendt, *Origins of Totalitarianism*, 68.

25. Arendt, *Origins of Totalitarianism*, 87.

26. Arendt, *Origins of Totalitarianism*, 68. This description is strikingly similar to the one she offers of Adolph Eichmann. "Eichmann remembered the turning points in his own career rather well, but that they didn't necessarily coincide with the turning points in the story of Jewish extermination" (Hannah Arendt, *Eichmann in Jerusalem: A Report on the Banality of Evil* (New York: Harcourt Brace, 1963), 53).

27. Arendt, *Origins of Totalitarianism*, 69.

28. Ibid., 68–79.

29. Kohn, "A Jewish Life," xix; Norma Claire Moruzzi, *Speaking Through the Mask: Hannah Arendt and the Politics of Social Identity* (Ithaca, NY: Cornell University Press, 2000), 73.

30. Arendt, *Origins*, 169.

31. Arendt, *Origins of Totalitarianism*, 69.

32. Ibid.

33. David Cesarani, *Disraeli: The Novel Politician* (New Haven, CT: Yale University Press, 2016), 236.

34. Arendt, *Origins of Totalitarianism*, 68.

35. Kevin Richards, "The Origins of Totalitarianism Part I—Anti-Semitism," May 3, 2018, https://u.osu.edu/richards.113/2018/05/03/the-origins-of-totalitarianism-part-i-anti-semitism-hannah-arendt.
36. Arendt, *Origins of Totalitarianism*, 68.
37. Ibid.
38. Hannah Arendt, "The Assets of Personality," in *The Jewish Writings*, eds. Jerome Kohn and Ron H. Feldman (New York: Schocken Books, 2007), 404.
39. Arendt, *Origins of Totalitarianism*, 68.
40. Ibid., 71.
41. Arendt, *Origins*, 169.
42. Arendt, "Action and the Pursuit of Happiness," Hannah Arendt Manuscripts Collection, Library of Congress, 1960, 1.
43. Ibid.
44. Arendt, *Origins of Totalitarianism*, 94.
45. Seyla Benhabib, *The Reluctant Modernism of Hannah Arendt* (New York: Rowman & Littlefield, 2000), 78–79.
46. Roy Tsao, "The Evolution and Structure of Arendt's Theory of Totalitarianism," *Social Research* 69 (2002): 584; Arendt, *Origins*, 317.
47. Arendt, *Origins of Totalitarianism*, 107.
48. Ibid.
49. Ibid., 328.
50. Ibid., 331.
51. Ibid., 332.
52. Ibid., 107.
53. Ibid., 329.
54. Ibid., 317.
55. Benhabib, *The Reluctant Modernism of Hannah Arendt*, 55.
56. Ibid., 66–67.
57. Arendt, *Origins of Totalitarianism*, 337.
58. Ibid., 356.
59. Hannah Arendt, "The Image of Hell," in *Essays in Understanding, 1930–1954*, ed. Jerome Kohn (New York: Schocken Books, 1994), 197–98.
60. Hannah Arendt, "Outline of 'Elements of Shame: Anti-Semitism, Imperialism and Racism,'" Hannah Arendt Manuscripts Collection, Library of Congress, 1.
61. Arendt, "Anti-Semitism," 97.

Chapter Five

Mitdasein II

Understanding *Imperialism*

Origins of Totalitarianism is another of Arendt's texts which is notoriously difficult to categorize. Seyla Benhabib describes it as "too systematically ambitious and overinterpreted to be a strictly historical account; it is too anecdotal, narrative, and ideographic to be considered social science, and although it has the vivacity and stylistic flair of a work of political journalism, it is too philosophical to be accessible to a broad public."[1] While the magnitude of the undertaking and the originality of the insights are often lauded, the text is also faulted for its ambiguous argument and methodology, as well as, the lack of internal coherence.[2] Bernard Crick argues that *Origins* is the text in which Arendt establishes herself as "the supreme example of a fox appearing to be a hedgehog," in so far as she constructs a series of brilliant essays which do not necessarily comprise a cohesive whole.[3] Part of the critique of *Origins* is that *Anti-Semitism* and *Imperialism* have little to do with *Totalitarianism*. The Heideggerian lens provides us with a way of understanding the linkage, not only between *Anti-Semitism*, *Imperialism* and *Totalitarianism*, but between the vignettes and the socio-political analysis, as well. In his often cited review of *Origins*, Eric Voegelin mentions *Imperialism* only briefly. He describes *Imperialism* as "theoretically the most penetrating" section of the book, appreciates Arendt's attempt to "create type concepts" and place these phenomena "in their proper, wider context."[4] In so much of the scholarly analysis of Arendt's work, *Imperialism* is either overlooked or prompts strikingly disparate interpretations.

The primary importance of *Imperialism* is itself a subject of considerable disagreement. Julia Kristeva concludes that Arendt favors the English two party system and the Rights of Englishmen over the Rights of Man enjoyed by the French.[5] Bernard Crick, on the other hand, asserts that the take away message is "[h]umanity is not a biological given; it is a cultural achievement that can become lost if we cease to re-enact it daily."[6] Whereas George Kateb finds that imperialism contributed to the possibility of totalitarianism since the Nazi version of totalitarianism, in particular,

> wears the appearance of earlier movements, racist and imperialist, in Europe. The appearance helps attract segments of a population already susceptible for generations—to racist and imperialist notions and fully developed ideologies.... The real continuity between the earlier movements and totalitarianism is found in the readiness of European peoples to think in racist and imperialist categories."[7]

Moreover, recent attempts to think Arendt through Heidegger have ignored *Imperialism* altogether.[8] It is my contention that this oversight, if it can be called that, contributes to the sense of *Origins* as an incoherent work. Alternatively, if we more fully flesh out the Heideggerian themes in Arendt's work the connections between *Anti-Semitism*, *Imperialism* and *Totalitarianism* become more readily discernible.

Imperialism, like *Anti-Semitism*, serves as an act of historicity. In other words, the first two sections of *Origins* disclose the structures that pressed upon imperialists, as well as natives, and the existential choices with which they grappled. Just as "modern anti-Semitism depends on the character of modern Jews,"[9] imperialism depends upon an "innate" imperialistic personality (as distinct from the *born* adventurer of colonialism).[10] Social and political structures both create and depend upon a particular, if not unique, ontological orientation. Arendt implicitly, if not explicitly, calls into question the "innate" personality associated with many stereotypes and challenges the dominant historical narrative, thus, inviting contestation. Throughout *Imperialism*, Arendt's focus remains ontic structures, yet she alludes to the nexus between the ontological and the political which will become the hallmark of her thought; in these moments, her experiential ontology becomes evident.

As we have previously seen, for both Arendt and Heidegger, remembering plays an integral part in thinking. Since care or concern is one of the constitutive structures of *Dasein* and care or concern emerges only through memory or in the act of remembering, memory serves as a precondition for transcendence. In other words, we can only become fully human in the act of remembering. Thus as Arendt transforms Heideggerian existentials for use in the public sphere, an important place must necessarily be reserved for the historical narrative, the public manifestation of memory. Moreover, as a phenomenologist, Arendt views the emergence of stories and their interpretation in shared spaces as constitutive. So vital is the shared story to our *Being-with* that Arendt finds its loss to be a major contributing factor to world alienation.

> In the situation of radical world-alienation, neither history nor nature is at all conceivable. This twofold loss . . . has left behind it a society of men who, without a common world which would at once relate and separate them, either live in desperate lonely separation or are pressed together in a mass . . . [they] have lost the world once common to all of them."[11]

Thus, she would likely agree with Michael Walzer and Sheldon Wolin that disparate interpretations of "historical moments when collective identity is collectively established" constitute questions of political importance.[12] This observation is perhaps particularly important in a post-genocidal context, since in these moments, the present is interpreted in light of the past in an attempt to forge a non-violent future. *The Origins of Totalitarianism* is a perplexing text because with it, Arendt strives to re-write Germany's future. In *Origins*, Arendt selects and illuminates those historical moments that, in light of the Final Solution, can now be understood to have been constitutive of our *Being-with*. In other words, she explores and re-interprets those historical moments when German collective identity was established, or at least those "subterranean streams" which led to genocide.[13]

In her attempt to abide by Heidegger's admonishment that the ontological can only be taken up through the ontic, Arendt attempts to understand the structures that press upon our individual, as well as, collective choices. In *Imperialism*, she develops the thesis that a temporary alliance between the political elite and the mob transformed racism from an idea, legitimated by the intellectual elite, to an ideology and a principle of political organization.[14] The move from idea to ideology was made possible only by the pervasive nature of ideological thinking as an ontological condition. Thus, Arendt again demonstrates that political phenomena (in this case—imperialism) derive from a particular ontological orientation. In so doing she discloses another ontic structure that prepared the way for the German genocide. As a work of historicity, *Imperialism* stands alongside *Anti-Semitism* as a companion piece in which Arendt calls attention to ontic conditions, as well as the subsequent ontological conditions that lay the groundwork for genocide.

ALLIANCE BETWEEN CAPITAL AND THE MOB

The most important concept at work in Arendt's discussion of imperialism is superfluousness. Superfluidity is used to describe people, wealth, goods and even collective entities such as a group of people or a nation. It is an economic, sociological, as well as metaphysical concept. The key trait shared by superfluous entities, according to Arendt, is idleness; they serve no productive function. Economically, gold and gems are superfluous goods. They have monetary value yet that value is not connected to any useful function.

Their only purpose is adornment or the advertisement of wealth. Sociologically speaking, groups of people can become superfluous if they cease to be productive members of a capitalist system. Moreover, Arendt argues that South Africa became superfluous in terms of international trade with the construction of the Suez Canal. It ceased to fulfill its previous function on the trade route from Europe to India. Thus perhaps ironically, the "owners of superfluous wealth were the only men who could use the superfluous men who came from the four corners of the earth. Together they established the first paradise of parasites whose lifeblood was gold. Imperialism, the product of superfluous money and superfluous men, began its startling career by producing the most superfluous and unreal goods."[15] Thus, imperialism is a political solution to an economic, as well as, a metaphysical problem.

It is as a metaphysical concept that superfluousness takes on its uniquely Arendtian quality with distinctly Heideggerian undercurrents and political consequences. Arendt refers to rootlessness, the lack of mooring or connectedness that renders superfluous men vulnerable to manipulation. In Heideggerian terms superfluous men project themselves forward without roots, without a sense of belonging to a place, a shared history, without taking the time to contemplate the implications of each venture. Their involvement in a foreign land is not grounded in either knowledge of or even curiosity about the history, language or cultures of the "new" place. Superfluous men, thus, succumb to calculative thinking; they view the foreign land as a resource, never stopping to consider the virtues of life in this place. They encounter locals as ready-to-hand, rather than as *Dasein*, already engaged in their own projection. As such they fall victim to inauthentic projects. The adventures offered by colonialism or imperialism are false projects, not grounded in an understanding of one's throw or a sense of cultural connectedness. They attempt to remedy an existential crisis with a distraction, an inauthentic project. To those suffering from a profound lack of connectedness, these adventures offered only a pseudo connection to other superfluous men in a foreign land. These foreign adventures held profound political appeal as they provided an outlet for superfluous wealth and men and in so doing, promise to stave off domestic conflict. Politically speaking, "such hopes still belonged with the old vicious practice of 'healing' domestic conflicts with foreign adventures. The difference, however, is marked. Adventures are by their very nature limited in time and space; they may succeed temporarily in overcoming conflicts, although as a rule they fail and rather tend to sharpen them."[16] Politically expedient, metaphysically costly, foreign adventures can take on disparate institutional structures: colonialism, imperialism and pan-imperialism.

COLONIALISM, IMPERIALISM AND PAN-IMPERIALISM

The colonialist chooses the life of the adventurer and within the institutional framework of the nation-state, rooted only in a skewed version of national identity, exploits the new land for its resources. Colonialists may be superfluous men, in a sense, though they are not rootless. Colonialism is based, at least to some degree, on respect for the Other's political autonomy. There may well be an implicit disregard for the Other in colonialism though the maintenance of political autonomy limits the scope of this disregard. The imperialist, on the other hand, is unconstrained by a sense of national identity, culture or connectedness and racism serves as his "ruling device."[17] Described by Arendt as rootless, the imperialist never chooses; in other words, he has "not stepped out of society but had been spat out by it."[18] He adapts to a new life in a new land by severing many of the ties that bound him to a human world. Imperialism differs from colonialism in two ways. First though there may be elements of superfluousness in colonialism, the "new fact in the imperialist era is that these two superfluous forces, superfluous capital and superfluous working power, joined hands and left the country together."[19] Second, these foreign investments came to require "political control" as a result of "an unparalleled orgy of swindles, financial scandals, and stock market speculation," though the critical distinction between colonialism and imperialism, according to Arendt, is that imperialism uses racism as an organizing principle. Imperialists adopt, as an official policy, a collective disregard for the Other's political autonomy, paving the way for a disregard of the Other's humanity. It is not clear whether political disregard for the Other leads to or depends upon disregard for the Other's humanity. Wherever racism appears "it is always closely tied to contempt for labor, hatred of territorial limitations, general rootlessness, and an activistic faith in one's own divine chosenness."[20] Thus, although the distinction between colonialism and imperialism is extraordinarily difficult to define, Arendt's tact, once again, is to disclose the social and political structures pressing upon existential choices, as well as the ontological core of the political phenomena. In order to do so, she describes the political and social context which led the Boers to *inadvertently* discover racism as a political tool.

One of the critical distinctions between colonialism and imperialism is the emergence of racism as a principle of political organization. As Arendt describes it "only peoples organized as races can be induced to 'expand' and seduced into assuming rulership everywhere over 'lower breeds.'"[21] Racism, as a political tool, requires as a deficient mode of *Being-with*. Despite the existence of some stereotypical depictions, Arendt's aim, again, is to reveal rather than blame. As with antisemitism, she seeks to disclose the appearance of racism as a political tool.

Ruling over tribes and living parasitically from their labor, they came to occupy a position very similar to that of the native tribal leaders whose domination they had liquidated. The natives, at any rate, recognized them as a higher form of tribal leadership, a kind of natural deity to which one has to submit; so that the divine role of the Boers was as much imposed by their black slaves as assumed freely by themselves.[22]

Finally, pan-imperialism began to link the disregard for an external Other to a disregard for an internal Other. Pan imperialists organized domestic, as well as, foreign policy around the conscious, purposeful and official policy of "looting . . . foreign territories" and permanently degrading "alien peoples."[23] If colonialism and imperialism provide an outlet for "superfluous forces," ideology is the process by which large segments of the population are mobilized.

RACE THINKING, SCAPEGOATS AND IDEOLOGY

An ideology, for Arendt, is to be understood as a literal etymology of the word—the logic of an idea. She attempts to reveal the processes by which a quasi-academic theory or hypothesis is transformed into an indisputable prophecy. She examines not only the political or sociological climate in which scapegoating is effective but also the process by which individuals succumb to the logic of the idea. For Arendt, the unique problem that occurs in genocide is that the logic takes precedence over the ideas, rendering the ideas mere—truisms. Thus, Arendt's examination of ideology explains not only the rhetoric or intent of leaders but the manner in which that rhetoric takes on a quasi-compulsory, even prophetic quality. Ideologies, for Arendt, "combine the scientific approach with results of philosophical relevance and pretend to be scientific philosophy . . . [they] pretend to know the mysteries of the whole historical process—the secrets of the past, the intricacies of the present, the uncertainties of the future—because of the logic inherent in their respective ideas."[24] For Arendt the notion of ideology which, along with a number of other factors, "crystallized" into totalitarianism and genocide is double faceted. She concerns herself, first, with historical scapegoating[25] and subsequently with the process by which scapegoating transforms into an ideology which transcends the idea itself, takes on a scientific or philosophical relevance, becomes imbued with a self-perpetuating motion and finally affects the thinking of individuals to the point where even individuals who do *not* subscribe to the idea, accept the historical process as not only valid but inevitable.

In *The Origins of Totalitarianism*, Arendt explored the crucial role of ideology in the German genocide. Subsequently in reporting on the Eichmann trial, she discovered that Eichmann never particularly subscribed neither to the regime's ideology nor to antisemitism. This development gave her pause and she confessed to Mary McCarthy that she might have overstated the importance of ideology in *Origins*.[26] The absence of antisemitism in Eichmann pushed her to examine the process by which the logic of the ideas comes to dictate the behavior of individuals who do not subscribe to the ideas. Herein lies Arendt's most notable contribution to the study of ideology. In terms of understanding ideology, the challenge is not to understand why an anti-Semite endorsed and even acted upon the Final Solution; the challenge, for Arendt, is to understand the sociological appeal of ideology, its political use and, finally, the active participation or quiet acquiescence of those who did *not* subscribe to the idea.

Ideologies, for Arendt, impose a single factor explanation, which interprets all of human history, contemporary challenges and, perhaps most importantly, decrees the future. This future vision is couched in terms of a natural process (i.e., an unavoidable progression), which is revealed by the laws of science or history. Thus, the ideology takes on its compulsory quality. Since the ideology claims as its basis a natural process, the shift to a claim of inevitability is a relatively simple one. Moreover, the *fact* that this process has been revealed through law of science or history, also, lends a certain amount of credence and renders challenges to the proscribed vision, futile. In short for Arendt, the defining features of an ideology are the claim to be able to explain all of human history, and to predict a future, which is preordained (thus, inevitable), according to some systematic law of nature or science. Although ideologies carry with them an element of inevitability, there is a crucial distinction to be made between an ideology and ideological thinking. An ideology refers to—the logic of an idea. The process by which individuals accept an ideology as representing truth, and requiring compliance, even facilitation,[27] is termed—*ideological thinking*.

Ideological thinking "orders facts into an absolutely logical procedure which starts from an axiomatically accepted premise, deducing everything from it; that is, it proceeds with a consistency that exists nowhere in the realm of reality."[28] As they engage in ideological thinking, individuals "become emancipated from the reality that we perceive with our five senses, and insist on a 'truer' reality concealed beyond all perceptible things."[29] This emancipation renders challenges to ideological thinking virtually impossible. Part of Arendt's concern lies in the detachment from a reality that is grounded in human experience and one of the crucial questions becomes— why do individuals succumb to ideological thinking? This question has a particular resonance for Arendt as she struggled to come to terms with Martin Heidegger's decision to support National Socialism and, in the later stage of her career, reported on the trial of Adolph Eichmann. In conventional terms, these two figures could not be more different. Heidegger was the brilliant existential philosopher, heir apparent to the legacy of German philosophy. Eichmann was the traveling salesman, released from his "humdrum life without significance . . . into History."[30] Yet they both ended up succumbing to National Socialism. Arendt did not believe either one was anti-Semitic; though they both actively supported an anti-Semitic regime. Additionally, both subscribed to the notion of a "truer" reality. Moreover, Arendt revealed the roles of the mob and the elite in galvanizing the public around an ideology, or in other words, in creating a political principle.

Race is a concept legitimated by an intellectual elite. Race thinking, as an individual phenomenon, is a perverted form of thinking that derives from a deficient mode of care. Racism is both an idea and a collective phenomenon that involves systematically exploiting an Other. Moreover, superfluous individuals may be particularly vulnerable to race thinking since they "have internalized their own superfluousness"[31] and racism provides a scapegoat for sociological superfluidity. Thus, anyone hoping to organize the superfluous for political purposes has an easy mechanism at his or her disposal. Social Darwinism becomes an ideology when it is employed for political purposes, by individuals who do not subscribe to the idea, yet accept the ends as a historical inevitability and act in accordance with those ends. The ideology had yet to fully emerge under imperialism since racism had not yet become a full-fledged historical inevitability. In an attempt to explore these "subterranean streams,"[32] Arendt examines the existential struggles of those caught in the throw of imperialism as well as the resulting political structures.

As such she challenges, as well as constructs a historical narrative; she relays the tales, factual as well as legendary, of individuals caught in the throw of imperialism and their subsequent struggles for an authentic existence. With *Kim* and Lawrence of Arabia, Arendt explores the existential struggles of those pressed upon by imperialism. Kim and Lawrence are both, to some degree, bouncing back and forth between two cultures, two traditions and two places. The difference is Lawrence maintains a strong sense of connection to England. His relationships with family and friends are firmly established; whereas Kim is connected to no one. The prominence of these characters in Arendt's analysis owes less to their factual or fictional nature and more to their accessibility as prototypes of the existential struggles perpetuated by imperialism and subsequent political implications. All the while Arendt heralds as heroic the assertion of Ludwig von der Marwitz that any nation aiming to expand "his frontiers should be considered a disloyal betrayer among the whole European republic of states."[33] As in *Rahel Varnhagen*, Arendt's heroes are those who recognize the political nature of the problem and advocate political solutions. In other words, she holds up as exemplars those who are cognizant of the political implications of an existential struggle.

KIPLING'S *KIM*

Nowhere perhaps is Arendt's notion of superfluousness more vibrantly revealed than in Rudyard Kipling's Kimball O'Hara: an orphan of Irish parentage, Kim is left alone to navigate the streets of Lahore, India. At issue with superfluous men "was not their morality or immorality, but rather that the decision to join this crowd . . . was no longer up to them."[34] A white child with papers, living on the streets of India, his only recourse was to beg for food, his only asset, his ability to pass either as a British or Hindu child. Thus, he drifted "like a detached leaf . . . without ever catching on to anything."[35] His size and dual identity presented him with the opportunity to move with relative ease across the country as well as among diverse groups. At the beginning of the eighth chapter, Kim changes his identity merely by changing the color of his turban from red to blue, "the change was made, and Kim stood up, externally at least, a Mohammedan."[36] In the ninth chapter, he alters his identity yet again and "flung himself wholeheartedly upon the next turn of the wheel. He would be a sahib again for a while."[37] Spat outside of society, Kim utilized whatever assets he could for his own survival. Firmly rooted nowhere and tethered to nothing, these superfluous people "were like living symbols of what had happened to them, living abstractions and witnesses of the absurdity of human institutions. They were not individuals . . . they were the shadows of events with which they had nothing to do."[38] They were not individuals, existentially speaking. Kim fascinates Arendt because he is clearly a character in search of his own identity, drawn to the lama's search for transcendence while increasingly emeshed in the Great Game.

Utterly rootless and lacking in a stable identity, Kim quite literally became a Hindu street urchin, *chela, sahib*. The rootless, according to Arendt are "game for anything . . . [t]hus they brought with them, or they learned quickly, the code of manners which befitted the coming type of murderer."[39] The point for Arendt is not a moral one; the point is that Kim beautifully represents the limited existential choice available to those "who had been spat out by" society.[40] Grounded in nothing, not a place, a language, a culture and tethered to no one, he had no stable basis from which to project himself forward, no clear identity from which to take himself up as a project. Instead he was swept along with each new opportunity, taking on a different Self with each new opportunity, each new turban. Throughout the novel, the search for transcendence is quite literally thwarted by Kim's desirability as an agent of the imperial regime. In many ways the message is a fairly simple one, in Heideggerian terms: the "they" impedes the search for transcendence or authenticity. Kipling succeeds though in placing Kim's struggle in a larger (i.e., political) context. The desperate, desolate Kim, rendered utterly rootless by the death of this father, has little choice but to offer himself in service to the Great Game, rendering authenticity a fleeting dream and placing Kipling's beautiful India at the mercy of the rootless in a senseless international power struggle, guaranteed to ruin all and, inadvertently, laying the groundwork for an even greater international catastrophe. The point for Arendt is that imperialism renders superfluousness the rule rather than the exception and in so doing serves as a precursor to totalitarianism.

As Arendt had previously demonstrated with *Rahel Varnhagen*, social and political strucures press upon our existential choices which, in turn, lead to an ontological condition or a manner of being in the world, revealing themselves in a personality type that Arendt refers to ironically throughout her work as "innate." This ontological condition, otherwise known as the innate personality or character, often takes on a political significance. Her description of the innate imperialist personality bears some resemblance to the innate Jewish personality.

> Deprived of political rights, the individual, to whom public and official life manifests itself in the guise of necessity, acquires a new and increased interest in his private life and personal fate. Excluded from participation in the management of public affairs that involve all citizens, the individual loses his rightful place in society and his natural connection with his fellow-men. He can now judge his individual private life only by comparing it with that of others, and his relations with his fellow-men inside society take the form of competition.[41]

Arendt's aim is to reveal the thread connecting existential choice, ontological condition (sometimes known as personality or character) and "those subterranean streams of Western history."[42] With such an undertaking it can be useful to pose the question what other choices existed, though it is senseless to blame individuals for collective outcomes, a point Arendt makes exceedingly clear in *Imperialism*.

> Somehow it was not the fault of the born adventurers, of those who by their very nature dwelt outside society and outside all political bodies, that they found in imperialism a political game that was endless by definition; they were not supposed to know that in politics an endless game can end only in catastrophe and that political secrecy hardly ever ends in anything nobler than the vulgar duplicity of a spy.[43]

Kim is the prototype, the classic illustration of an imperialist character. T. E. Lawrence, on the other hand, represents the born adventurer of colonialism. Quick to adapt though not thoughtful, particularly in the collective sense, Kim's dual identity, combined with his preoccupation with his own self-interest creates the ideal secret agent. Conversely, Lawrence of Arabia combined self-awareness and thoughtfulness. The difference was that Lawrence "still clung fast to a morality which, however, had already lost all objective bases and consisted only of a kind of private and necessarily quixotic attitude of chivalry."[44] With the illustrations of Kimball O'Hara and T. E. Lawrence, Arendt contrasts rootlessness and rootedness, thoughtlessness and thoughtfulness. Kimball O'Hara represents the imperialistic personality, whereas T. E. Lawrence personifies the adventurer. Just as George Kateb notes that antisemitism relied upon the innate Jewish personality, imperialism, as distinct from colonialism, relied upon the development of the imperialist character, someone who internalized his or her own superfluousness.

LAWRENCE OF ARABIA

Both Kim and Lawrence shifted roles as the Game demanded. The distinction between them is that Kim found himself shifting back and forth tethered to nothing, save perhaps the lama. Lawrence, in contrast, was firmly tethered to a moral system, as well as a support system of friends and family. Moreover, he developed not only a familiarity with and respect for Arab culture but a profound personal commitment to one Arab friend: Dahoum. This personal friendship provided Lawrence not only with the perspective to approach his interactions with Arab leaders, mindful of the other. Lawrence's friendship with Dahoum required him to assume the role of other in thinking about his own actions and the actions of the British Empire. In a 1919 letter to G. J. Kidston, Lawrence described his motivation during the war by beginning with Dahoum: "I liked a particular Arab very much and I thought that freedom for the race would be an acceptable present."[45] In other words as Lawrence became increasingly convinced that the British were not dealing sincerely with the Arabs, particularly in regard to the promise of self-governance, he pressed forward mindful of Dahoum's future and happiness.

In contrast to Kim, Lawrence does not view the British fomentation of the Arab National Movement as a game. His correspondence is littered with evidence of his own struggle to do his job and engage the Other out of concern, in other words, to remain an authentic Self despite his increasing fame. In contrast to Kim's fascination with the Game for its own sake, Lawrence examined his role in the Game from a critical perspective. Moreover, he views his Self, in the Great Game, not as superfluous but as playing a role and struggling for authenticity within the confines of that role. In a letter to Vyvyan Richards he describes the toll that service had taken on him. "I have been so violently uprooted and plunged so deeply into a job too big for me, that everything feels unreal. I . . . live only as a thief of opportunity, snatching chances of the moment when and where I see them . . . it's a kind of foreign stage, on which one plays day and night, in fancy dress, in a strange language with the price of failure on one's head."[46] In this passage Lawrence expressed awareness of a distinction between his Self and the role that he had come to play. Moreover, in *Seven Pillars of Wisdom*, Lawrence challenges the dominant cultural narrative by exposing the duplicity of the British and in the process opening his actions, as well as, British policy to contestation. "The Cabinet raised the Arabs to fight for us by definite promises of self-government afterwards."[47] Yet as he gradually realized that the promise of self governance was merely a sham, "instead of being proud of what we did together, I was continually and bitterly ashamed."[48] At the same time he acknowledges determining that it was "better we win and break our word than lose."[49] In so doing he provides insight into his own thought process, and the British role in the rebellion and invites the world to stand in judgment. He also judged himself: "[t]he only thing to do was to refuse rewards for being a successful trickster."[50] Lawrence remains rooted and authentic, in the Heideggerian sense: he thinks and acts, in the Arendtian sense and, in short, provides a striking contrast to Joseph Conrad's Mr. Kurtz, who exemplifies full-fledged racist imperialism.

CONRAD'S *HEART OF DARKNESS*

Joseph Conrad's *Heart of Darkness* depicts Charles Marlow's journey up the Congo River to a Belgian trading station in search of the legendary, Mr. Kurtz. In his classic work, Conrad provides us with "the most illuminating work on actual race experience in Africa."[51] He reveals the many complex layers of the race problem in Africa. He depicts the vacuity of life in Belgium, the motives for joining an imperialist expedition, as well as, the nearly unfathomable regard with which Africans appear to hold Mr. Kurtz. Moreover, Conrad explores the tumultuous internal struggles of both Kurtz and Marlow. Racism became a problem not only for the Africans who "quickly became the only part of the population that actually worked."[52] Arendt's point, following Conrad, is that racism also dehumanizes the racist. Not only is the exploited race forever changed; but "this absolute dependence on the work of others . . . transformed the Dutchman into a Boer."[53] That Kurtz epitomizes the individual who is "spat out" by society[54] is clear, as are the economic motives, particularly, once we learn that his fiancé's family disapproved of their relationship because of his lack of financial means. Marlow understands, if not precisely how Kurtz got to this point, the profound nature of his transformation. Marlow also obviously conceals Kurtz's transformation from his compatriots, as well as from his "Intended." Thus, racism clearly dehumanizes both victim and perpetrator, while the political bureaucracy conceals its true nature. Like Marlow, himself, the nature of this concealment remains opaque. Unlike T. E. Lawrence, the adventurer or colonialist, who remained rooted in and deeply connected to his homeland, Kurtz, the race imperialist, is "[e]xpelled from a world with accepted social values . . . thrown back upon [himself] and still had nothing to fall back upon except . . .

a streak of talent."[55] The myriad of different conceptual approaches to Conrad's work resemble the perspectives brought to bear on Arendt's work.

Leo Gurko suggests that Conrad, fully cognizant of imperialism's ill effects, ends up justifying the institution, whereas Avrom Fleishman insists that Conrad is highly critical of the European innovation.[56] Bruce Johnson, on the other hand, views Conrad's contribution as a primarily philosophical one. "Conrad anticipated existentialist thought by showing how the alienated self, when confronted with the meaninglessness of existence, has both the freedom and the responsibility to create its own values and even reality."[57] Peter Glassman suggests that the truly disconcerting thing about Kurtz, for Marlow, is that "Kurtz has shown Marlow that he *is* what Marlow has come to the Congo to become: a completed Self."[58] Though this interpretation certainly warrants examination the concerning thing is that in a Heideggerian sense, Glassman may be right. Kurtz resolutely and with spirit takes up a project by stepping outside social conventions imposed by the "they." In short, *The Heart of Darkness* provides Arendt with a familiar illustration of racism as a full-fledged ideology, complete with its existential dilemmas, as well as catastrophic, collective implications.

Another of the born adventurers of whom Arendt writes is Denys Finch Hatton, Isak Dinesen's lover. Finch-Hatton "belonged to the generation of young men whom the First World War had made forever unfit to bear the conventions and fulfill the duties, of everyday life."[59] Since marriage was among the duties Finch-Hatton was unfit to fulfill, Dinesen could only "lure" him back with an endless supply of original stories. Arendt does not explicitly develop the connection between the born adventurer and colonialism, as she does between the imperialist and racism. Although the restlessness of Denys Finch Hatton or T. E. Lawrence is a far cry from the ruthlessness of Mr. Kurtz, the characteristic they all share is superfluousness. Finch Hatton and Lawrence maintain significant cultural ties: personal ties to family and friends, a commitment to certain social values. Kim and Mr. Kurtz are considerably more disconnected. Neither Kim nor Mr. Kurtz struggles to reconcile their actions with their principles in the way T. E. Lawrence does. Denys Finch Hatton may prove a more interesting case than Arendt develops in her fleeting mentions. Though an adventurer and a playboy in many respects and certainly not rooted in his geographical place of origin in the way that Heidegger imagines, Finch Hatton nonetheless finds his project by reflecting on the world he encounters. Famous for his inability to commit to a lover and his tendency to use Africa as his own personal playground, Finch-Hatton also contemplated the big questions—what would all the big game hunting mean for Africa, the way of life, the livelihood of Africans? In short, he engaged in the kind of meditative thinking that Heidegger associates with rootedness. The result of this contemplation was that he discovered his project, pressured local administrators and the House of Commons to confront the issue of big game hunting.⁶⁰ His efforts culminated in the establishment of national parks in Kenya, Uganda and Tanzania.⁶¹

In thinking through *Imperialism*, Arendt develops the thesis that the alliance between the mob and the elite transforms an idea into a principle of political organization as, first, the intellectual elite transform the idea into an ideology by imbuing it with a sense of scientific determinism and historical inevitability. The political elite, then, use fear to transform the ideology into a political principle, while the support of the intellectual elite justifies its political use to external audiences.⁶² The shift from idea to ideology was made possible only by the pervasive nature of ideological thinking as an ontological condition. Just as modern Jews assimilated by internalizing anti-semitism, imperialists, as well as natives, lost their roots and acculturated themselves to imperialism by accepting racism, as a principle of political organization and ideological thinking as an ontological condition. In order to illustrate the subtle shift in existential choice from colonialism to imperialism, she drew on the readily accessible characters: Kimball O'Hara, Lawrence of Arabia and Mr. Kurtz. The adventurer of colonialism, personified by T. E. Lawrence, remained firmly rooted in his English Self, committed to traditional moral standards, cognizant of his role playing. He agonized over the duplicity of the British and his own moral and ethical obligations. The "innate" imperialist character, on the other hand, exemplified by Kimball O'Hara played the roles of *chela*, *sahib* and street urchin without setting down roots in a place, culture, language or moral system, cognizant of his own superfluity; whereas it is Mr. Kurtz who illustrates full-fledged racist imperialism. It becomes clear in Conrad's *Heart of Darkness* that it is not only the exploited Africans who are profoundly dehumanized. In so doing, Arendt reveals a subtle shift in the ontic structures that pressed upon perpetrators, as well as victims, of the German genocide. Thus, *Imperialism* and *Anti-Semitism* stand together as companion pieces in which Arendt seeks to understand the ontic structures, prior to taking up the ontological, both of which are critical to her ultimate aim of "leaping ahead . . . not in order to take "care" away . . . but . . . to give it back."⁶³ Again, with this approach, the historian pursues his or her own project in a mode of *being-with* that hands down to others their "inherited possibility" as such, historicity is an act in which the historian not only challenges a dominant interpretation of past events but in so doing retrieves possibilities. Thus, historicity serves as a precursor to both transcendence and, perhaps, as we shall soon see, to authenticity in the public realm.

NOTES

1. Seyla Benhabib, *The Reluctant Modernism of Hannah Arendt* (New York: Rowman & Littlefield), 63.

2. Benhabib, *The Reluctant Modernism of Hannah Arendt*; Margaret Canovan, *Hannah Arendt: A Re-interpretation of Her Political Thought* (New York: Cambridge University Press, 1992); Eric Voegelin, "The Origins of Totalitarianism," *Review of Politics* 15 (1953): 68–76.

3. Bernard Crick, "Arendt and *The Origins of Totalitarianism*: An Anglocentric View," in *Hannah Arendt in Jerusalem*, ed. Steven E. Ascheim (Berkeley: University of California Press, 1999), 96.

4. Eric Voegelin, "The Origins of Totalitarianism." It is not clear, however, that Voegelin and Arendt share a similar notion of either the proper or the wider context. He seems to grant secularization a place of primacy in terms of contextual factors, a contention with which Arendt does not agree.

5. Julia Kristeva, *Hannah Arendt* (New York: Columbia University Press, 2001), 5.

6. Crick, "Arendt and *The Origins of Totalitarianism*," 97.

7. George Kateb, *Hannah Arendt: Conscience, Evil and Politics* (Totowa, NJ: Rowman & Allanheld, 1983), 56.

8. Jacques Taminiaux, *The Thracian Maid and the Professional Thinker: Arendt and Heidegger* (Albany, NY: SUNY Press, 1997); Dana Villa, *Arendt and Heidegger: The Fate of the Political* (Princeton, NJ: Princeton University Press, 1996).

9. Kateb, *Hannah Arendt*, 59.

10. Arendt puts the term innate in quotation marks because she is using the term ironically. Her sincere reflection on whether or not characteristics can be considered innate is found in *Anti-Semitism*. "Each society demands of its members a certain amount of acting, the ability to present, represent and act what one actually is. When society disintegrates into cliques such demands are no longer made of the individual but of members of cliques. Behavior then is controlled by silent demands and not by individual capacities, exactly as an actor's performance must fit into the ensemble of all other roles in the play" (Hannah Arendt, *The Origins of Totalitarianism* (New York: Harcourt Brace, 1958), 84–85).

11. Hannah Arendt, "The Concept of History," in *Between Past and Future* (New York: The Viking Press, 1968), 89–90.

12. Michael Walzer, *Spheres of Justice* (New York: Basic Books, 1983), xiv; Sheldon Wolin, *The Presence of the Past* (Baltimore, MD: Johns Hopkins University Press, 1989), 140.

13. Hannah Arendt, "Outline of 'Elements of Shame: Anti-Semitism, Imperialism and Racism,'" Hannah Arendt Manuscripts Collection, Library of Congress, 1.

14. See in particular Max Weinreich's *Hitler's Professors: The Part of Scholarship in Germany's Crimes Against the Jewish People* (New Haven, CT: Yale University Press, 1946[1999]): 22–36.

15. Arendt, *Origins of Totalitarianism*, 151.

16. Ibid., 152.

17. Ibid., 195.

18. Ibid., 189.

19. Ibid., 150.

20. Ibid., 197.

21. Hannah Arendt, "Draft Research Outline of 'Elements of Shame: Anti-Semitism, Imperialism and Racism' Hannah Arendt Manuscripts Collection," Library of Congress, 4.

22. Arendt, *Origins of Totalitarianism*, 193.

23. Ibid., 155.

24. Ibid., 468–69.

25. The role of scapegoating in the development of genocide is examined by Peter Uvin (*Aiding Violence: The Development Enterprise in Rwanda* [West Hartford, CT: Kumarian Press, 1998]) and Ervin Staub (*The Roots of Evil: The Origins of Genocide and Other Group Violence* [Cambridge: Cambridge University Press, 1989]).

26. Hannah Arendt to Mary McCarthy, September 20, 1963, in *Between Friends: The Correspondence of Hannah Arendt and Mary McCarthy 1949–1975*, ed. C. Brightman (New York: Harcourt Brace, 1995), 147.

27. Martin Heidegger, "Memorial Address," in *Discourse on Thinking*, trans. John M. Anderson and E. Hans Freud (New York: Harper and Row, 1966), 46–47.

28. Arendt, *Origins of Totalitarianism*, 471.

29. Ibid., 470–71.
30. Hannah Arendt, *Eichmann in Jerusalem: A Report on the Banality of Evil* (New York: Harcourt Brace, 1963), 33.
31. Dana R. Villa, *Politics, Philosophy and Terror: Essays on the Thought of Hannah Arendt* (Princeton, NJ: Princeton University Press, 1999), 20.
32. Arendt, "Draft Research Outline of 'Elements of Shame,'" 1.
33. Arendt, *Origins of Totalitarianism*, 170.
34. Ibid., 189.
35. Ibid., 190.
36. Rudyard Kipling, *Kim*, intro. Edward Said (New York: Penguin Classics, 1987), 179.
37. Ibid., 196.
38. Arendt, *Origins of Totalitarianism*, 189.
39. Ibid.
40. Ibid.
41. Ibid., 141.
42. Arendt, "Draft Research Outline of 'Elements of Shame,'" 1.
43. Arendt, *Origins of Totalitarianism*, 217–18.
44. Ibid., 218.
45. T. E. Lawrence to G. J. Kidston, November 14, 1919, in *Lawrence of Arabia: The Selected Letters*, ed. Malcolm Brown (London: Little Books, 2007), 178.
46. T. E. Lawrence to Vyvyan Richards, July 15, 1918, in *Lawrence of Arabia*, 158.
47. T. E. Lawrence, *Seven Pillars of Wisdom: A Triumph* (Blacksburg, VA: Wilder Publications, 2011), 10. Moreover, in the spirit of challenging the dominant historical interpretation, Lawrence ironically subtitled his text: A Triumph (T. E. Lawrence to Vyvyan Richards, early 1923, in *Lawrence of Arabia*, 237).
48. Lawrence, *Seven Pillars of Wisdom*, 11.
49. Ibid.
50. Ibid.
51. Arendt, *Origins of Totalitarianism*, 185.
52. Ibid., 193.
53. Ibid.
54. Ibid., 189.
55. Ibid.
56. Leo Gurko, *Joseph Conrad: Giant in Exile* (New York: Macmillan, 1962), 148; Avrom Fleishman, *Conrad's Politics* (Baltimore, MD: Johns Hopkins University Press, 1967), 89.
57. Bruce Johnson, *Conrad's Models of Mind* (Minneapolis: University of Minnesota Press, 1971), 71.
58. Peter J. Glassman, *Language and Being: Joseph Conrad and the Literature of Personality* (New York: Columbia University Press, 1976), 228.
59. Hannah Arendt, *Men in Dark Times* (New York: Harcourt Brace, 1968), 101.
60. Finch Hatton engaged Chief Secretary to the Government of Tanganyika (Tanzania), Douglas Jardine, in a debate about enforcement of restrictions on hunting game from vehicles during June and July of 1929 (Denys Finch Hatton, "Hunting from Motorcars," *The Times*, July 3, 1929, 17; Douglas Jardine, "Hunting from Motorcars: The Law and Public Opinion," *The Times*, July 8, 1929; Denys Finch Hatton, "Hunting from Motorcars: The Affected Area," *The Times*, July 10, 1929, 12; Douglas Jardine, "Hunting from Cars," *The Times*, July 18, 1929).
61. While it is certainly risky to comment on Finch Hatton's thought process, particularly since he left so little in the way of a written record, he moved from promoting hunting to photography and engaged in an active public relations campaign (contrary to his inclinations) to preserve and protect African wildlife (Denys Finch Hatton, "Lions at their Ease: Stalking by Car," *The Times*, January 21, 1928, 11; Denys Finch Hatton, "Stalking with a Camera: The New African Sport," *The Times*, June 29, 1929, 13; Sara Wheeler, *Too Close to the Sun* (New York: Random House, 2006), 217–19).
62. Weinreich, *Hitler's Professors*, 36–40; Yvonne Sherratt, *Hitler's Philosophers* (New Haven, CT: Yale University Press, 2013), 92–126.

63. Martin Heidegger, *Being and Time*, trans. Joan Stambaugh (Albany, NY: SUNY Press, 1997), 115.

Chapter Six

Vorspringen (Leaping Ahead)

Understanding *Totalitarianism*

Though Heidegger elevates ontological questions over ontic ones, he also cautions that ontological questions can only be taken up through the ontic, which is to say once one has developed a sense of belonging to a particular place and time. For Heidegger this rootedness need not be either intellectual or historical in nature. In other words, though Heidegger may well be an elitist, the essential components of authenticity are not by any means reserved for intellectuals. In this vein, Arendtian authenticity, despite its dependence on a public self-revealing, remains a viable option for common folk. In her own project, her public self-revelation began with an examination of the ontic characteristics (jewish and female) in the biography of Rahel Varnhagen. In *Anti-Semitism* and *Imperialism*, she examines the ontic structures within which individuals make their existential choices, take up an ontological condition and, to some degree, the collective implications of those choices. Her focus shifts in *Totalitarianism* to the political and sociological structures that press, in an immediate sense, on both victims and perpetrators. In the process she begins to view the mob-elite alliance, ideology and secrecy as ontic structures that pressed upon Germans and Russians alike, regardless of the particular ideological orientation. Finally, in "Ideology and Terror," she reveals that the ontological core of totalitarianism, whether from the left or right, is loneliness. Arendt's unique contribution to the study of totalitarianism lay in her examination of the ontic circumstances under which loneliness translates into a deficient mode of care as a collective norm.

While Arendt embraces Heidegger's critique of historiography, she is not content to offer an abstract analysis. Thus, *The Origins of Totalitarianism* reflects her attempt to undertake a historically oriented study mindful of all the risks and limitations of historiography; the brilliance of her text lies in the attempt to reveal the complex intertwining of political, economic, sociological, as well as ontological factors contributing to the "crisis of our time."[1] While several scholars have noted the importance of the breakdown of traditional forms of social connectedness into a mass mentality[2] or the unique leadership style of Hitler or Stalin,[3] still others raise the question of whether Marxism is innately totalitarian.[4] Arendt reveals that the reason a leader such as Hitler or Stalin found a following is that ideology provided both the mob and the mass with two things they desperately needed, while a bewildering array of front organizations, shadow governments and legal obfuscation shielded perpetrators and victims from reality. In so doing Arendt reveals the ontological underpinnings of genocide, as well as the collective implication of a deficient mode of care, all for the purpose of handing back to *mitdasein* their "ownmost" possibilities.

In the 1964 interview, Günter Gaus, at one point, posed the question to Hannah Arendt, "[d]o you want to achieve extensive influence with these works?" Arendt responded with a brief reproach, "that is a masculine question . . . [m]en always want to be terribly influential, but I see that as somewhat external." In drawing the gendered distinction Arendt offered insight not only into her own intellectual process, but the role of scholarship in a public space.

> What satisfies me is the thought process itself. As long as I have succeeded in thinking something through, I am personally quite satisfied. If I then succeed in expressing my thought process in writing, that satisfies me also. . . . Do I imagine myself being influential? No. I want to understand. And if others understand—in the same way that I have understood—that gives me a sense of satisfaction.[5]

In this formulation, writing and scholarship are cast as nothing more than part of the process of achieving understanding, as part of the thinking process. Satisfaction lies in promoting or provoking thought, rather than imposing the results of one's thinking on others. The provisional nature of Arendt's work is perhaps nowhere more readily discernible than in *The Origins of Totalitarianism*.[6] Moreover, it is consistent with the Heideggerian notion of writing as a way of releasing one's discovery for further examination and critique by others.[7]

UNDERSTANDING TOTALITARIANISM

As previously noted the notion of causality is virtually non-sensical in the context either of historicity or as a phenomenological approach to historical inquiry. As such there may be only one aspect of *Totalitarianism* that generates unanimous agreement: Arendt eschews causal analysis and instead sought to identify "subterranean streams" that came together or elements that crystallized into totalitarianism, in the hope that this revelation would prove destructive.[8] Thus in the text of *Totalitarianism*, Arendt approaches the phenomena by breaking it down into its constituent parts: masses, functionaries and leadership.[9] She examines the process by which the Nazi regime destroyed, first, the juridical person, then the moral person and finally, "human individuality itself."[10] Yet it is the conflation of these elements that continued to intrigue her. In *Totalitarianism*, she devotes the lion share of her efforts to describing either totalitarianism as it appeared in Germany, Russia or to a description of the constituent parts of her concept of totalitarianism.[11] Over time it is the interaction between these constituent parts that fascinates her. These subsequent or follow-up questions lead Bernard Crick to contend that "most of her other works are like huge footnotes to resolve the difficulties left behind" by *Origins*.[12] Arendt starts to move from the description of specific political structures and development of an ideal type or conceptual description to an examination of ontological questions with the addition of "Ideology and Terror." As with *Imperialism* the lasting importance of the text remains a matter of some dispute. George Kateb and Seyla Benhabib focus on the role of concentration camps[13]; whereas Margaret Canovan and Roy Tsao argue that Arendt's primary contribution is in redefining totalitarianism as a movement rather than a structure.[14] Jerome Kohn finds the merit, as well as the challenge, of Arendt's text derives from the conflation of her description of totalitarian regimes with her development of the concept—totalitarianism. Her description of the Nazi and Stalinist regimes raises questions about the nature of totalitarianism at the same time that her discussion of totalitarianism, as a conceptual matter, raises questions about her assessment of the regimes.[15]

Both Kateb and Benhabib note Arendt's peculiar invocation of historical forces. She attempts not to "establish some inevitable continuity between the past and the present" since she views the future as "radically undetermined."[16] Despite her view that there was nothing predetermined, inevitable or fated in the totalitarianism that emerged, Europe did experience "something it had prepared for itself."[17] For Kateb and Benhabib, contra Canovan, the concentration camps epitomize totalitarianism or "reveal the elementary truths" particularly in so far as they "served no 'utilitarian' purpose ... they were needed neither to intimidate and subdue the opposition nor to provide for 'cheap and disposable' labor."[18] For Kateb this senselessness is part and parcel of the uniqueness of totalitarianism which is less a political structure than a "methodical killing of certain populations on a large scale ... undertaken deliberately and as a matter of policy by those in power, whose overriding aim is to kill them even though they are not hostile or even dissident, or even unwitting obstacles to any purpose of utility, or practicality, or even in possession of worldly goods of any sort that their killers need, want or covet."[19] Though Margaret Canovan takes issue with this assertion, Kateb's analysis is noteworthy for its contention that Arendt is most essentially interested in genocide. As we shall soon see she identifies and describes with striking prescience a multitude of factors that have only recently found support in the comparative genocide literature. As such I contend that Arendt's text which once occupied an important place in the literature on totalitarianism may yet prove fertile ground for genocide research.

Moreover in contrast to those who label her later work as her return to philosophy, Benhabib describes *Origins* as the "work in which the legacy of German *Existenz* philosophy and the political catastrophes of the twentieth century are brought into fateful synthesis. . . . It is also in this work that Martin Heidegger's continuing influence upon Arendt is most visible."[20] In short, I argue with Benhabib that Arendt's debt to Heidegger is readily discernible in *Origins*. Contra Benhabib I find the lasting value of Arendt's theory of totalitarianism in the ontological comparability of Nazi Germany and Stalinist Russia. Arendt obviously does not assert that antisemitism and imperialism "crystallized" in the same way in these two cases.[21] Rather she contends that political structures and conditions created similar existential choices among segments of the population, hence similar ontological conditions which facilitated the emergence of genocide.

Margaret Canovan and Roy Tsao argue that Arendt's primary contribution lay in redefining totalitarianism as a movement rather than a political structure. Canovan highlights the role of the masses, in particular the parallel between the masses and the leaders in a totalitarian movement. The masses proved fertile ground for recruitment due to "a mixture of gullibility and cynicism."[22] The masses were mobilized by propaganda which provided them a

> reassuring claim to infallibility, prophecy based on a supposed insight into the inevitable forces of history. Although the theories and predictions that the movement offered were contrary to common sense, this was no deterrent to belief, since common sense was precisely what the masses no longer possessed. Bereft of social status and communal relations by unexpected catastrophes, they had lost their ability to distinguish reality from unreality and had become hungry for any doctrine, however preposterous, that would reveal some kind of consistent pattern within the bewildering events of their time.[23]

In this way the masses were remarkably similar to the leaders of the totalitarian movement, not only in the "mixture of gullibility and cynicism," but in their reliance on the inevitability of historical forces as justification for their actions. Canovan views Arendt's unique contribution to the literature on totalitarianism as redefining it from an institutional structure to a movement.

"These were not states protecting specific interests, but movements interested in remaking reality ... on a global scale," intent on reducing human beings to "bundles of reactions" devoid of spontaneity or creativity, thus individuality.[24] In contrast to Benhabib and Kateb, Canovan does find a purpose in the dehumanization of the camps. The purpose was to eliminate spontaneity, not only in the prisoners, but in the troops and rest of the population as well.

THE MOB—ELITE ALLIANCE

Among the elements that, according to Arendt, *crystallize* in a genocidal regime is the curious alliance between the mob and the elite. This purported relationship becomes all the more perplexing once we realize that she has two separate and distinct elite in mind (political and intellectual) and they perform multifarious tasks. Moreover, it is impossible to discuss the function of the mob without differentiating it from the supporting role played by the masses. In describing the relationship between the elite and the mob, Arendt uses the phrase—*temporary alliance*. The *temporary* nature of the alliance refers to the contribution of the intellectual elite and the mob. The part played by the masses, on the other hand, is not temporary; their willingness to take up the work of killing constitutes an enduring and necessary condition for the execution of genocide. As such the role of the masses can probably best be described as a subordinate one, though this characterization runs the risk of understating their importance.

One wonders if Arendt may have Heidegger in mind when she asserts that the appeal of the alliance for the elite lay in watching the excluded (among whom they feel at home) destroy the hypocrisy of society. The elite "did not object at all to paying a price, the destruction of civilization, for the fun of seeing how those who had been excluded unjustly in the past forced their way into it. They were not particularly outraged at the monstrous forgeries in historiography.... They had convinced themselves that traditional historiography was a forgery in any case."[25] Moreover, the alliance is described by Arendt as temporary because the intellectual elite are needed only to justify the movement en route to power. Once they acquire power, the political elite have no need for intellectual justification. For that reason, their "obsession ... with 'scientific' proof ceases once they are in power."[26]

In *Origins* the mob served as agitators of violence during the Dreyfus Affair and proved to be amenable both to manipulation and co-ordination by the political elite. It was the mob that escalated the Dreyfus controversy from an unfortunate political scandal to a series of violent political episodes by publicly calling for Jewish blood. For Arendt the mob is a necessary by-product of capitalism. It contains shades of a criminal underworld and is characterized by rootlessness and contempt for respectable society.[27] The mob are the "denizens of the frankly criminal milieu that thrived in the bowels of nineteenth- and early-twentieth-century capitalism, a motley assortment of 'armed bohemians' who share the respectable bourgeoisie's possessive individualism without the latter's inhibited propriety, and who bypass the much-vaunted ethic of work in favor of more or less organized violence."[28] Often mistaken for the people, by those who hope to organize it, as well as by its victims, Arendt states clearly that this is an incorrect supposition; instead the mob is an angry, violent "caricature of the people."[29] It "hates the society from which it is excluded."[30] On its own, the mob's predisposition to violence presents a limited concern since it is inherently resistant to organization. The antagonism toward respectable society, however, is a predisposition shared by both the mob and the elite; whether she refers to the intellectual elite, the political elite or both remains unclear.

Arendt emphasizes that there is a striking resemblance between the mob and the elite. The "present totalitarian rulers and the leaders of totalitarian movements still bear the characteristic traits of the mob."[31] The elite are "completely absorbed by their desire to see the ruin of this whole world of fake security, fake culture, and fake life."[32] Their frustration was genuine, their pursuit of change, desperate. They had been "touched by misery . . . [and were] deadly hurt by hypocrisy."[33] They sought solace in the feeling of belonging afforded by the totalitarian movement. The elite embraced violence in order to put an end to hypocrisy, while the mob wanted "access to history even at the price of destruction."[34] Thus, the only real common ground between the mob and the elite could be found in the depth of their malevolence and their sense of despair at their exclusion from respectable society. While this shared animus does not provide an enduring basis for a long-term alliance, the intensity of their enmity serves as a catalyst. In the context of totalitarianism, the mob drew upon and gave focus to the frustration of the masses. This mob differed from the nineteenth-century mob insofar as the twentieth-century mob "could no longer escape into exotic lands, could no longer afford to be dragon-slayers among strange and exciting people."[35] Though these foreign adventures may have represented false projects, they did provide an outlet for widespread animosity, in their absence

> this feeling of being caught again and again in the trappings of society—so different from the conditions which had formed the imperialist character—added a constant strain and the yearning for violence to the older passion for anonymity and losing oneself. Without the possibility of radical change of role and character, such as the identification with the Arab national movement. . . . These people felt attracted to the pronounced activism of totalitarian movements.[36]

Vorspringen *(Leaping Ahead)* 99

In short, Arendt provides an overview of the emergence of a genocide. The intellectual elite, first, offers both domestic and international audiences a palatable explanation for the regime's policies. Second, the political elite triggers and co-ordinates episodic violence, which is in fact carried out by the mob. Finally, the routinized "work" of extermination is turned over to the masses.

Among the ontic features that pressed upon both perpetrators and victims, Arendt begins with the emergence of a classless society. She notes both the existential angst, as well as the political implications. While individuals struggled with "[s]elflessness in the sense that oneself does not matter" as well as the "feeling of being expendable,"[37] collectively "[m]asses are not held together by a consciousness of common interest and they lack that specific class articulateness which is expressed in determined, limited and obtainable goals."[38] Thus individuals fail to take themselves up as projects, cease to experience themselves as future directed beings. They are not conscious of shared interests; thus no commonality can be articulated and expressed in a political sense, adding weight to the angst and enmity.

The role of the intellectual elite may be among Arendt's least developed assertions. She not only draws attention to the intellectual elite's exclusion from and distain for the hypocrisy of respectable society but she also distinguishes between two different sets of motives. She identifies one group who *merely* co-operated with the regime, presumably in the interest of their own career advancement, and another who volunteered its services out of a genuine commitment to National Socialism. Moreover, she goes on to list the genuine Nazis; the list does not include Martin Heidegger, leading one to surmise that perhaps Heidegger falls into the former category—merely cooperative. She takes both the time to develop the connection and then dismisses its significance almost immediately by arguing that the intellectual elite may have played a role in legitimizing the totalitarian movement for external audiences, though it had no impact on the totalitarian regime.[39] "[I]t must be stated that what these desperate men of the twentieth century did or did not do had no influence on totalitarianism whatsoever, although it did play some part in earlier, successful attempts of the movements to force the outside world to take their doctrines seriously."[40] Though it is unclear to what earlier efforts Arendt is referring, she notes that these intellectual supporters were "shaken off even before the regimes proceeded toward their greatest crimes."[41] Given that the intellectual elite, as well as the mob, retain an element of unpredictability, the very characteristic that predisposes them to initiate violence may render their long-term reliability doubtful, since spontaneity makes individuals "unpredictable and therefore get[s] in the way of attempts to harness [them] for collective motion."[42] In short, while the political elite co-ordinate outbreaks of violence, the intellectual elite provide a theoretical justification which serves, perhaps temporarily, to legitimate the regime, deflect criticism from it and perhaps deter intervention.

If the mob hated the "society from which it [was] excluded,"[43] the mass demonstrated no such potent animosity, no contempt, no self-interest. Rather the masses "yearn for anonymity, for being just a number and functioning only as a cog."[44] The main trait of the "mass man is not brutality and backwardness, but isolation and a lack of normal social relationships."[45] Rendered atomized and isolated by the virtually simultaneous "breakdowns of civic, political, [and] cultural associations,"[46] the mass man has lost "a stable space of reference, identity . . . a particular social perspective from which to view the world."[47] If the mob man's outlook is characterized by anger and resentment, the mass man's condition is one of isolation and loneliness. The masses can fulfill various supporting roles though on their own they lack the spontaneity necessary to initiate violence; additionally, they lack the perspective necessary for judgment that might enable them to resist ideological thinking. The troubling thing for Arendt is that the mass man proves more amenable to manipulation, though the lack of animosity means that this manipulation will require both a catalyst and a justification. The mob man will undertake violence with only the slightest of provocations. Ultimately, however, it is the mass man who is capable of the greatest crimes, "provided that these crimes were well organized and assumed the appearance of routine jobs."[48]

The point for Arendt is that just as there are two different groups of elite serving different functions, genocidal violence is perpetrated by two distinct groups. The mob, whose disaffection requires little in the way of provocation, initiates the violence; the masses, whose existential despair predisposes them to manipulation, take up the work with a peculiar devotion, born of a desperate desire to belong to something, anything that might lend meaning to their existence. "Nazi propaganda . . . gave the masses of atomized, undefinable, unstable and futile individuals a means of self-definition and identification which not only restored some of the self-respect they had formerly derived from their function in society, but also created a kind of spurious stability which made them better candidates for an organization."[49] In short, while Arendt warns of explosive potential created by the temporary alliance between the elite and the mob, it is the mass man, utterly lacking in spontaneity, who proves to be the more reliable executioner over the long term, as long as he is carefully prepared and motivated, hence manipulated, by an effective elite. According to Arendt only "the mob and the elite can be attracted by the momentum of the totalitarianism itself; the masses have to be won by propaganda."[50] Mob mobilization requires little in the way of provocation; mass mobilization requires an ideology.

The Arendtian ideology, which imposes a single factor explanation, interprets all of human history, including contemporary challenges, in terms of a natural process, an unavoidable progression which has a scientific explanation. This natural process or scientific explanation soon gives way to a theory of world conspiracy which is the key to both scapegoating a particular Other and transforming the mob's anger and propensity for violence into actual violence. That same violence is then used as evidence that the inevitable historical processes are, in fact, underway. This explanation, according to Arendt, appeals to the masses in that the escape from reality into a consistent, predictable, logic fantasy "grants them a minimum of self-respect."[51] It offers an explanation by which their plight, their hopelessness, belongs not to any of their own culpability but rather to a grand, evil world conspiracy that can be avenged. It was only when colonialism, imperialism and the First World War ceased to provide an outlet in the form of foreign adventures that the elite hit upon an explanation to trigger the mob's malevolence and persuade the masses. Moreover they employed a sophisticated bureaucratic apparatus and invoked a tradition of secret societies in order to scapegoat the Other, in this case, the Jews.

SECRECY, REALITY AND FICTION

Among the factors which press upon existential choices in a totalitarian movement, secrecy features prominently, operates somewhat differently with different audiences and contributes to dubious notions of reality and fantasy. Secret societies, front organizations, shadow governments and a "fluctuating hierarchy" in which additional layers were added without ever dissolving the previous layer, new units were added, ostensibly fulfilling the same function, made it impossible for party members to know their true status within the organization. Duplicate agencies were often presented with conflicting orders, making it impossible for insiders to know which orders were real, or what the meaning of the order actually was. The camps themselves were shrouded in secrecy. Neighbors and family members did not know what happened to the arrested. Locals did not know what happened at the camps. Oftentimes party members did not know what happened to the arrested and no one knew, particularly in Stalinist Russia, who would be arrested next. As the notion of reality, that which one can perceive with one's five senses, of which the intellectual elite had always been skeptical, became dubious for the masses as well, a totalitarian personality developed, characterized by "extraordinary adaptability" the "absence of continuity," gullibility and cynicism.[52] In other words, the resulting personality was amenable not only to manipulation and shifting loyalties but it was sufficiently skeptical of any objective reality that all falsehoods became equally plausible.

Totalitarian movements constructed numerous fictional tales that various groups preferred to reality for different reasons. The masses preferred the logical simplicity of ideology to the inconsistency of reality. It suited their desire for "a completely consistent, comprehensible world." According to Arendt in their "essential homelessness they can no longer bear its accidental, incomprehensible aspects . . . [the] fictitious consistency . . . grants them a minimum of self-respect."[53] Though the connection between homelessness and fantasy remains unclear, Arendt seems to be suggesting that in the absence of a grounding or rootedness in time and place, the rootless may seek a sense of belonging to anything. The logical, fictitious consistency of an ideology grants them a sense of comfort and purpose. As we can see, Arendt has clearly begun to explore the link between the sociological phenomena and its existential roots. Outsiders also believe the fiction over the reality albeit for different reasons. When offered the fiction of front organizations, the non-totalitarian world

> refuse to believe their eyes and ears in the face of the monstrous. . . . This common sense disinclination to believe the monstrous is constantly strengthened by the totalitarian ruler himself, who makes sure that no reliable statistics, no controllable facts and figures are ever published, so that there are only subjective, uncontrollable, and unreliable reports about the places of the living dead.[54]

In short, the non-totalitarian world believed fiction over reality because the reality was both horrifying and implausible.

As with her other discussions of the elite, Arendt leaves the role of the totalitarian elite underdeveloped, which is to say she never clarifies whether she has in mind a political or intellectual elite. She notes only that without their "artificially induced inability to understand facts as facts, to distinguish between truth and falsehood, the movement could never move in the direction of realizing its fiction."[55] Though it is never clear what exactly it means to say the elite's "inability to understand" was "artificially induced," she seems to view it almost as a willful disregard for facts and truth. The only illustration of the "artificially induced inability to understand" appears as Arendt's interpretation of public reaction to Brecht's *Dreigroschenoper* and Celine's *Bagatelles pour un Massacre*. The *Dreigroschenoper* portrayed "gangsters as respectable businessmen and respectable businessmen as gangsters."[56] The irony, Arendt argues, "was somewhat lost when respectable businessmen in the audience considered this a deep insight into the ways of the world."[57] Simply put, the bourgeoisie enjoyed the play and understood it as conveying a profound insight since "it had been fooled by its own hypocrisy for so long that it had grown tired of the tension."[58] It was quite simply easier, then to subscribe to this "artificially induced inability to understand."[59] It was easier to accept untruths than to do the difficult work of reflecting on what Brecht was suggesting. Thus the effect was open acceptance of that which Brecht had intended as irony. Similarly, Celine's play proposed to massacre all the Jews. One review "delighted . . . in the blunt admission of such a desire" as it pointed out the "hypocritical politeness" of respectable society.[60] These two episodes, according to Arendt, demonstrate the elite's inability to place a valid observation in a proper context so as to understand its proper meaning, as well as its importance.

Suffice it to say that one of the cultural phenomena pressing upon victims, as well as perpetrators was the challenge of discerning reality from a carefully constructed fiction that was in many ways more plausible than the truth.[61] Since objective reality was itself impossible, all fiction was preferable to reality, for elites, as long as it could claim to reveal the hypocrisy of society and, for the masses, as long as it afforded a sense of belonging to something. Under these conditions, the resulting "totalitarian" personality, which may well have characterized both victims and perpetrators, was amenable not only to manipulation and shifting loyalties but profoundly skeptical of the existence of an *objective* reality. For party members, once a leader's false statements had been revealed, the totalitarian personality not only stood by the leader but admired "their superior tactical cleverness."[62] Though the conceptual value of totalitarianism is widely considered marginal at this point, the lasting value of Arendt's text may well lie in the area of genocide studies, as the empirical evidence from Rwanda supports several of her assertions.

UNDERSTANDING GENOCIDE: THE EVIDENCE FROM RWANDA

In her effort to understand the German genocide, Hannah Arendt does not speak about genocide explicitly but rather discusses the emergence of a novel form of government—totalitarianism which she defines as a system in which "genocide was the *raison d'etre*."[63] She describes a system that required by its very logic and for its perpetuation, "an unending supply of innocent victims."[64] The Nazi regime manufactured these victims by first destroying the juridical person, then the moral person, and finally "human individuality itself."[65] Dehumanization proceeded in an orderly and systematic fashion from the elimination of political and human rights, to ghettoization and finally concentration camps. Yet in Rwanda there were no camps, no ghettos and the legal status of the Tutsi never changed. Even in the absence of a camp system however, dehumanization occurred and terror thrived.[66] In the absence of some of the formal developments Arendt deemed important in the German case, the mob-elite alliance mobilized a willing mob through the use of a highly effective ideology. Thus, though the term for Arendt's area of interest was totalitarianism, her primary interest was genocide and it may well be in the area of genocide research that *Totalitarianism* finds its most enduring impact.

Most explanations of the Rwandan genocide discuss the role of ideology. Verwimp argues that the Habyarimana regime employs a Marxist interpretation of the Hamitic myth, casting the Tutsi as an intellectual bourgeois who refused to do the difficult work of tilling the soil.[67] Mamdani views the Kayibanda regime as primarily responsible for imbuing the Hamitic myth with racist overtones and casting the Tutsi as malicious and manipulative invaders, depriving the Hutu of the rewards of their work.[68] While these accounts recognize the political potency of scapegoating an ethnic group, they employ the term ideology haphazardly to denote a set of controlling, quasi-hegemonic ideas. In other words, Verwimp and Mamdani are primarily interested in the ideas underlying the ideology. For Arendt, one of the unique elements of a genocide is that a logical manner of thinking takes over the ideas, rendering the ideas—truisms. Thus, Arendt's examination of ideology explains not only the rhetoric or intent of leaders but the process by which that rhetoric takes on a quasi-compulsory, even prophetic quality.

The role of the Hamitic *hypothesis* in the Rwandan genocide has been well documented.[69] It derives from sociological and political questions regarding the construction of Hutu and Tutsi identity, as well as anthropological investigation of the Tutsi migration hypothesis. The term Hamitic *hypothesis* is used in the literature to refer both to the anthropological hypothesis regarding Tutsi migration and the value laden myths that were used in the construction of Tutsi and Hutu as political identities, thus laying the groundwork for a bifurcated society and ultimately, a genocide. The Tutsi migration hypothesis is, in fact, an anthropological hypothesis, linked to questions of whether Tutsi exists as a genetic group. The myth of Hamitic peoples in Africa appropriates the label hypothesis inappropriately; thus, lending an air of scientific validity to a value laden and socially constructed myth.

The Tutsi migration hypothesis finds support across a variety of academic disciplines. Simply put the hypothesis is that the Tutsi of East Africa, primarily Rwanda and Burundi, migrated to the Great Lakes region around the fifteenth century from southern Ethiopia and southern Somalia.[70] This migration ostensibly occurred because the Tutsi sought a climate more suitable to cattle. This hypothesis finds support, though certainly not unequivocal support, in genetic studies, fossil records and historical accounts.[71] The Tutsi migration hypothesis shifts in the direction of a socially constructed, value laden myth when it begins to suggest that the physical features common to the Tutsi are genetically closer to Caucasian.[72] Moreover, the supposition of genetic similarity is further co-opted by the suggestion that the physical features are co-terminus with higher levels of intelligence and a greater propensity toward civilization. These so-called scientific findings were utilized by colonial powers in the construction of a Tutsi race, invested with social and political privilege, similar to that of the Court Jews of which Arendt writes.

The Hamitic myth, on the other hand, derives from competing interpretations of Judeo-Christian myths and begins to take the form of an ideology in the colonial era. Ham was a son of Noah, who was cursed by his father for his disrespect. The curse, seemingly, led to the emergence of the Negroid race, which explains not only physical features—hair texture, skin tone, lip shape, but also character traits. The Negroid race, by virtue of Noah's curse was commanded "to love theft and fornication, to be banded together in hatred . . . and never to tell the truth."[73] To the degree that this myth comprised part of a hypothesis, in keeping with the Tutsi migration hypothesis, it was a non-scientific hypothesis proclaimed by colonial powers as justification for the social and political identity they constructed with respect to the Tutsi. The colonists claimed that "wherever in Africa there was evidence of organized state life, there the ruling groups must have come from elsewhere. These mobile groups were known as Hamites, and the notion that they were the hidden hand behind every bit of civilization on the continent was known as the 'Hamitic hypothesis.'"[74] As such the Hamites, occupied a netherland between Caucasian and Negroid, sometimes referred to as "Caucasians under a black skin." Ostensibly exhibiting the superior intelligence and organizational skill of Caucasians, yet "hopelessly mongrelized by the native and inferior blacks" the Hamites were perfectly positioned targets either as nearly white aliens or intruders, hence as oppressors, or as mongrels, inferior to true Africans. Thus a legitimate academic hypothesis was co-opted by colonial powers, transformed into a myth or pseudo-hypothesis and gradually began to morph into an Arendtian ideology, in so far as it purported to explain, not only the history of Rwanda, East Africa and power relations with the European powers but also "claimed to explain all signs of civilization in Bantu Africa—from monotheism to the use of iron and other material artifacts to the development of statecraft."[75] The Hamitic *hypothesis* accomplishes the first two objectives of an Arendtian ideology—explaining human history and contemporary challenges, though it was not until the 1990s that it took on a prophetic quality.

In short, the so-called Hamitic hypothesis was used to suggest to the Hutu the inevitability of a future in which they would find themselves once again subordinated to the Tutsi, unless they took it upon themselves to do the "work" of defending themselves against the ambitious, conniving, ruthless invaders. In the context of this multi-faceted threat, Habyarimana utilized rhetoric designed to consolidate the Hutu, in a unified effort to resist the encroaching Rwandan Patriotic Front (RPF). In this sense as an ideology, the Hamitic myth was used differently in the Rwandan genocide than it was in the German genocide. In the German genocide, the Darwinian triumph of the Aryan race was posited as an inevitable outcome and the Final Solution merely served to accelerate this natural progression. Whereas in the Rwandan case, the future predicted by the Hamitic myth was one of restored Tutsi dominance and Hutu were exhorted to ensure that this outcome did not come to pass. It was precisely the purported inevitability which rendered extreme measures such as *self-defense* necessary. In both cases, a group that had enjoyed privileged social position and was deprived of that privilege under conditions of the modernity (modern nation-state or colonial independence) saw itself scapegoated, and in both cases, that scapegoating took similar forms. Based on previous privileged status, both groups were accused of serving as a "hidden hand" and in both cases, leaders used a myth of inevitability, cloaked in scientific terminology to re-enforce the futility of non-compliance and encourage logical thinking. The intellectual elite in Rwanda appear to have played a more direct role in exhorting the mob to acts of violence than did German intellectuals.

Ferdinand Nahimana, a French trained historian, served as advisor and speechwriter to the Habyarimana regime. In some respects, Nahimana bears a striking resemblance to Martin Heidegger. Nahimana served as Dean of the College of Letters at the National University before he became a speechwriter for the Habyarimana regime. Like Heidegger, Nahimana's role raises questions about his scholarly work. In his early work, *Le Blanc Est Arrive, Le Roi Est Parti*, Nahimana challenges the Tutsi-centric historical narrative, by attempting among other things, to re-introduce Hutu leaders into Rwandan history. His later work, *Rwanda: les virages* (missed opportunities), has been less well received and its academic merit called into question. In contrast to the German intellectuals, Nahimana had an impact on the regime though the full extent of his influence is still unknown. He was responsible for educating military personnel on the extent of the Tutsi threat, though the degree to which he may also have educated the Habyarimana regime remains a question.[76] Additionally, when an international commission warned of human rights violations under the Habyarimana, Nahimana was sent to Brussels to speak on behalf of the regime.[77] Nahimana was not only among the founders of Radio Télévision Libre des Mille Collines (RTLM); he proposed its creation, hired the staff and, along with Jean-Bosco Barayagwiza controlled the finances.[78] Moreover as Director of ORINFO (Rwandan Bureau of Information) and member of the RTLM Steering Committee, he was in a position to make editorial and programming decisions, virtually unilaterally. In March 1992, Nahimana ordered a broadcast stating that a Tutsi plan to kill Hutu leaders had been revealed in Nairobi. RTLM's editorial team decided against the broadcast because it was unable to confirm the information. Nahimana overruled the editorial staff and the broadcast aired four or five times between March 3rd and 4th 1992. In the aftermath of these broadcasts, over three hundred Tutsi were killed in Bugesera alone.[79] Finally on March 28th of 1994, Nahimana sent a letter to members of the political and intellectual elite urging that "young people, especially those displaced by the RPF advance, be trained as part of the 'civil defense operation.'"[80] Additionally, he encouraged the elite not to "remain 'unconcerned' but rather work . . . to rouse the population to the danger of war."[81]

Though the German political elite certainly benefitted from the support of the intellectual elite, it is not clear that the political elite sought either their support, or their counsel. In Rwanda, on the other hand, the support of the intelligentsia was more deliberate and purposeful. Unlike Heidegger, Nahimana was not only in a position to influence the decisions and strategy of the regime, but the creation of RTLM was likely his idea. One other distinction between these two cases may involve the mob. In the Rwandan case, there were multiple mobs at work initiating violence at the behest of the political elite. As Scott Straus notes, attempts to identify the *interahamwe* have been rendered virtually futile by the conflation of the terms *interahamwe* and *genocidaire*. The *interahamwe*, properly speaking, was the youth group associated with the National Republican Movement for Development and Democracy (MRND). They were in many cases joined by the *impuzamugambi*, the youth group and armed militia, associated with the Coalition for the Defense of the Republic (CDR). Linda Melvern reports that the *interahamwe* was initially recruited from a soccer club.[82] Subsequently, its recruits came from unemployed young men, young men displaced by the encroaching RPF, along with Hutu refugees from Burundi.[83] As such the *Interahamwe* shared much in common with Arendt's mob. Anger, resentment and unemployment were prevalent, as was statelessness. The mob of which Arendt writes, however, while subject to the co-ordination of the political elite, was certainly never trained by the military.

Both Scott Straus and Philip Verwimp examine the local dynamics in the Rwanda case. Though neither explicitly distinguishes between initiators of violence or the mob and perpetrators who joined the effort over time, Verwimp culls characteristics of peasant perpetrators from rural household surveys.[84] He finds that typically one male member of the household participated. The combination of father and son participating was rare and in female headed households, the oldest son typically participated, suggesting that participation of the masses was treated as an *umuganda* style obligation.[85] In analyzing cross-sectional patterns of violence, Straus finds that at the local level, "[i]nfluential rural elites . . . organized, legitimized and directed the killing within their communes . . . Next were a relatively small group of aggressive and often young men. . . . These aggressive men killed and . . . mobilized as many adult Hutu males as possible to join the attacks. They were the elites' principal enforcers."[86]

Straus also examines one commune in which no genocide occurred: Giti. In some sense Giti was an anomaly. Despite statistical evidence suggesting that onset of violence correlates with support for the MRND, Giti was an

MRND stronghold. Yet there was no armed *Interahamwe* in Giti. Straus attributes the absence of genocide in Giti to two primary factors: a burgomaster, who actively resisted violence, and the arrival of the RPF in a neighboring region. When the cattle belonging to a Tutsi family were killed, the burgomaster had the young men arrested and jailed because he was concerned that an escalation of violence would follow. When asked about his decision to stand against the violence, the burgomaster simply replied, "One cannot fight for one's country by killing people."[87] In the case of Giti, attempts to mobilize the mob were thwarted by the local political elite who were able to hold out long enough for re-enforcements to arrive in a bordering region.

Similarly, Longman examined the role of the church in the local culture, governance structure and, ultimately, in the execution of the genocide in two rural towns: Kirinda and Biguhu. In Kirinda, church leaders and the political elite constituted a small group that often overlapped, lived extravagantly and exploited local peasants. On the other hand, church leaders in Biguhu viewed empowering the peasants as their responsibility. They lived modestly and instituted numerous grass roots development programs. As a result of these various development projects, there was no disaffected group of unemployed youth which could be easily organized into a mob. Moreover, church leaders in Biguhu used church doctrines and formal communications to discourage violence, rather than re-enforce the messages of the national, political elite. Thus Longman argued as a result of role of local leaders, the church and the absence of a mob, Tutsi from Biguhu had to be lured out of Biguhu to be killed, rather than being killed by their neighbors.[88] In short, taken together Verwimp, Straus and Longman find empirical evidence to support not only Arendt's distinction between the mass and the mob but also a pivotal roles played by the elite.

Moreover, Arendt's distinction between the political and intellectual elite warrants further examination. In both the German and Rwandan genocides, a select group of academics used their status in order to justify a genocidal regime. The intimate connections between and the multitude of roles played by the intellectual and political elite in Rwanda justify further examination of Arendt's contentions. Some members of the intellectual elite explicitly utilized scholarship to lend credence to the regime while others simply used the credibility associated with their status as members of the *intelligentsia*. Léon Mugesera's status as an intellectual, for example, lent credibility to his efforts though there was no connection between his training and his ideological commitment. Nahimana's scholarship, on the other hand, dealt with the underrepresentation of the Hutu in the Rwandan historical narrative. He used his scholarly work to justify the regime's policies and his status as an expert on Rwandan history to teach military personnel that the Tutsi would return to power unless the regime's policies were enforced.[89] While Mugesera and

Nahimana would have to be classified as convicted members of Hutu Power, the notion of mere co-operation also warrants re-examination. Recent genocide studies support a re-appraisal on this point. Manus Midlarsky, for example, concludes that victim vulnerability constitutes a necessary condition for genocide to occur.[90] In cases in which a sympathetic, external audience can be expected to intervene, victim vulnerability is diminished. Midlarsky also contends that previous unpunished violent outbursts prepare both internal and external communities for a non-response in the early stages of the genocide. Again, impunity contributes to a perception of victim vulnerability, thus increasing the likelihood of genocide. In light of Midlarsky's conclusions, even the *temporary* legitimization of a genocidal regime, warrants serious examination.

CONCLUSION

With *Totalitarianism*, Arendt continues to reveal the ontic features that press, this time in an immediate sense, upon both victims and perpetrators of the atrocities in Germany and Russia. As with *Anti-Semitism* and *Imperialism* she illustrates the emergence of a totalitarian personality. Only in the subsequently added "Ideology and Terror" does she explicitly connect ontic conditions with the ontological orientation. As such *Origins* constitutes a work of historicity in which Arendt approaches the ontological through the ontic. In other words, since ontological questions can only be taken up once one has undertaken an unconcealment of some concrete aspect of one's existence, Arendt devotes most of *Origins* to creating a familiarity with historical developments before taking up the ontological questions. Though the prevailing scholarly term for Arendt's interest may have been totalitarianism, as Dana Villa points out she is interested in understanding a system that required "an unending supply of innocent victims" for both its logic and its perpetuation.[91] In other words, she examines a system in which "genocide was the *raison d'etre*."[92] Ultimately it may well be in the area of comparative genocide studies that *Totalitarianism* finds its most enduring impact.

Arendt engages in a bit of a debate with Eric Voegelin regarding one of his critiques of *Totalitarianism*. Voegelin disputes Arendt's claim that totalitarianism dehumanizes since the essence of humanity cannot change.[93] As chapter outlines, letters and some early essays demonstrate, Arendt is clearly in the process of "thinking something through" with *Totalitarianism* in particular.[94] She is working through the relationship between the ontic and the ontological. She more or less accepts Heidegger's proposition that the mode of care is a constitutive feature of *Dasein*. Contra Heidegger she cannot dismiss or even marginalize the ontic. In *Anti-Semitism* and *Imperialism*, she notes that ontic phenomena can fundamentally affect one's manner of being in the world. The crucial task for Arendt is to understand how. In light of the primacy of this task, the question of whether human nature can change or human nature is necessarily unchangeable, Voegelin's question, resembles a matter of semantics, though she is clearly interested in whether something fundamental is altered under conditions of modernity. In keeping with the Heideggerian importance of projection, she views spontaneity and creativity as constitutive features of the nature of being and she has argued that ontic conditions can create an "innate" Jewish or imperialist personality. The question with respect to totalitarianism, thus, becomes does totalitarianism alter something more profound than personality, something intrinsic or perhaps even eliminate spontaneity itself? Would "normal people" under conditions of modernity, eschew spontaneity for security? Or does personality, perhaps particularly when it comes to characterize a group, serve as an indicator of something more profound or intrinsic, such as one's manner of *being* in the world?

She concludes "Totalitarianism in Power" with the query—have conditions of modernity created such dire living conditions that normal people would rationally opt for security and certainty at the cost of spontaneity and creativity? And can the techniques of total domination eliminate human spontaneity itself? In "Ideology and Terror," she more or less accepts that the answers to both questions are—yes. However, in the Eichmann trial, she finds hope in the stories of Anton Schmidt and the Danish shipbuilders. Normal people might rationally prefer security and certainty but some people will, perhaps irrationally, act in unpredictable ways even under the most desperate of circumstances. The reason she wrote *Eichmann* in a state of euphoria is that she discovered that totalitarianism cannot eliminate human spontaneity itself.

NOTES

1. Hannah Arendt, *The Origins of Totalitarianism* (New York: Harcourt Brace, 1958), 478.
2. Gustave LeBon, *The Crowd: A Study of the Popular Mind* (New York: Viking Press, 1960).
3. Roy A. Medvedev, *Let History Judge: The Origins and Consequences of Stalinism* (New York: Vintage, 1974); Isaac Deutscher, *Stalin: A Political Biography* (New York: Vintage, 1960).
4. Robert C. Tucker, "The Dictator and Totalitarianism," *World Politics* 17 (1965): 555–83; Leonard Shapiro, *Totalitarianism* (New York: Praeger, 1972).
5. Hannah Arendt, "'What Remains? The Language Remains': A Conversation with Günter Gaus" in *The Portable Hannah Arendt*, ed. Peter Baehr (New York: Penguin Putnam, 2000 [1964]), 5.
6. The evolving nature of Arendt's thought around *Origins* is apparent both in the continued additions of prefatory material, as well as the concluding chapter, which first appeared in the second edition. If the evolving nature of Arendt's thought is clear, the overarching argument and cohesion of the text is somewhat less readily discernible. Moreover, the availability of her prospectus makes apparent certain changes in her plan for the book.

7. Martin Heidegger, *Being and Time*, trans. Joan Stambaugh (Albany, NY: SUNY Press, 1997), 205.
8. Hannah Arendt, "Outline of 'Elements of Shame: Anti-Semitism, Imperialism and Racism,'" Hannah Arendt Manuscripts Collection, Library of Congress, 1.
9. George Kateb, *Hannah Arendt: Conscience, Evil and Politics* (Totowa, NJ: Rowman & Allanheld, 1983), 69–70.
10. Dana Villa, *Politics, Philosophy, and Terror: Essays on the Thought of Hannah Arendt* (Princeton, NJ: Princeton University Press, 1999), 21–29.
11. Jerome Kohn, "Arendt's Concept and Description of Totalitarianism," *Social Research* 69 (2002): 621–56.
12. Bernard Crick, "Arendt and *The Origins of Totalitarianism*: An Anglo-Centric View," in *Hannah Arendt in Jerusalem*, ed. Steven E. Ascheim (Berkeley: University of California Press, 1999), 99.
13. Seyla Benhabib, *The Reluctant Modernism of Hannah Arendt* (Thousand Oaks, CA: Sage Publications, 1996), 64; Kateb, *Hannah Arendt*, 57.
14. Margaret Canovan, *Hannah Arendt: A Re-Interpretation of Her Political Thought* (Cambridge: Cambridge University Press, 1992), 55; Roy Tsao, "The Evolution and Structure of Arendt's Theory of Totalitarianism," *Social Research* 69 (2002): 579–619.
15. Kohn, "Arendt's Concept and Description of Totalitarianism."
16. Benhabib, *The Reluctant Modernism of Hannah Arendt*, 64.
17. Kateb, *Hannah Arendt*, 57.
18. Benhabib, *The Reluctant Modernism of Hannah Arendt*, 65.
19. Kateb, *Hannah Arendt*, 76; Dana Villa (*Politics, Philosophy and Terror: Essays on the Thought of Hannah Arendt* [Princeton, NJ: Princeton University Press, 1999]) similarly views genocide as the crucial concept of interest.
20. Benhabib, *The Reluctant Modernism of Hannah Arendt*, 62.
21. While Benhabib (*The Reluctant Modernism of Hannah Arendt*, 67–68) challenged the conflation of the German and Russian cases into totalitarianism, Kateb (*Hannah Arendt*, 74–75) finds that most of Arendt's analysis applies to the German case, at times misrepresents the Russian case and Arendt, herself, thought the totalitarian aspects of Marxism required its own, book length treatment, Stephen Whitfield (*Into the Dark: Hannah Arendt and Totalitarianism* [Philadelphia: Temple University Press, 1980]) defends Arendt's argument that these cases are conceptually similar.
22. Canovan, *Hannah Arendt: A Re-Interpretation of Her Political Thought*, 55; Arendt, *Origins of Totalitarianism*, 382.
23. Canovan, *Hannah Arendt: A Re-Interpretation of Her Political Thought*, 55.
24. Ibid., 58–60.
25. Arendt, *Origins of Totalitarianism*, 332–33.
26. Ibid., 345.
27. Benhabib, *The Reluctant Modernism of Hannah Arendt*, 78–79.
28. Tsao, "The Evolution and Structure of Arendt's Theory of Totalitarianism," 584.
29. Arendt, *Origins of Totalitarianism*, 107.
30. Ibid.
31. Ibid., 326.
32. Ibid., 328.
33. Ibid., 331.
34. Ibid., 332.
35. Ibid., 331.
36. Ibid.
37. Ibid., 315.
38. Ibid., 311.
39. Ibid., 339.
40. Ibid.
41. Ibid.
42. Canovan, "Arendt's Theory of Totalitarianism," 27.
43. Arendt, *Origins of Totalitarianism*, 107.

44. Ibid., 329.
45. Ibid., 317.
46. Benhabib, *The Reluctant Modernism of Hannah Arendt*, 55.
47. Ibid., 66–67.
48. Arendt, *Origins of Totalitarianism*, 337.
49. Ibid., 356.
50. Ibid., 341.
51. Ibid., 352.
52. Ibid., 306.
53. Ibid., 352
54. Ibid., 436–37.
55. Ibid., 385.
56. Ibid., 335.
57. Ibid.
58. Ibid.
59. Ibid., 385.
60. Ibid., 335.
61. In thinking through the problem of a discerning reality from a carefully constructed fiction, Arendt turns to common sense. Common sense relies on "the intersubjectivity or 'presence of others'" allows us to trust in our own "sense experience" as a reliable and valid source of information about the world (Marieke Borren, "'A Sense of the World': Hannah Arendt's Hermeneutic Phenomenology of Common Sense," *International Journal of Philosophical Studies* 21 (2013): 225–55). See also Sandra K. Hinchmann, "Common Sense & Political Barbarism in the Theory of Hannah Arendt," *Polity* 17 (1984): 317–39.
62. Arendt, *Origins of Totalitarianism*, 382.
63. Kateb, *Hannah Arendt*, 80.
64. Villa, *Politics, Philosophy, Terror*, 18.
65. Ibid., 27.
66. Jean Harzfeld describes the dehumanization of running for one's life (*The Antelope's Strategy: Living in Rwanda after the Genocide* [New York: Picador, 2010], 37–47). Whereas, Carl Wilkens argues that a version of a concentration camp did exist in which Rwandans were invited to take refuge in schools, churches and then abandoned by their protectors (*I'm Not Leaving* [Spokane, WA: World Outside My Shoes, 2011]).
67. Philip Verwimp, "Development Ideology, the Peasantry and Genocide: Rwanda Represented in Habyarimana's Speeches (1973–1994)," *Journal for Genocide Research* 2 (2000): 325–61.
68. Manhood Mamdani, *When Victims Become Killers: Colonialism, Nativism, and the Genocide in Rwanda* (Princeton, NJ: Princeton University Press, 2001).
69. Ibid.
70. The questions of from where and when this migration occurred remain the subject of scholarly debate.
71. For a balanced discussion of both the evidence supporting a genetic distinction, as well as the counter evidence, see Mamdani, *When Victims Become Killers*, 43–62.
72. This conclusion is most likely based on the prevalent small facial features, yet it ignores skin pigmentation and hair texture, which are not at all Caucasian.
73. R. Graves and R. Patai, *Hebrew Myths: The Book of Genesis* (New York: Doubleday, 1964), 121, as cited in Mamdani, *When Victims Become Killers*, 81.
74. Mamdani, *When Victims Become Killers*, 80.
75. Ibid., 85.
76. Linda Melvern, *Conspiracy to Murder: The Rwandan Genocide* (New York: Verso, 2004), 41
77. Ibid., 62.
78. Ibid., 54.
79. Ibid., 26–27; Alison Des Forges, *Leave None to Tell the Story: Genocide in Rwanda* (New York: Human Rights Watch, 1999), 68.
80. Des Forges, *Leave None to Tell the Story*, 110.

81. Ibid., 170.
82. Melvern, *Conspiracy to Murder*, 118.
83. Mamdani, *When Victims Become Killers*.
84. Since this study is based on household surveys and members of the *Interahamwe* were hypothesized to be landless, it may systematically exclude the mob.
85. *Umuganda* is a tradition of community work in which, historically, each family provides one person to help with community projects, usually either the father or oldest son. Philip Verwimp, "An Economic Profile of Peasant Perpetrators of Genocide: Micro-Level Evidence from Rwanda," *Journal of Development Economics* 77 (2005): 297–323.
86. Scott Straus, *The Order of Genocide: Race, Power, and War in Rwanda* (Ithaca, NY: Cornell University Press, 1995), 94.
87. Ibid., 86.
88. Timothy Longman, "Genocide and Socio-Political Change: Massacres in Two Rwandan Villages," *Issue: A Journal of Opinion* 23 (1995): 18–21; Timothy Longman, *Christianity and Genocide in Rwanda* (Cambridge: Cambridge University Press, 2009), 288.
89. Melvern, *Conspiracy to Murder*, 42.
90. Manus I. Midlarksy, *The Killing Trap: Genocide in the Twentieth Century* (Cambridge: Cambridge University Press, 2005).
91. Villa, *Politics, hilosophy, Terror*, 18.
92. Kateb, *Hannah Arendt*, 80.
93. Peter Baehr, "Debating Totalitarianism: An Exchange of Letters Between Hannah Arendt and Eric Voegelin," *History and Theory* 51 (2012): 374.
94. Arendt, "What Remains? The Language Remains," 5.

Chapter Seven

On the Political Importance of a Normative Ontology

Eichmann in Jerusalem

The trial of Adolph Eichmann has often been described as a point of transition in the *oeuvre*, as well as the life of Hannah Arendt.[1] First, it marks a transition in the way she talks about and thinks about evil.[2] Second, it is thought to serve as a point of departure in her return to philosophy, as she shifts from political sociology to political ontology.[3] Additionally, it marks the beginning of her career as a pariah.[4] Though Arendt had often touted the virtues of the conscious pariah, it was not until after the Eichmann trial that she experienced the full sting of ostracism. While *Eichmann in Jerusalem* is often viewed as a point of disjuncture, I argue that it represents a point of continuity in the development of Arendt's normative experiential ontology, both with and against Heidegger. With Heidegger, she accepts both the validity and the significance of his *existentials*; contra Heidegger she worries that while it may be empirically valid to talk about the deficiency of *existentials*, the use of non-normative ontological categories in the public realm constitutes an unthinking, hence irresponsible, political act. Adolph Eichmann exemplifies the use of a deficient mode of care in the public sphere.

In defending *Eichmann in Jerusalem* against the barrage of criticism, Hannah Arendt noted on multiple occasions that she had not proffered a theory of evil but merely written a factual account of Adolph Eichmann's trial. In the context of a trial report, she opined it would have been inappropriate to develop a theory of evil. While Arendt clearly did not explicate a philosophical account of evil, neither did she confine herself to a factual account of Eichmann's trial. At several points she laments the inclusion of testimony from witnesses who neither met nor even saw Eichmann. They were called upon merely to tell their stories. Arendt both criticizes such testimony as it contributed nothing to the legal question of Eichmann's guilt or innocence and mused "how utterly different everything would be today in this courtroom, in Israel, in Germany, in all of Europe, and perhaps in all countries of the world, if only more such stories could have been told."[5] This remark in the context of Arendt's other, legally astute, misgivings seems misplaced. Additionally, it contradicts her assertion that she merely reported on the trial as a factual matter. If only more such stories could have been told, then what? They would have been equally irrelevant to the proceedings and contributed to the political nature of the trial which Arendt abhorred. Yet she also wrote, "everyone should have his day in court."[6] It remains somewhat ambiguous whether this statement refers to victims, perpetrators or both. In what follows I argue that *Eichmann* represents a continuation of Arendt's project of attempting to concretize Heidegger, which is to say, as illuminating Heideggerian concepts by illustrating their appearance in socio-historical context. In the process she often transforms these concepts beyond recognition, as Dana Villa aptly demonstrates.[7] In *Eichmann in Jerusalem*, Arendt normatizes the Heideggerian notion of being-with (*Mitdasein*), which is to say, she takes a purely descriptive concept and considers the normative implications by identifying both benevolent and malevolent forms of care in socio-historical context.

For Heidegger the mode of *being-in-world*, the manner of *being-with*, of interacting with others, is one of care or concern. He uses two different words to describe this mode of being: *besorgen* and *fürsorge*. *Besorgen* usually refers to tasks which can be resolved or completed, errands. *Fürsorge*, on the other hand, refers to matters of concern related to human issues or human interaction.[8] Additionally for Heidegger, *existentials* are non-normative, which is to say they can take a form that is proficient, deficient or indifferent. Heidegger notes in *Being and Time* that *Being* is always *being-with*, though he devotes little time to explicating *being-with* except in so far as he develops a troubling portrait of the "they" and "idle chatter," leaving the impression that the role of *Mitdasein* in achieving transcendence is a predominantly negative one. If *Mitdasein* can facilitate the development of one's true self, as it does for Karl Jaspers, one finds no evidence of it in Heidegger. In this chapter I argue that *Eichmann in Jerusalem* can be read as normatizing *being-with* for political purposes. In other words, Arendt offers illustrations of the collective implications of both *proficient and deficient* modes of *being-with*. In Denmark, for example, she finds *fürsorge* employed as a normative, political concept. In short, she demonstrates the importance of a normative ontology in the public sphere by illustrating the political implications of various forms of care.

A more apt, though perhaps no less inflammatory, subtitle for the book might have been *the banality of evildoers* since Arendt found nothing banal in the evil she had previously described as absolute and radical. Rather it is the intent, in the legal sense, of Adolph Eichmann, that warrants the term: banal. Simply put, the potential for evildoing emerges from engaging others in a mode of *fürsorge* which is deficient. Eichmann exemplifies this point, particularly in his treatment of Bertold Storfer. Conversely, Arendt also demonstrates that the potential for heroism consists in engaging others in a mode of *fürsorge*. A point aptly illustrated by Anton Schmidt. Though as previously stated, Arendt is not content simply to illustrate Heideggerian existentials in socio-historical context. She, additionally, sought to reveal the collective implications of the transference of non-normative *existentials* into the public sphere. Again, she allows Eichmann to represent the collective implications of a deficient mode of *fürsorge*, while Dr. Warner Best, General von Hannecken and Denmark exemplify the collective implications of engaging others in a mode of *fürsorge* which is proficient. As such Arendt attempts to show the political importance of the Heideggerian notion of care by demonstrating not only the collective consequences of a deficient mode of care but the process by which a deficient mode of *being-with* can transform into the collective experience of genocide. In short, since in her early work Arendt uses the term, radical evil, albeit not in a Kantian sense, her debt to Kant on this issue is obvious. Previous interpretations of the banality of evil, however, have neglected her Heideggerian roots. Heidegger's non-normative modes of *being-with* provide us with a way of understanding not only Arendt's concern with Adolph Eichmann and her peculiar trial report, but her critique of Heidegger as well.

KANT: ON RADICAL EVIL AS AN INVERSION OF MAXIMS

Some, including Arendt, have argued that Kant's concept of radical evil is neither radical, nor useful as a tool for understanding genocide. My purpose here is not to contribute to this debate, though I will briefly explore its contours, but rather to argue that regardless of the academic debate surrounding Kant's notion of radical evil, Arendt's debt to him is considerable, as is the Heideggerian inspired modification she offers. Moreover, the academic disagreement surrounding Kant's notion of radical evil tends to focus on the analytical value of radical evil, rather than on the distinctions that Kant draws between different stages or gradations of evil. Kant posits that all forms of evil derive, not from a natural inclination to evil, but rather from human free will. More specifically, evil can result from three conditions: human frailty, impurity of maxims or the reversal of maxims. These three gradations of evil represent the increasing likelihood that unconscionable acts of depravity will result. Moreover, as the individual moves from the first level to the third, the choice to deviate from a moral maxim becomes increasingly a conscious one. For Kant maxims constitute the underlying and unobservable principles that guide our decision-making and behavior. In order to have moral value, actions must not only be in accord with a moral maxim, they must also derive from a sense of duty to the moral maxim, as the sole motivating factor.

The first form of evil, human frailty, occurs when an individual subscribes to moral maxims, prioritizes moral maxims but out of human weaknesses, succumbs either consciously or unconsciously to a maxim of self-love. Secondly, evil can result from the impurity of maxims. In this case action is not based on a moral maxim "alone as its all-sufficient incentive." Rather one's action "stands in need of other incentives beyond this."[9] In other words, good action undertaken on the basis of moral responsibility albeit not on the basis of moral responsibility alone constitutes a form of evil. In this case, the moral maxim and additional incentives point toward the same act. Thus, in the case of impurity, the act undertaken is in keeping with one's moral duty. According to Kant,

> when incentives other than the law itself (such as ambition, self-love in general, yes, even a kindly instinct such as sympathy) are necessary to determine the will to conduct conformable to the law, it is merely accidental that that these causes coincide with the [moral maxim], for they could equally well incite its violation. The maxim, then, in terms of whose goodness all moral worth of the individual must be appraised . . . despite all his good deeds, is nevertheless evil.[10]

In short, a person may be evil, for Kant, despite good deeds if the motivation for those good deeds is ambition or self-interest, rather than a sense of moral duty. Interestingly, not only does the second degree of evil, result in a good deed, but as Claudia Card points out, impurity represents a greater degree of evil than frailty despite the fact that the outcome in the case of impurity is consistent with the requirements of moral duty; whereas the outcome in the case of frailty runs contrary to one's moral obligation.[11]

Despite the outcome disparity, impurity represents a higher degree of evil than does frailty because the consistent invocation of non-moral maxims creates the structural mechanism for a far greater evil: radical evil. As Kant says, the fact that the outcome is consistent with moral duty is "merely accidental." Finally, Kant's notion of radical evil, which he characterizes as existing when "the cast of mind is corrupted at the root" refers to the prioritization of non-moral maxims over moral ones as an enduring rather than fleeting condition.

> [T]he wickedness or if you like the corruption of the human heart is the propensity of the will to maxims which reflect the incentives springing from

the moral law in favor of others which are not moral. It may also be called the perversity of the human heart, for it reverses the ethical order among the incentives of a free will; and although conduct which is lawfully good may be found within it, yet the cast of mind is thereby corrupted at its root (so far as the moral disposition is concerned), and the man is hence designated as evil.[12]

In other words, radical evil occurs when individuals succumb to the temptation of employing self-love as a maxim. These individuals have given up on moral responsibility as the underlying principle that guides human behavior. Not all of the acts that result from this inversion of maxims will necessarily constitute grossly evil acts. But in accepting self-love as a maxim which takes priority over moral duty, the deliberative context, in which the most hideous acts of evil can occur has been created.

Kant's critics, including Arendt, dispute either the contention that all evil acts result from self-love or self-interest, or the assertion that diabolic evil does not exist. Richard Bernstein finds the reliance on self-love or self-interest "shallow" which is to say in his attempt to create a theory of evil which *always* holds individuals responsible for their actions and explains *all* evil acts, regardless of how insignificant, Kant crafts a notion of evil that borders on a truism and fails to explain the most egregious forms of evil in the world.[13] Kant's "aim is to bring all cases of [evil]—whatever their degree—under a single concept, a single maxim of evil, a maxim that applies in the same way to minor evils as it does to the worst evils."[14] It does not account for acts of evil that Claudia Card characterizes as *gratuitous suffering*.[15] Consideration of this criticism, first, requires an examination of what is meant by self-love. Second, are the most egregious forms of evil or suffering accounted for in Kant's tri-part schema? Do even the most horrific evil acts have self-love or self-interest as their motivation? In Kantian terms, is the will to conduct behind, even the most disturbing of evil acts, determined by self-love or self-interest? Is there possibly, in Card's terms, *gratuitous suffering* without *gratuitous evil*? Kant, like Arendt, "rejects the claim that serious evils require a distinctly diabolical motivation."[16] Moreover, Bernstein and Card take issue not only with Kant's reliance on self-love but also question his premise that diabolical acts do not require diabolical motivation.

In other words, our propensity to evil has its roots in the ability of human beings, given free will, to prioritize self-interest over moral duty, though according to Sharon Anderson-Gold, diabolically evil acts require the conscious acceptance of self-interest over moral duty as a maxim in a collective context. The frequency of exercising free will in this manner increases under competitive conditions prevalent in organized society. As Anderson-Gold observed unsociable sociability is another name for radical evil, in so far as unsociable sociability represents the collective manifestation of the prioritization of self-love over moral duty as a determinant of the will to conduct.

As such, the most egregious forms of evil may arise from the collective manifestation of the individual inversion of maxims. Thus, the radical nature of Kant's third stage of individual evil is fully realized only in its collective manifestation. Though both Kantian and Arendtian approaches to evil disavow the notion of some kind of diabolical evildoer and place evildoing within the realm of the ordinary, their approaches also diverge on a critical point. Kant's inversion of maxims suggests a conscious choice; whereas Arendt's ultimately offers an indictment of decisions without judgment. In other words, for Arendt both the most profound forms of evil and heroism have a mundane quality, in the sense that sources of both are found in the everyday decisions of common folk.

ARENDT: ON THE BANALITY OF EVILDOERS

Bernstein notes that the first to use the term banality in reference to Nazi atrocities was Karl Jaspers,[17] though it seems to have been Heinrich Blücher who suggested the phrase "banality of evil" as a subtitle for the Eichmann book.[18] While Arendt is certainly best known for the phrase "banality of evil," she also at various points, characterizes evil as *radical, absolute* and, finally, *extreme*.[19] While Arendt refers to Kant in her use of the term, radical evil, she does not appear to have ever used the term radical evil, in a Kantian sense.[20] Card argues that Arendt used the Kantian term "not to mark deep culpability . . . but to mark the radical harm of being turned into a 'living corpse.'"[21] In other words, her use of the term *radical evil* characterized the result, rather than the perpetrator or the perpetrator's motives. Arendt uses the term, first, in conjunction with the death camps. Only later does she use it to describe the socio-political phenomena: superfluousness. Thus as Bernstein argues, Arendt uses the term radical evil differently than Kant did. Arendt uses radical evil to refer to the purposeful transformation that occurs to human beings under conditions of totalitarianism. She refers to the destruction of the "plurality, spontaneity, natality and individuality" that are necessary to live a human life.[22] Dana Villa argues that this transformation is complete only when the victims of totalitarianism, both executioners and prisoners alike "have internalized their own superfluousness," since that is when both submit "mutely to power."[23] In other words, Arendt uses the term radical evil to refer to the existential harm of accepting one's own superfluousness. Her use of the term *absolute evil* is closer to the Kantian at least in so far as absolute evil concerns itself with the perpetrator's motives. As she says in *Origins*, "in the first stages of totalitarianism an absolute evil appears (absolute because it can no longer be deduced from humanly comprehensible motives)."[24] Total domination may not be a comprehensible motive though she does view it as stemming from a desire to dominate.

Though Arendt is best known for characterizing evil as banal, a more apt subtitle might have been: the banality of evildoers. As she explained to Mary McCarthy, although the book certainly contained philosophical insights and interpretations, it was primarily a trial report. As such, it "is a report and therefore leaves all questions of why things happened as they happened out of account." The real issue, she asserts, is "what kind of man was the accused and to what extent can our legal system take care of these new criminals who are not ordinary criminals."[25] In other words, she intended the subtitle to serve as a description of the character of Adolph Eichmann, not as a statement about either the nature of evil perpetrated by the Nazis, nor as a statement about the nature of harm suffered by the Jewish people. Thus, a more apt subtitle might have been the banality of evildoers, since as Karl Jaspers noted, "[w]hat evil stands behind your phrase characterizing Eichmann."[26] Arendt is clearly interested not only in the character and thought process of Eichmann but also the collective processes that resulted in genocide.

The banality of evildoers, of which Arendt offers Eichmann as a prime example, rests with the inability to think, which in turn leads to a lack of understanding and judgment. He personifies logical thinking at its most troubling because he does not experience the two-in-one dialogue. As we have already seen, for Arendt, thinking is a dialectical and critical process, an ongoing, soundless dialogue with oneself, a "habit of examining whatever happens to come to pass or to attract attention," that reveals the inherent duality in human nature.[27] Thinking reveals the disconnect or disharmony between our appearance, or what we reveal of who we are in the public realm, and our consciousness, our true selves, which we may or may not reveal in the public realm. Thinking requires solitary time and space. "To be in solitude means to be with one's self, and thinking, therefore, though it may be the most solitary of all activities, is never altogether without a partner and without company."[28] Thinking is an activity that can only be engaged in by oneself and with oneself as the only partner, the process of going home to face the "partner who comes to life when you are alert and alone."[29] Without the inner dialogue to force him to reconcile his actions with his inner critic, the lonely individual is vulnerable to what Arendt refers to as deductive reasoning or logical thinking: the cornerstone of ideology.

> The tyranny of logicality begins with the mind's submission to logic as a never-ending process, on which man relies in order to engender his thoughts. By this submission, he surrenders his inner freedom as he surrenders his freedom of movement when he bows down to an outward tyranny.[30]

Moreover, logical thinking occurs when "[t]he idea [of class or race] becomes a premise in the logical sense from which a process is being deduced . . . [According to this approach, thinking involves] conclusions instead of judgment, [and becomes subsumed] under certain rules."[31]

Herein lies the key to the appeal of totalitarianism, and the relationship between existential loneliness and a totalitarian form of government. Without the opportunity for self-reflection, lonely individuals find "comfort and consolation" in rules, logical and deductive reasoning.[32] In short, Adolph Eichmann illustrates existential loneliness. He lacked the ability to divide into the two-in-one, to engage in self-reflective thinking and instead sought validation in the rules, logic, clichés, euphemisms and the hierarchical structure offered by National Socialism.[33] As Arendt noted, "[t]he longer one listened to him, the more obvious it became that his inability to speak was closely connected with an inability to think, namely to think from the standpoint of somebody else."[34] Thus Eichmann serves as a prototypical case of the banality of evildoers. Their inability to connect to their own inner critics and engage in a self-reflective form of thinking leads them to seek acceptance and connectedness in whatever social movement may come their way. They seek solace in the feeling of belonging afforded by the social movement, any social movement.

> [A] thinking being, rooted in his thoughts and remembrances, and hence knowing that he has to live with himself, there will be limits to what he can permit himself to do, and these limits will not be imposed on him from the outside, but will be self-set. These limits can change considerably . . . but limitless, extreme evil is possible only where these self-grown roots, which automatically limit the possibilities are absent. They are absent where men skid only over the surface of events, where they permit themselves to be carried away without ever penetrating into whatever depth they may be capable of.[35]

This lack of depth or rootedness may not create an obvious problem *until* in a context of multiple losses, uncertainty and fear become politicized.[36] Under these conditions, the unmoored individual may be swept up in the pseudo-connections that social movements provide. In other words, complicity in genocide requires neither malicious intent nor malevolent character. Evil is neither deep nor profound, rather it is common and mundane, spreading "like a fungus on the surface."[37] At an ontological level, it requires only simple failure to think, "namely, to think from the standpoint of someone else" and "remember what they did."[38]

Kant and Arendt both view the personification of diabolical evil as philosophically indefensible and politically problematic. Moreover, they both locate the essence of diabolically evil acts in the core of our humanity. For Kant, our propensity to evildoing derives from free will, perhaps its collective manifestation. Whereas for Arendt, the tendency toward evil acts may originate in an ontological condition that precludes the self-reflective thought that necessarily precedes either judgment or action. In both cases, perpetrators are responsible for all acts in which they participated. As such the political implications of Kantian, as well as Arendtian, approaches to evil share much common ground. In their respective approaches to evil, Kant and Arendt diverge on two questions. First, does all evil operate in the same way? Kant argues that it does; whereas Arendt believes it may take different forms. Second, is evildoing a conscious act? Again for Kant the answer is—yes. The gradual slide from the first to the third phase of evil includes a corresponding shift from an unconscious to a conscious diminution of moral duty as the controlling maxim. For Arendt, on the other hand, the answer is—no. The lack of thought personified by Eichmann presupposes that the decision to do evil is lacking in deliberation and therefore, lacking in consciousness. Part of Arendt's concern is the western legal system, requiring both *actus rea* and *mens rea* is ill-equipped to process a crime like Eichmann's.[39]

FÜRSORGE: PROFICIENT AND DEFICIENT

Amidst the historical context, estimations of victims, cutting commentary on the judges, attorneys and her often sardonic tone, Arendt's point occasionally becomes muddled. Since the importance of storytelling in the Arendt canon has been well document, it is not surprising that the most memorable and poignant moments in the text are those in which Arendt recounts stories from the trial that while irrelevant in the legal sense nonetheless bring conceptual clarity.[40] It is also these moments as Deborah Lipstadt notes, for which Arendt reserves her most elegant prose.[41] Two of the most compelling tales involve Anton Schmidt and Bertold Storfer. Anton Schmidt was a sergeant in the German army in Lithuania, assigned to rescue Nazi personnel, disconnected from their units. In the process, he witnessed the inhumane treatment of Jewish victims and decided to rescue them as well, providing papers and, in some cases, transportation for approximately 250 potential victims. In his last letter to his family before his execution, he wrote simply, "I have only acted as a human. I never wanted to hurt anyone."[42] Regarding this testimony, which had absolutely no legal bearing on the Eichmann case, Arendt found her most poetic prose.

> During the few minutes it took Kovner to tell of the help that had come from a German sergeant, a hush settled over the courtroom; it was as though the crowd had spontaneously decided to observe the usual two minutes of silence in honor of the man named Anton Schmidt. And in those two minutes, which were like a sudden burst of light in the midst of impenetrable, unfathomable darkness, a single thought stood out clearly, irrefutably, beyond question—how utterly different everything would be today in this courtroom, in Israel, in

Germany, in all of Europe, and perhaps in all countries of the world, if only more such stories could have been told.[43]

As a legal matter, Schmidt's actions had no bearing on the question of Eichmann's guilt or innocence. As a human matter, juxtaposed with Eichmann, Schmidt's response captured Arendt's attention. Upon witnessing the mass murder of other human beings, Schmidt "could not think and had to help them."[44] In other words, faced with the ultimate form of human suffering Schmidt responded with great empathy, with care and concern for others. He did not see a political solution to a political problem. He did not see a task completed, an item on his list of things to do; he saw human suffering and took steps to alleviate it, despite the fact that those actions put himself and his family at risk. Moreover, he does not seem to have viewed his response as heroic or extraordinary, it was simply the only thing he could *do* under the circumstances. In short, in response to the claim that collaborators were forced to carry out orders, Arendt offers us the story of Anton Schmidt. Adolph Eichmann also witnessed firsthand the murder of innocent civilians.

Eichmann was sent to report on the extermination of Jews in Poland. At Chelmo, he saw firsthand the use of mobile killing units and described his own reaction.

> The truck was making for an open ditch, the doors were opened, and the corpses were thrown out, as though they were still alive, so smooth were their limbs. They were hurled into a ditch, and I can still see a civilian extracting the teeth with tooth pliers. And then I was off—jumped into my car and did not open my mouth any more. After that time, I could sit for hours beside my driver without exchanging a word with him. There I got enough. I was finished. I only remember that a physician in white overalls told me to look through a hole into the truck while they were still in it. I refused to do that. I could not. I had to disappear.[45]

Despite Eichmann's self-described aversion to the Final Solution, one of the striking things about his reaction is that unlike Schmidt, it could not be characterized as *fürsorge* or concern for the other. He does not describe concern for the suffering of Jewish victims; rather he describes his own revulsion. He does not express concern for the victims, rather his concern is for the perpetrators. His only objection, "[w]e are bringing up people to be sadists."[46] Interestingly, Eichmann exhibits an awareness that perpetrators are not unaffected by their role in the atrocities. While strikingly absent from Eichmann's reaction is any evidence of care or concern for the suffering of the Jewish victims. Also absent is any sense, such as that conveyed by Anton Schmidt, of an impulse to act, to assist the victims. Anton Schmidt "had to help": Adolph Eichmann "had to disappear." These two disparate impulses and the corresponding responses, highlighted by Arendt, reflect modes of

Being-with. Schmidt exhibited a mode of *Being-with* that might be described as *fürsorge*. Eichmann's *Being-with*, on the other hand, was deficient. He recounts only that seeing victims of mass murder was an unpleasant experience for him. Eichmann's *Being-with* of Jewish victims was deficient in *fürsorge* and more accurately captured by the term—*besorgen*. He conveys no empathy, no concern and approaches them in the mode of a task. Accounts of him approaching Jewish victims as a task to be completed (*besorgen*) are plentiful; Bertold Storfer was one such task.

Bertold Storfer was a Jewish functionary in Vienna and as such was immune from deportation. Apparently Storfer either tried to flee or went into hiding and as a result was deported to Auschwitz. Since he had worked closely with Eichmann, it was Eichmann that he requested to see. Eichmann reported telling Storfer that he could not do anything to get him out of Auschwitz, though he could alter his work duty. He explained to the trial court that it was a matter of great satisfaction to him that he was able to help Mr. Storfer, who was shot six weeks later, by seeing to it that his work duty was sweeping a gravel path, a job in which he was occasionally able to sit on a bench.[47] Despite the appearance of Bertold Storfer and a matter of human concern, Eichmann's focus on tasks remained unaltered. Again instead of reacting with human concern, Eichmann recounts his own satisfaction: he and Storfer had a "normal, human encounter."[48] That Storfer was immune from deportation and yet felt sufficiently threatened to attempt an escape does not permeate Eichmann's thought process. Eichmann reports having asked Storfer why he tried to escape; as for Storfer's response, Eichmann could not recall. That Storfer was shot to death, six weeks after receiving Eichmann's *help* does not comprise even a small part of his tale. He did, however, relay to the Court that it was "a great inner joy" that he could see Storfer and that they "could speak with each other."[49] Again, Eichmann is only capable of recalling his response.

Among the most controversial points in Arendt's text, her discussion of the Jewish councils (*Judenrate*) draws the most virulent criticism even though it comprises a small part of the text. The topic emerges in Arendt's coverage of the trial because several of the witnesses comment on the cooperation of either ghetto police or *Judenrate*. The commentary which proved to be the most controversial was Arendt's assessment that "[w]herever Jews lived, there were recognized Jewish leaders, and this leadership, almost without exception, cooperated in one way or another, for one reason or another, with the Nazis . . . if the Jewish people had really been unorganized and leaderless, there would have been chaos and plenty of misery but the total number of victims would hardly have been between four and a half and six million people."[50] The criticism itself[51] is of little interest for the purpose of this essay though it bears noting that the Jewish councils may be the quintessential illustration of the collective manifestation of relating to others in a mode of *besorgen*, which is to say as a task to be completed. The Nazis carefully selected Jewish leaders for the *Judenrate* and charged them with, among other things, the task of selecting fellow Jews for deportation. Their position was clearly an impossible one, which is precisely the reason that Arendt's judgment was viewed as harsh. However, the ontic structures and the way that they pressed upon both victims, as well as, perpetrators of the German genocide was consistently a phenomenon that Arendt sought to reveal. The Jewish councils constitute one such structure, ambiguously located between victim and perpetrator.

THE MODE OF BEING IN THE PUBLIC SPHERE

Arendt is certainly interested in exploring the manifestation of one's ontological condition in socio-historical context, though it is her preoccupation with the political implications of different modes of *Being* that constitutes the unifying thread throughout her otherwise eclectic *oeuvre*. In *Eichmann*, she not only relays the tales of individuals engaging with others in modes of concern which are either deficient or proficient; she documents the political outcome associated with particular ontological conditions. She explores, for example, the curious cases of Dr. Werner Best and General von Hannecken, German military commanders in a collective space characterized by concern for Jewish victims, who became in Arendt's word—unreliable. Arendt points out that the spirit of resistance to German authority served both to limit German ambitions in Denmark, and led to some creative forms of resistance. She notes, first, that when the Nazis inquired about the imposition of the yellow star, they were told that the King would be the first to wear it. Additionally, when instructed to repair German ships set to deport Jewish victims, Danish dockworkers refused and subsequently went on strike. In this context, the Nazi commanders not only failed to carry out orders from Berlin but used their authority in Denmark to protect potential victims.

As a descriptive matter, Arendt more or less agrees with Heidegger that traditional moral and ethical standards have broken down under conditions of modernity; she concurs as well with his observation that individuals can act toward others either with great care or with extreme carelessness. She is ill at ease, however, with the non-normative or the purely descriptive since from the perspective of the political, whether care takes a form that is deficient or proficient is a matter of considerable interest. Moreover, her criticism of Heidegger is that having offered his fundamental ontology as a descriptive matter, he leaves us with utterly no standards by which to judge, which becomes particularly problematic when the brilliant philosopher decides to enter the public realm. In the absence of any standards of judgment, Heidegger lends his support to Hitler, since "action and authenticity were what mattered."⁵² Arendt more or less concurs that both action and authenticity belong in public life though along with them she would reserve a crucial place for self-reflective thought and judgment. In other words, Heidegger took what purported to be a purely descriptive and non-normative framework and used it as a basis from which to enter the political realm with disastrous consequences.

Part of Arendt's task is to reveal the conditions under which an individual will relate to others in a mode of concern or *fürsorge*. In order to complete certain tasks, I must necessarily cease to relate to other beings. I cannot prepare a lecture while simultaneously listening to a student's dilemma. I can elect, however, to set aside my lecture when a matter of some urgency arises, requiring me to switch from a mode of *besorgen* to *fürsorge*. I divide into the two-in-one, engage myself in dialogue and decide to set aside my lecture notes and act out of concern for the student. Arendt's term for this process is thought. A being will relate to other beings in a mode of *fürsorge* if he or she engaged in an Arendtian form of thinking which requires rootedness, in "thoughts and remembrances."⁵³ For both Arendt and Heidegger remembering plays an integral part in thinking, particularly meditative thinking. Heidegger notes that one's innermost essence, "the heart's core . . . the gathering of all that concerns us, all that we care for" can only "unfold in memory."⁵⁴ In other words, since care or concern is one of the constitutive structures of Dasein and our care or concern emerges only through memory or in the act of remembering, memory not only becomes a precondition for transcendence but it constitutes a necessary but not sufficient condition for engaging others in a mode of care that is proficient. Arendt repeatedly notes Eichmann's inability to recall events of considerable significance and subsequently grants remembrance a crucial place in both thought and judgment. "[A] thinking being, rooted in his thoughts and remembrances, and hence knowing that he has to live with himself, there will be limits to what he can permit himself to do, and these limits will not be imposed on him from the outside, but will be self-set."⁵⁵ Arendtian thought requires one to remember what one has done and to engage in a self-reflective form of thinking, which is to say to think "from the standpoint of someone else."⁵⁶

As an ontological matter, according to Arendt, Eichmann's failure lay simply in the inability to engage in a self-reflective form of thinking in which the Other, personified in the two-in-one, required him to examine the disconnect between his actions and his conception of Self. In the absence of self-reflection, Eichmann insulated himself from the sound of his own voice, experienced a profound sense of disconnection from his own self and sought solace and a sense of belonging in a mass movement in which he substituted rhetoric, cliques and euphemisms for self-reflective thought. As a political matter there is nothing simple about the consequences associated with one's manner of *being-in-the-world*. Engaging the other in self-reflective thinking might have enabled Eichmann (or Heidegger) to connect his actions to world events, render judgment and imagine a course of action either heroic (Anton Schmidt) or creative (Danish dockworkers). In a recent reappraisal of Eichmann in Jerusalem, Villa suggests that the most important, ongoing question about the German genocide is "how could so many people . . . lend their best, most conscientious efforts to the manufacture of horror."[57] Eichmann stands in for this phenomena in Arendt's text.

For Arendt, thinking exists as a viable opportunity for the masses, as it does not require formal education, familiarity with German philosophy or hours spent in contemplation of big questions. Arendt's transcendent being, contra Heidegger, must squarely face his or her own self, reflect on his or her experiences, render judgment and then speak and act in accordance with that judgment in the public sphere. Arendt's authentic political actor bears a striking resemblance to the burgomaster from Giti.[58] He exemplifies Arendt's hope for preventing violence and the spread of evil when confronted with an approaching RPF, an irate mob and instructions to kill, he engaged in a self-reflective form of thinking, considered the relationship between his actions and the violence occurring in other regions, rendered judgment and acted out of concern for a Tutsi family and his community. As Arendt demonstrates in *Eichmann*, whether one *has to help* or *has to disappear* may tell us something about the nature of evil, and it obviously has profound implications for our living together. In short, Arendt does not blame the Jews; she certainly does not exonerate Adolph Eichmann. She simply suggests that, ontologically speaking, both the Nazis and the Jewish functionaries experienced and exhibited a manner of being in the world that was deficient in *fürsorge* (concern) and could possibly best described as *besorgen* (task oriented).

NOTES

1. Jerome Kohn, "A Jewish Life: 1906–1975," in *The Jewish Writings*, eds. Jerome Kohn and Ron H. Feldman (New York: Schocken Books, 2007), xxviii.

2. Though Bernstein responds to the question (did Hannah Arendt change her mind "about the meaning of evil?") in the negative, he also notes that superfluousness played a more significant role in the conception of evil that appears in Origins, whereas thoughtlessness takes on a pivotal role post-Eichmann (Richard J. Bernstein, *Hannah Arendt and the Jewish Question* (Cambridge, MA: MIT Press, 1996), 152).

3. Julia Kristeva, *Hannah Arendt* (New York: Columbia University Press, 2001), 154.

4. Jennifer Ring, *The Political Consequences of Thinking: Gender and Judaism in the Work of Hannah Arendt* (Albany, NY: State University of New York Press, 1997); Elizabeth Young-Bruehl, *Hannah Arendt: For Love of the World* (New Haven: Yale University Press, 1982), 367.

5. Hannah Arendt, *Eichmann in Jerusalem* (New York: Penguin Books, 1963), 231.

6. Ibid., 229. Arendt also describes this thought as foolish.

7. Dana Villa, *Arendt and Heidegger: The Fate of the Political* (Princeton, NJ: Princeton University Press, 1996).

8. Joan Stambaugh, "Translator's Preface," In *Being and Time*, trans. Joan Stambaugh (Albany, NY: SUNY Press, 1997).
9. Immanuel Kant, *Religion Within the Limits of Reason Alone*, trans. T. M. Greene and H. H. Hudson (New York: Harper & Row, 1793[1960]), 26.
10. Ibid.
11. Claudia Card, "Kant's Moral Excluded Middle," in *Kant's Anatomy of Evil*, eds. S. Anderson-Gold and P. Muchnik (Cambridge: Cambridge University Press, 2010), 79.
12. Kant, *Religion Within the Limits of Reason Alone*, 25.
13. Richard J. Bernstein, *Radical Evil: A Philosophical Interrogation* (Oxford: Blackwell Publishers, 2002).
14. Allen W. Wood, "Kant and the Intelligibility of Evil," in *Kant's Anatomy of Evil*, eds. S. Anderson-Gold and P. Muchnik (Cambridge: Cambridge University Press, 2010), 156.
15. Claudia Card, *The Atrocity Paradigm: A Theory of Evil* (New York: Oxford University Press, 2002), 76.
16. Sharon Anderson-Gold, "Kant, Radical Evil and Crimes Against Humanity," in *Kant's Anatomy of Evil*, eds. S. Anderson-Gold and P. Muchnik (Cambridge: Cambridge University Press, 2010), 200.
17. Bernstein, *Radical Evil*, 215.
18. Karl Jaspers to Hannah Arendt, December 13, 1963, in *Hannah Arendt-Karl Jaspers Correspondence, 1926–1969*, eds. Lotte Kohler and Hans Saner (New York: Harcourt Brace, 1992), 542.
19. Arendt uses the term *radical evil* in *Origins of Totalitarianism*. See especially Hannah Arendt, *Origins of Totalitarianism* (New York: Harcourt Brace, 1958), 459. The term *absolute evil* appears in the preface to *Totalitarianism* (Arendt, *Origins of Totalitarianism*, viii-ix). Arendt notes in a letter to Mary McCarthy that the Eichmann case did cause her to change her mind about the nature of evil and she uses the term *extreme evil* (Hannah Arendt to Mary McCarthy, October 3, 1963, in *Between Friends: The Correspondence of Hannah Arendt and Mary McCarthy, 1949–1975*, ed. C. Brightman (New York: Harcourt Brace, 1995), 152).
20. Though both Kant and Arendt dispute the existence of diabolical motives, Arendt also dismisses Kant's contention that self-love is the source of all evil. Rather she argues that extreme forms of evil may arise from humanly incomprehensible motives (Arendt, *Origins of Totalitarianism*, viii-ix.).
21. Card, *The Atrocity Paradigm*, 75.
22. Richard J. Bernstein, "Did Hannah Arendt Change her Mind? From Radical Evil to the Banality of Evil," in *Hannah Arendt: Twenty Years Later*, eds. L. May and J. Kohn (Cambridge, MA: MIT Press, 1996), 135.
23. Dana R. Villa, *Politics, Philosophy and Terror: Essays on the Thought of Hannah Arendt* (Princeton, NJ: Princeton University Press, 1999), 20.
24. Arendt, *Origins of Totalitarianism*, viii-ix.
25. Arendt to McCarthy, October 3, 1963, *Between Friends*, 152.
26. Jaspers to Arendt, December 13, 1963, in *Hannah Arendt-Karl Jaspers Correspondence*, 542.
27. Hannah Arendt, *Life of the Mind: Thinking* (New York: Harcourt Brace, 1978), 5–6.
28. Hannah Arendt, *The Human Condition* (New York: Harcourt Brace, 1958), 76.
29. Arendt, *Life of the Mind: Thinking*, 188.
30. Hannah Arendt, "Ideology and Terror: A Novel Form of Government," *Review of Politics* 15 (1953): 320.
31. Hannah Arendt, "The Great Tradition and the Nature of Totalitarianism" (Hannah Arendt Manuscripts Collection, container #74, Library of Congress, 1953), 8.
32. Jeffrey C. Isaac, *Arendt, Camus and Modern Rebellion* (New Haven, CT: Yale University Press, 1992).
33. Ibid., 56.
34. Arendt, *Eichmann in Jerusalem*, 49; Seyla Benhabib invokes Heidegger in an alternative interpretation of Eichmann's thoughtlessness, as she suggests that for Heidegger thoughtlessness "stems from being all too beholden to what other may think" (Seyla Benhabib, "Who's Trial? Adolph Eichmann's or Hannah Arendt's: The Eichmann Controversy Revisited," in *The*

Trial That Never Ends: Hannah Arendt's Eichmann in Jerusalem in Retrospect, eds. Richard J. Golsan and Sarah M. Misemer (Toronto: University of Toronto Press, 2019), 218).

35. Arendt, "Some Questions of Moral Philosophy," 101.

36. Manus I. Midlarsky, *The Killing Trap: Genocide in the Twentieth Century* (Cambridge: Cambridge University Press, 2005).

37. Hannah Arendt, "A Letter to Gershom Scholem," in *The Jewish Writings*, eds. Jerome Kohn and Ron H. Feldman (New York: Schocken Books, 2007), 471.

38. Arendt, *Eichmann in Jerusalem*, 49; Arendt, "Some Questions of Moral Philosophy," 112.

39. *Actus rea* and *mens rea* derive from the Latin "Actus non facit reum nisi mens sit rea" (an act does not make a person guilty unless the mind is also guilty).

40. Lisa J. Disch, "More Truth than Fact: Storytelling as Critical Understanding in the Writings of Hannah Arendt," *Political Theory* 21 (1993): 665–94; Lisa J. Disch, "Please Sit Down but Don't Make Yourself at Home: 'Visiting' and the Prefigurative Politics of Consciousness-Raising," in *Hannah Arendt and the Meaning of Politics*, eds. Craig Calhoun and John McGowan (Minneapolis: University of Minnesota Press, 1997), 132–65; Ernst Vollrath, "Hannah Arendt and the Method of Political Thinking," *Social Research* 44 (1977): 160–82; David Luban, "Explaining Dark Times: Hannah Arendt's Theory of Theory," *Social Research* 50 (1983): 215–47.

41. Deborah Lipstadt, *The Eichmann Trial* (New York: Schocken Books, 2011), 138.

42. Arno Lustiger, "Feldwebel Anton Schmid," in *Retter in Uniform*, ed. Wolfram Wette (Frankfurt: Frankfurt Main, 2002), 63.

43. Arendt, *Eichmann in Jerusalem*, 231.

44. Lustiger, "Feldwebel Anton Schmid," 62.

45. Arendt, *Eichmann in Jerusalem*, 88.

46. Ibid.

47. Ibid.

48. Ibid., 51.

49. Ibid.

50. Ibid., 125. Seyla Benhabib suggests that one reason Arendt's tone, particularly in Eichmann, is frequently misinterpreted is that her critics fail to see her as a trauma survivor, who quite possibly used irony, sarcasm and mockery as defense mechanisms (Benhabib, "Who's Trial? Adolph Eichmann's or Hannah Arendt's," 210–11)

51. For a detailed account of the controversy, see Michael Erza, "The Eichmann Polemics: Hannah Arendt and Her Critics," *Democratiya* 9 (2007): 141–65.

52. Richard Wolin, "An Affair to Remember: Hannah and the Magician," *The New Republic*, October 9, 1995, 36.

53. Arendt, "Some Questions of Moral Philosophy," 101.

54. Martin Heidegger, "What Is Called, What Calls for, Thinking," in *Martin Heidegger: Philosophical and Political Writings*, ed. Manfred Stassen (New York: Continuum, 2003), 83.

55. Hannah Arendt, "Some Questions of Moral Philosophy," 101.

56. Arendt, *Eichmann in Jerusalem*, 49.

57. Dana Villa, "*Eichmann in Jerusalem*: Conscience, Normality, and the 'Rule of Narrative,'" in *The Trial That Never Ends: Hannah Arendt's Eichmann in Jerusalem in Retrospect*, eds. Richard J. Golsan and Sarah M. Misemer (Toronto: University of Toronto Press, 2019), 62.

58. Scott Straus, *The Order of Genocide: Race, Power and War in Rwanda* (Ithaca, NY: Cornell University Press, 2006) 86.

Chapter Eight

The Politics of Existential Loneliness

Loneliness, as conceptually distinct from isolation, is a central, unifying problem in the work of Hannah Arendt. The primary concern for Arendt is that loneliness, understood as an existential crisis experienced by an individual, exacerbates the breakdown of traditional forms of connectedness and, thus, contributes to a variety of troubling results in contemporary political life. As such both the existential crisis and the collective manifestations resulting from it are likely to increase rather than decrease under conditions of modernity. Loneliness is particularly noteworthy since it is the defining existential experience of refugees and stateless persons. Moreover, it is loneliness among the white, male, party elite that creates the conditions in which Eichmann accepts orders in an uncritical manner. Accordingly, Arendt says towards the end of *Origins of Totalitarianism* that totalitarianism is but one manifestation of the crisis of our time. This crisis isn't totalitarianism, concentration camps, National Socialism or even, genocide. The crisis of our time is the existential crisis, loneliness, which gives rise to a variety of collective outcomes—with catastrophic potential. In short, Arendt's unique reflections at the intersection of ontology and democratic theory are fully comprehensible only once we recognize that for Arendt one's way of being in the world does not simply inform one's politics, but rather one's way of *being-in-the-world* may preclude the possibility of becoming a fully actualized Self. While Heidegger's fundamental ontology may imply an elitism, his politics certainly lean toward the autocratic, since authenticity requires not only an understanding of the call but resoluteness, as well. Arendt, on the other hand, recasts political action as residing within the sphere of the everyday as she shifts from the Heideggerian notion of the inauthentic to existential loneliness. As such she transforms authenticity from a tool of autocracy into a dim hope for democracy.

Isolation appears as a key concept of interest in both *Rahel Varnhagen* and *Origins of Totalitarianism*, loneliness is first defined in the final chapter.[1] It is not until *The Human Condition* that a clear conceptual distinction emerges between these two terms. Finally, in "Some Questions of Moral Philosophy" she posits two distinct varieties of isolation, as well as loneliness—an existential, as well as a categorical. In what follows, I examine the discussion of isolation and loneliness in Arendt's work as she transforms Heideggerian authenticity into an explicitly political concept since the complex intertwining of ontology and democratic theory cannot be fully worked out without understanding loneliness.

ISOLATION AND LONELINESS: SYNONYMS

Maurizio Passerin D'Entrèves uses the terms, *loneliness* and *isolation*, more or less interchangeably as preconditions for the emergence of totalitarian man, as well as numerous, troubling developments of modernity. The synonymous use of these terms for D'Entreves shows itself most clearly in his discussion of alienation, which consists in "being thrown back upon ourselves means also losing ourselves, losing the faith in our senses and ultimately, in our reason. . . . The result is that, alienated from ourselves and from others, we become doubtful of our experiences and of the reality of the world. Such a situation is conducive, in Arendt's eyes, to mass manipulation and totalitarian indoctrination, if only as a way of relieving individuals of their anxiety and their sense of isolation."[2] D'Entreves speaks here of isolation yet the reference to losing ourselves and becoming doubtful of the world and reality bears a striking resemblance to loneliness, as we shall soon see. While Arendt's emerging thought on the subject leads her to periodically offer contradictory and misleading descriptions of loneliness, she never describes isolation as a loss of oneself—that phrase applies exclusively to loneliness.

Seyla Benhabib explains the connection between loneliness and ideology though isolation goes unmentioned. Of individuals in a state of loneliness she says, "[t]hey are worldless in the sense that they have lost a stable space of reference. . . . Not having a . . . perspective from which to view the world, they are particularly open to ideological manipulation: they can believe anything and everything for they have no definite perspective which is tied to having a certain place in the world."[3] In other words, loneliness leads to a lack of perspective or worldlessness which can serve as a precursor to totalitarianism. Benhabib examines neither the ontological foundations of loneliness, nor the political implications. In the *Reluctant Modernism of Hannah Arendt*, she uses nearly the same exact explanation of the implications of isolation that she had previously attributed to loneliness. "We can say," she asserts, "that the radical isolation of the individual makes this individual susceptible to being sucked in by collectivities that falsely promise solidarity and companionship."[4] In other words, Benhabib uses the term *radical isolation* as a synonym for *loneliness*. Arendt, herself, uses the term *utter loneliness*. However, as we will soon see, Arendt uses qualifiers such as *utter* and *radical* not simply to denote a more severe case of emotional distress, as Benhabib suggests, but to distinguish between an ontic reality and an ontological condition.

A CONCEPTUAL DISTINCTION EMERGES

Margaret Canovan argues that Arendt has laid out a three pronged distinction between isolation, solitude and loneliness. Individuals who spend much of their time in either solitude (philosophers or artists) or isolation (craftsmen or laborers) run the risk of slipping into loneliness. The real danger, inherent in both solitude and isolation, is that if one ceases to re-emerge occasionally to rejoin the world, he or she may succumb to the truly dangerous phenomena of loneliness.[5] According to Canovan, Arendt's notion of loneliness is characterized by "not belonging to the world at all."[6] Since Arendt uses the terms *world* or *worldliness* to refer to politics, "a place fit for action and speech," and also the experience of human plurality, loneliness represents a lack of attention to the political and the absence of genuine, authentic, human interaction.[7] It would seem, therefore, that although solitude and isolation might be unavoidable components of productive life, one's identity may become so thoroughly subsumed in the productive enterprise that one neither reconnects with other human beings nor considers the political and/or collective implications of one's work. The danger is that the laborer fails to reconnect with other human beings once the work day is over and does not recognize the collective interests he or she shares with others. Similarly, the philosopher fails to emerge from the solitude of his own thoughts to consider the implications of his work for real people, struggling in the world. Here we can see that even if solitude and isolation are unavoidable, they are, again, not synonymous. Though both imply time and space without the company of others, isolation suggests an inability to connect with others, albeit temporarily; whereas solitude is a highly valued and enormously important state in which one engages with oneself.

Jacques Taminiaux focuses on two of Canovan's tripartite categories (solitude and loneliness), arguing that in the background of *Origins* Arendt is taking sides in an ontological debate between Heidegger and Jaspers. Heidegger views fellow humans as "an impediment to the Being of Self" since transcendence requires solitude and thought[8]; whereas for Jaspers man's essence lies in "communicative plurality."[9] In *Origins*, as in her 1946 article on existential philosophy and perhaps most clearly in *The Human Condition*, Arendt sides with Jaspers. Given this point of departure, Taminiaux then contrasts solitude and loneliness. Solitude, while clearly a solitary activity, is still characterized by a plurality since others are represented in the two-in-one dialogue. No such dialogue occurs in a state of loneliness; hence loneliness is characterized by the absence of plurality.

LONELINESS AS AN *EXISTENTIAL*

Lewis P. and Sandra K. Hinchman argue that just as Heidegger develops an array of *existentials*, as opposed to categories, for the purpose of understanding ontology, Arendt creates political existentials. While labor, work and action have long been recognized as constituting Arendtian existentials, Hinchman and Hinchman add loneliness to the list.[10] Thomas Dumm concurs and argues that since the Arendtian experience of loneliness is the experience of a profound conformity "[i]t is in conformity that we become ghostly, uncertain of ourselves because we are unable to think about how we are alone, even as we realize that we are alone. We lose ourselves in ourselves."[11] Given the seemingly inescapable nature of Arendtian loneliness, Dumm is left to ponder whether we are "living in a vestibule of the totalitarian possibility."[12]

George Kateb connects the existential experience of loneliness with political existence. In his early work, he focuses on the connection to totalitarianism. Kateb argues both that the lonely individual is more susceptible to totalitarianism "because loneliness disposes a person seek relief in the rigidity of an ideological system" and also that loneliness "facilitates self-discovery, which nourishes self-loathing" without exploring either the metaphysical basis for loneliness or a wider array of political implications.[13] Simply put, subscribing to an ideological system relieves the need to expend effort thinking and provides a false, though reassuring, sense of connectedness. Moreover, blind adherence to ideology frees the individual to devote mental energy (not to be confused with actual, or authentic, thought) to his or her own self. Kateb asserts that this inward focus translates into self-loathing and prepares the individual to take on a variety of roles in a totalitarian system, such as either victim or executioner. In short, he explores both the roots and implications of ideological thought, though the connection between inwardness and self-loathing remains tenuous at best. Is self-loathing one among a number of potential outcomes that might result from inwardness? More recently, Kateb has devoted considerable attention to the dangers of using political outlets or causes to alleviate existential distress. Just as Arendt worries about political movements based only on "shared victim status," or *isms* that claim to offer comprehensive, single factor explanations and simple solutions to complex socio-political phenomena, Kateb finds much cause for concern in culturally distinct communities or identity groups, which promise to alleviate loneliness through the use of a uniform, pre-determined narrative, effectively minimizing genuine individuality.[14]

This brief review of the literature can be summarized as follows: Margaret Canovan's work represents a substantial step forward in so far as she recognizes isolation and loneliness are conceptually distinct. Moreover, she addresses the collective importance of loneliness. Taminiaux, Hinchman and Hinchman trace loneliness to Arendt's existential roots and though they do not address isolation specifically, this move nonetheless implies a conceptual distinction. Similarly, Kateb focuses on the myriad of troubling collective outcomes associated with loneliness from the perspective of democratic theory. In the remainder of this chapter, I will attempt to build upon these contributions by developing the existential foundations of loneliness, distinguishing between ontic and ontological varieties of both isolation and loneliness, left implicit in Arendt's work, and explaining the political implications of conceptualizing isolation and loneliness as both *existential* and *categorical* phenomena.

SELF-NEGATION

Hannah Arendt often uses the terms isolation and loneliness in conjunction with one another. In *Origins of Totalitarianism*, isolation emerges as a major theme since it is a precondition of totalitarianism. Loneliness, on the other hand, is not mentioned until the last chapter ("Ideology and Terror") which first appeared in the second edition and is developed more fully in *The Human Condition*. She refers to a peculiar though consequential tenet of loneliness in her description of the process by which solitude can become loneliness. Loneliness is at its most profound, she proffers, "when all by myself, I am deserted by my own self." It is a brief, often overlooked, yet significant distinction between isolation and loneliness which is critical in understanding Arendt's existential take on feminism. Some have read this to suggest that isolation is a precursor of loneliness,[15] or that both isolation and loneliness are preconditions of totalitarianism.[16] Certainly individuals who are both isolated and lonely are particularly vulnerable to totalitarian exploitation. In other words, they are particularly likely to seek out meaning with such zeal that they then impose that meaning and "try to remake the world in its image with a total devotion and a total lack of restraint."[17] Yet Arendt emphasizes that isolation and loneliness are two separate and distinct phenomena. While the absence of human companionship may be common in *existential* loneliness, self-desertion is the pivotal and most poignant component.

> What makes loneliness so unbearable is the loss of one's own self which can be realized in solitude, but confirmed in its identity only by the trusting and trustworthy company of my equals. In this situation, man loses trust in himself as the partner of his thoughts and that elementary confidence in the world which is necessary to make experiences at all. Self and world, capacity for thought and experience are lost at the same time.[18]

So crucial is the two-in-one partnership that the loss of "trust in himself" renders one incapable of engaging in thought, incapable of self-reflection, incapable of even processing the meaning of one's experiences. Isolation involves being deserted by others; whereas loneliness involves a form of self-desertion. As for which is worse, Arendt leaves no doubt. It is "[b]etter to be at odds with the whole world than be at odds with the only one you are forced to live together with when you left the company behind."[19]

The most succinct statement regarding loneliness can be found in Arendt's 1965 essay "Some Questions of Moral Philosophy." Written in the aftermath of the Eichmann trial and subsequent controversy, this essay represents the culmination of Arendt's political existentialism. In it she captures the experience of loneliness as an ontological phenomenon and connects it to three distinct, collective (i.e., political) phenomena. As an ontological experience, she posits that loneliness "is precisely this being deserted by oneself, the temporary inability to become two-in-one as it were, while in a situation where there is no one else to keep us company."[20] As an individual experience the inability to engage oneself in an inner dialogue triggers not only a profound and uncomfortable sense of disconnectedness; the loss of the two-in-one means that "I become one, possessing of course, self-awareness, that is, consciousness, but no longer fully and articulately in possession of myself."[21] Interestingly, this exploration of loneliness as an ontological phenomena is the only place Arendt refers to loneliness as a temporary experience. In fact, it directly contradicts the portrait of loneliness that emerges from the totalitarian context, in which "[t]otalitarianism takes care that loneliness remains and that solitude cannot develop."[22] One suspects she may be indebted to Heidegger and the distinction between an ontic reality and an ontological state. In other words, intermittent loneliness resembles an ontic reality, in and out of which, a person may move; whereas *existant* loneliness is perhaps a matter of how one inhabits one's very ontological condition. As such, *existant* loneliness affects one's political existence.

Over time the inability to connect with one's inner partner renders thought and the validation of one's experiences (and therefore understanding) utterly impossible. In short, the loss of the two-in-one results in the subsequent loss of thought, experience and judgment. In other words, "[t]his is the thinking of loneliness where I preserve a hollow identity through avoiding contradictions and remain in contact with others only because all others are like me literally." Engaging only with others who are "like me literally" ensures a hollow existence since it renders thinking and understanding virtual impossibilities. Thinking, for Arendt, is an iterative experience of recalling experiences and making sense of them in the two-in-one. Understanding, at least in a general sense, derives from the experience of reflecting on one's experiences in conjunction with a partner (either one's inner self or another individual) and placing them in some kind of larger context. Thus, in a state of loneliness individuals not only experience a profound sense of despair and hollowness but they also become ineffectual politically. Metaphysically speaking they cease to be able to divide into the two-in-one, which in turn makes thinking impossible. Moreover, they "preserve a hollow identity," become utterly unable to uncover meaning in their own life experiences and hence to attain some kind of understanding or cognizance of the context in which those experiences occur. In short, lonely individuals lose the ability to think, to derive understanding from their experiences and, therefore, to judge—all of which are important components of a political existence.

Arendt explains the importance of the two-in-one, with respect to thinking, but what exactly does it mean to deny oneself to one's own self? Though she never elaborates, in *The Human Condition*, on how it is that one experiences the loss of his or her own self, she describes in "We Refugees," the means by which individuals engage in self-denial (negation). Arendt uses the phrase, the *insane optimism* of assimilationists, which she describes as "next door to despair."[23] She describes the process of self-negation, "as soon as we were saved—and most of us had to be saved several times—we started our new lives and tried to follow as closely as possible all the good advice our saviors passed on to us. We were told to forget and we forgot quicker than anyone could imagine."[24] Denial of oneself to one's own self occurs when an individual is placed in the undesirable position of renouncing a component of his or her own uniqueness, a part of the self that is crucial to recognizing his or her own humanity. Arendt does not clearly develop how it is that the Self achieves "uniqueness," though one suspects she may, again, be indebted here to the Heideggerian notion of authenticity. It may be an individual project in which one's talents and experiences become the subjects of thinking. Talents and experiences may be conditioned by collective traits, but can only be understood individually. Thus, the denial of either experiences or traits, not only deprives the collective of one's lived experiences but renders the experience of authenticity of the development of uniqueness an impossibility.

Thus, individuals who are placed in the position of renouncing language, culture or experiences cease to be able to present themselves in the world with authenticity, cease to be able to act and speak in the world, which is to say—politically. For example, refugees are placed in the position of having to renounce language, culture and even deny, as a factual matter, the events that led to their refugee status. Similarly, women face considerable social pressure to find in marriage and motherhood an immense and profound satisfaction, which is often at odds with the lived experience since tasks associated with *animal laborans* are rarely deeply satisfying. Women, like refugees, face a series of paradoxical choices. Women, like refugees, experience a profound social compulsion to deny their real experiences. These pressures leave both women and refugees struggling to recover their own uniqueness, in other words, leave them struggling to attain humanness. Women must renounce either social equality or economic independence; they must accept either enslavement in their own home or the dissolution of their families; women must either be constrained by biologically grounded tasks or renounce reproduction and family life entirely. Women must proclaim motherhood the most satisfying experience of a lifetime, despite chronic sleep deprivation and the prevalence of depression. This denial of lived experiences is often accompanied by an escape into the private realm. Though the private realm and the activities that take place there (e.g., thinking) are important pre-conditions for a public presentation, there is a profound danger in occupying either the private or the public realm to the exclusion of the other. In the case of refugees, Arendt references the escape into astrology and palm reading, "[t]hus we learn less about political events but more about our own dear selves."[25] Eventually, Arendt does explicitly establish the connection between refugees and women.

> We are like people with a fixed idea who can't help trying continually to disguise an imaginary stigma. Thus we are enthusiastically fond of every new possibility which, being new, seems able to work miracles. We are fascinated by every new nationality in the same way a woman of tidy size is delighted with every new dress which promises to give her the desired waistline. But she likes the new dress only as long as she believes in its miraculous qualities, and she will throw it away as soon as she discovers that it does not change her stature—or, for that matter, her status.[26]

Both women and refugees, having denied something fundamental about their own uniqueness, cease to confront the two-in-one. Both women and refugees, having denied a fundamental component of their own unique distinctiveness, turn away from the "partner who comes to life when you are alert and alone" and busy themselves with fashion, soap operas or other mind-numbing experiences.[27]

AUTHENTIC CONNECTION

There is perhaps an irony in describing our contemporary political lives as lacking connection since it often feels like we cannot avoid the political, even for 24 hours. The crucial distinction between an overabundance of inane interactions and the kind of authentic connections required for Arendtian action lies in thoughtfulness. One of the challenges of the authentic life for Arendt is the necessity of moving back and forth between the world of thought and the world of appearances. The conscience is a byproduct or a result of thinking which results once one has restored or created harmony with one's inner partner. The conscience must necessarily precede judgment and should, but need not necessarily precede action. It is through acts of conscience that "the liberating effect of thinking . . . [is] manifest in the world of appearances, where I am never alone and always too busy to think."[28] As one prepares to share the product or the results of thinking, to identify and express the useful byproducts of the thinking activity to others, the products of one's thinking are *crystallized* in the form of thoughts, which can then be shared with others. It is in the process of sharing thoughts with others that one not only enters into the realm of action, but achieves the distinction of being fully human. Since for Arendt it is the activity of being seen and heard by others that validates one's existence, this interaction serves as a tether of sorts between the individual and the world.

A lack of thinking is troubling to Arendt for several reasons. It increases the prospects of evildoing since "most evil is done by people who never made up their minds to be or do either evil or good."[29] There is something in the thinking process itself which may prevent evildoing. Perhaps, she suggests, evildoing represents a lack of inner harmony. "The manifestation of the wind of thought is not knowledge; it is the ability to tell right from wrong, beautiful from ugly. And this at the rare moments when the stakes are on the table, may indeed prevent catastrophes, at least for the self."[30] Not all thoughtlessness results in evildoing, however. Arendt also describes a more mundane outcome, which may be particularly applicable to contemporary politics. "A life without thinking is quite possible; it then fails to develop its own essence—it is not merely meaningless; it is not fully alive. Unthinking men are like sleepwalkers."[31] Thoughtlessness or a lack of "intercourse with oneself" may result in a nearly undetectable emptiness, a surreal existence or hollowness that consists primarily in going through the motions of a fully human life, a shadow existence or an inauthentic life.

If isolation involves being deserted by others, labor and work both require isolation, at least in the short term. In order for tasks to be completed, for a play or poem to be written, one must have time alone with his or her own thoughts and tools, to create a tangible product. In fact, isolation may be beneficial in terms of productivity and the creation of wealth. Arendt writes that the "arts may flourish under these conditions if the ruler is 'benevolent' enough to leave his subjects alone in their isolation."[32] Action, on the other hand, can never occur in isolation, since action is plural by its very nature. Acting, for Arendt, requires interaction. Action requires an audience since action necessarily takes place in the space between.[33] Isolated individuals cannot act; to be isolated is to be deprived of the capacity to act.

Labor is not only inherently isolated, but also inherently lonely. It is not commonly recognized as lonely since many forms of labor are performed in physical proximity to others. However, the performance of labor in proximity to others "has none of the distinctive marks of true plurality. It does not consist in the purposeful combination of different skills and callings."[34] The loneliness one finds among laborers may be yet another example of *existant* loneliness, which differs profoundly from ontic loneliness. In *The Human Condition*, Arendt uses the term utter loneliness, to describe the experience of the physical laborer and to explain the inability of laborers to organize effectively into a political movement.

> [The] 'collective nature of labor,' far from establishing a recognizable, identifiable reality for each member of the labor gang, requires on the contrary the actual loss of all awareness of individuality and identity . . . the actual experience of this sameness, the experience of life and death, occurs not in isolation but in *utter loneliness*, where no true communication, let alone association and community is possible [emphasis added].[35]

Arendt uses the term utter loneliness to describe the ontological condition. Since communication and shared experiences are at the heart of the human experience, under conditions of utter or *existant* loneliness, individuals cease to be fully human. In her conversation with Günter Gaus, Arendt connects the experience of loneliness with an emphasis on consumption in a way that is reminiscent of Betty Freidan's notion of the feminine mystique.[36] This loneliness, she asserts, "consists in being thrown back upon oneself a state of affairs in which, so to speak, consumption takes the place of all the truly relating activities," precisely the process she described afflicting refugees.[37]

Thus for Arendt, one's manner of *being-in-the-world* is inextricably linked to the prospects of self-governance. Fear and loneliness are fundamentally anti-political experiences, rendering political engagement all but impossible. "Just as fear and the impotence from which fear springs are anti-political principles and throw men into a situation contrary to political action, so loneliness and the logical-ideological deducing the worst that comes from it represent an antisocial situation and harbor a principle destructive for all human living-together."[38] Again, isolation is not the same as being alone. One can be alone and not isolated. Moreover, one can be together with others, in a physical sense, and still be deserted by them. The immediate, physical presence of others may render the experience of desertion, whether by others or by oneself, all the more poignant. Work, on the other hand, may be isolated and in no way lonely, since the critical distinction is whether or not one has been deserted by him or herself, whether one has denied some crucial aspect of him or her own Self. If the worker finds, in work, an outlet for genuine self-expression, the task of working may be isolated and not lonely. Action, however, as Arendt uses the term, a self-revealing, public presentation, is fundamentally inconsistent with both isolation and loneliness. An isolated individual cannot act. A lonely individual cannot act in a self-revealing manner, having already been deserted by him or herself since acting requires not only engagement with other human beings, but an authentic *re-presentation* of oneself. Action can propel one out of loneliness since it is only in action that a person discloses her or his "who" nature: it is only in action that we come to know ourselves, and are able to let ourselves be known to others.[39]

CONCLUSION

For Arendt, one's manner of *being-in-the-world* is inextricably linked to the prospects of self-governance since one's being is conditioned in part by political rights, engagement, or the lack thereof. Moreover, one's prospects of ensuring political rights, hence some measure of security, are dependent upon the ability to *act*. For this reason, she views fear and loneliness as antipolitical experiences, rendering political engagement all but impossible. "Just as fear and the impotence from which fear springs are anti-political principles and throw men into a situation contrary to political action, so loneliness and the logical-ideological deducing the worst that comes from it represent an antisocial situation and harbor a principle destructive for all humans living-together."[40] Isolation is not the same as being alone. One can certainly be alone and not isolated. Moreover, one can be together with others, in a physical sense, and still be deserted by them. In fact, the immediate, physical presence of others may render the experience of desertion, whether by others or by oneself, all the more poignant. Work, on the other hand, may be isolated and in no way lonely, since the critical distinction is whether or not one has been deserted by him or herself, whether one has denied some crucial aspect of him or her own self. If the worker finds, in work, an outlet for genuine self-expression, the task of working may be isolated and not lonely. Action, however, as Arendt understands it, is a self-revealing, public presentation, and is fundamentally inconsistent with both isolation and loneliness. An isolated individual cannot act since action requires an audience. A lonely individual cannot act in a self-revealing manner, having already been deserted by him or herself since acting requires not only engagement with other human beings, but an authentic *re-presentation* of oneself. Action can propel one out of loneliness, as we have seen with Rahel Varnhagen, since it is only in action that a person discloses her or his "who" nature: it is only in action that we come to know ourselves, and to let ourselves be known by others.[41]

These concerns, particularly as ontological phenomena, are troubling in and of themselves. Yet for Arendt the ontological reality comprises only half the problem. In her experience one's way of being profound affects one's prospects for political existence. The mechanism by which political rights can be assured is *action*. Therefore, if individuals belonging to a marginalized political group find themselves in a state of utter or *existant* loneliness, the prospects of either recognizing or remedying the lack of political rights are slim. But ontological loneliness also affects white men, who have been "spat out" by society.[42] Thus, when she says, "the true predicaments of our time will assume their authentic form—though not necessarily the cruelest—only when totalitarianism has become a thing of the past," it is loneliness, as an ontological condition, as a manner of *being-in-the-world*, to which she refers. She could not dismiss Heidegger, despite his shortcomings, philosophical antisemitism and his political missteps because his work, including his own errors, help us understand "the crisis of our time."[43] His work helps us understand, despite his own political ineptitude, why "organized loneliness is considerably more dangerous than the unorganized impotence" of arbitrary dictatorships or despotisms.[44]

The democratizing moves Arendt makes are, first, to locate the possibility of authentic political action within the scope of the everyday and, second, to require that Heidegger's self-disclosure occur in the public sphere. Arendt's political action exists as a viable opportunity for the masses, as it does not require formal education, familiarity with German philosophy nor hours spent in contemplation of big questions. Moreover, Arendt's authentic political actor, contra Heidegger, must simply exhibit a willingness to squarely face his or her own Self, reflect on his or her experiences and render judgment. Finally, in connecting one's manner of *being-in-the-world* to the political, Arendt forges a democratic ontology; in which self-actualization requires a collective purpose and public disclosure while democracy requires individuals who are willing to risk a public revealing, in the pursuit of authenticity.

NOTES

1. "Ideology and Terror" first appeared as a stand-alone article in the *Review of Politics* in 1953 and was added to *Origins* as the concluding chapter in the 1958 edition.
2. Maurizio Passerin D'Entreves, *The Political Philosophy of Hannah Arendt* (London: Routledge, 1994), 38.
3. Seyla Benhabib, "Hannah Arendt and the Redemptive Power of Narrative," in *Hannah Arendt: Critical Essays*, eds. Lewis P. Hinchman and Sandra K. Hinchman (Albany: State University of New York Press, 1994), 117–18.
4. Seyla Benhabib, *The Reluctant Modernism of Hannah Arendt* (New York: Rowman & Littlefield, 2000), 105.
5. Margaret Canovan, *Hannah Arendt: A Reinterpretation of Her Political Thought* (Cambridge: Cambridge University Press, 1994), 91–93, 261.

6. Hannah Arendt, *Origins of Totalitarianism* (New York: Harcourt Brace, 1958), 495; Canovan, *Hannah Arendt: A Reinterpretation*, 92.

7. Hannah Arendt, *The Human Condition* (New York: Harcourt Brace, 1958), 173; Canovan, *Hannah Arendt: A Reinterpretation*, 92.

8. This interpretation of Heidegger, though common, may understate the importance of *Mitsein* (Villa, *Arendt and Heidegger*). In other words, for Heidegger, *being* is always *being-with*, though the role of *Mitsein* in achieving transcendence seems to be a predominantly negative one.

9. Jacques Taminiaux, "The Philosophical Stakes in Arendt's Genealogy of Totalitarianism," *Social Research* 69 (2002): 423–69.

10. Lewis P. and Sandra K. Hinchman, "In Heidegger's Shadow: Hannah Arendt's Phenomenological Humanism," *The Review of Politics* 46 (1984): 183–211.

11. Thomas Dumm, *Loneliness as a Way of Life* (Cambridge, MA: Harvard University Press, 2008), 40.

12. Ibid., 45.

13. George Kateb, *Hannah Arendt: Conscience, Evil and Politics* (Totowa, NJ: Rowman & Littlefield Publishers, 1984), 175.

14. George Kateb, *Patriotism and Other Mistakes* (New Haven, CT: Yale University Press, 2006).

15. Kateb, *Hannah Arendt: Conscience, Evil and Politics*.

16. Michael Bittman, "Totalitarianism: The Career of a Concept," in *Hannah Arendt: Thinking, Judging, Freedom*, eds. G. T. Kaplan and C. S. Kessler (Sydney: Allen and Uwin, 1989); Benhabib, *The Reluctant Modernism of Hannah Arendt*.

17. George Kateb, "Ideology and Storytelling," *Social Research* 69: 324.

18. Arendt, *Origins of Totalitarianism*, 477.

19. Hannah Arendt, *The Life of the Mind: Thinking* (New York: Harcourt Brace, 1978), 188.

20. Hannah Arendt, "Some Questions of Moral Philosophy," in *Responsibility and Judgment*, ed. Jerome Kohn (New York: Schocken Books, 2003 [1965]), 96.

21. Ibid., 98.

22. Hannah Arendt, "The Great Tradition and the Nature of Totalitarianism," Lecture, presented at the New School for Social Research, 1953. Hannah Arendt Papers, Manuscript Division, Library of Congress, Container #74, 10.

23. Hannah Arendt, "We Refugees," *The Menorah Journal* 31: 72.

24. Ibid., 69.

25. Ibid., 70.

26. Ibid., 76.

27. Arendt, *The Life of the Mind: Thinking*, 188.

28. Ibid., 193.

29. Ibid., 180.

30. Ibid., 193.

31. Ibid., 191.

32. Arendt, *The Human Condition*, 203.

33. Ibid., 180.

34. Ibid., 212.

35. Ibid., 213–15.

36. Friedan's most compelling chapter reveals that ironically it is the advertisers themselves who understand the woman problem. "Time and time again, the surveys shrewdly analyzed the needs, and even the secret frustrations of the American housewife; and each time if these needs were properly manipulated, she could be induced to buy more 'things.' In 1957, a survey told the department stores that their role in this new world was not only to 'sell' the housewife but to satisfy her need for 'education'—to satisfy the yearning she has, alone in her house, to feel herself a part of the changing world. The store will sell her more, the report said, if it will understand that the real need she is trying to fill by shopping is not anything she can buy there. . . . The buying of things drains away those needs which cannot really be satisfied by home and family—the housewives' need for something beyond themselves with which to identify" (Betty Friedan, *The Feminine Mystique* (New York: Norton, 1963) 320–22).

37. Hannah Arendt, "Interview with Günter Gaus," in *The Portable Hannah Arendt*, ed. Peter Baehr (New York: Penguin Putnam, 2000 [1964]), 20.
38. Arendt, *Origins of Totalitarianism*, 478.
39. Maria Markus, "The Anti-Feminism of Hannah Arendt," in *Hannah Arendt: Thinking, Judging, Freedom*, eds. G. T. Kaplan and C. S. Kessler (Sydney: Allen and Unwin, 1989), 121.
40. Arendt, *Origins of Totalitarianism*, 478.
41. Markus, "The Anti-Feminism of Hannah Arendt," 121.
42. Arendt, *Origins of Totalitarianism*, 189.
43. Ibid., 478.
44. Ibid.

Chapter Nine

Experiential Ontology

Implications for Identity Politics

Both Heidegger and Arendt are often read as either indifferent or hostile to identity politics. In the case of Heidegger, this interpretation is based on an essentialist reading that fails to adequately take into account the roles of *thrownness* and *projectivity* in *Being and Time*. As we have seen while it is certainly true that Heidegger places most facets of historical identity into a category he refers to as ontic and rather summarily dismisses as irrelevant to the project of fundamental ontology, he also acknowledges that ontological questions must necessarily be taken up through the ontic. Similarly, Arendt warns of potential dangers associated with political movements based only on shared victim status. Despite such warnings, it has never been clear what role she imagines for identity in political action. In this chapter, I suggest that both thinkers are productive resources for considering contemporary identity politics in the context of continental philosophy and political theory. For example, Heidegger's leaping—in/leaping—ahead distinction is an important ethical supplement to contemporary debates in identity politics. In particular, this distinction allows us to remain sensitive to the complicated ways in which identity is never something stable such that it could be taken over and handed back to a person or group, even with the best of intentions. Instead, identity is itself a project that allows a person to find his or her own possibilities in the task of taking him or herself up as a project.

Though conventional wisdom regarding Heidegger's work would tend to regard any claim that he was attentive to otherness as dubious,[1] more recent scholarship notes the conceptual debt that feminist approaches owe to Heidegger. It questions whether gender is an ontic characteristic[2] and re-examines Heidegger's claim to non-normativity in ways that illuminate the trap, from which Heidegger cannot escape. These attempts to re-think Heidegger are productive, for feminist theory, as well as, identity politics. Moreover, using Heidegger's approach to transcendence as a jumping off point, Arendt ends up anticipating someone like Judith Butler, by pointing us toward a phenomenological approach to identity, in which one facet of identity politics should be the unconcealment of a set of structures that press upon individuals and their existential choices.[3] Moreover, anticipating someone like Adriana Cavarero, Arendt alerts us to the importance of taking seriously concrete political identities and listening to historical narratives of such identities. In ways that will be picked up and expanded by thinkers such as Jean-Luc Nancy, both Heidegger and Arendt attend to the ontological stakes of such identity.[4] Namely, thrownness and the aim of projecting oneself into the future are not results of history, but characteristics of how historicity is the ontological condition for the ontic practice of history itself. Nancy, along with Cavarero, turns our attention to listening as a productive orientation toward the *being-with* that remains attentive to the *in-between* (in other words, treats the role of the other as genuinely constitutive of meaning). In short, Nancy, Butler and Cavarero not only extend the work of and illustrate the contemporary relevance of Arendt and Heidegger for philosophical debates in identity politics, they provide alternative responses to the question—what would a construction of *Being-with* look like that is genuinely constitutive of Being? As such, they each, implicitly, provide alternative answers to the question—for what is Arendt's trap a metaphor? In the process, they point us toward the possibility of grounding democratic theory in a dynamic and evolving plurality.

In light of an existentially attentive reading of Heidegger, Arendt's work can be understood as an attempt to take the Heideggerian notion of historicity seriously as a constitutive feature of lived existence. As we have seen, in her first two major works, *Rahel Varnhagen* and *Origins of Totalitarianism*, Arendt situates herself as a historical *Being-with-others*. Through Varnhagen, she struggled with the throw of a German, Jewess. With *Origins*, she examined existential choices amidst the development of modern antisemitism and capitalism. Only once she has grappled with these ontic questions, does she move to her own ontological questions: if we are to take democracy seriously as a proposition under conditions of modernity, with what political existential reality must we contend? Her response to such questions, in *The Human Condition* the posthumously published *Life of the Mind* and *Responsibility and Judgment*, stands as an important contribution to debates concerning identity politics. Ultimately, then, against interpretations that focus on Arendt and Heidegger's animosity to identity politics, I argue that not only are Arendt and Heidegger relevant to contemporary debates about identity in continental philosophy and political theory, but also that subsequent thinkers, such as Nancy, Butler, and Cavarero, complete Arendt's project of transforming fundamental ontology with an eye to its use in the public sphere.[5]

Despite Patricia Huntington's claim that Sandra Lee Bartky was the first to examine Heidegger's importance for feminist scholarship, Günther Stern noted in 1947 that in Heidegger's fundamental ontology "[a]ll want is wanting; thus sex too."[6] In other words, Heidegger failed to take into account any ontic barriers to transcendence, thus denying the role of social relations in *Existenz*. Stern accuses Heidegger of ignoring the impact of economics and particularly the fact that the tools which reveal *DaSein* are simultaneously alienating. Stern points out that any self-revealing act has the potential to be simultaneously alienating and raises the question: are self-revealing acts inherently alienating? In what follows I explore the ways in which Jean-Luc Nancy, Judith Butler and Adriana Cavarero extend Arendt's critique of Heidegger, and in so doing, contribute to a plural, ontological grounding of democratic theory.

JEAN-LUC NANCY

Jean-Luc Nancy attempts to move beyond the Self-Other dichotomy by taking seriously the notion of *Being-with* as a constitutive feature of *Being*. Nancy posits that *Being-with* is equiprimordial with *Being*. However, unlike Heidegger, Nancy attends to what this would require. In order for this assertion to take on concrete value, otherness must be part and parcel of the experience of Self. Jean-Luc Nancy and Judith Butler hash this out in different ways. Butler, following Adorno, examines the role of other in creating a notion of morality which then presses upon the Self.[7] Conversely, Nancy uses Heidegger explicitly to develop an approach to ontology that privileges plurality. In the process he shifts us away from a Cartesian epistemology, challenges the privilege of ocularity in western philosophy in favor of an auditory approach. Additionally, he goes beyond problematizing the notion of other as external to the Self by exploring ways in which otherness or foreignness is central to the experience of ipseity.

Nancy develops not only the importance of listening but he provides a conceptual approach to listening that when overlayed on his notion of spatiality provides a unique supplement to the Heideggerian concept of leaping-ahead for the purpose of handing back, which could inform, albeit in complicated ways, our approach to identity politics. If Heidegger gives us a type of thinking that requires "coming into the nearness of distance"[8] and Arendt creates a dialectical thinking,[9] Nancy reminds us of the shortcomings of the subject-centered approach which Heidegger epitomizes and Arendt fails to entirely escape. Both Heidegger and Arendt utilize an epistemological approach that can only be described as subject-centered. Heidegger reserves no role for the Other at all, save one, distracting the thinker from his or her project with "idle talk." Arendt reserves a role for the Other, in the sense that understanding or meaning derives from a dialogue between the Self and the inner partner, but since the other who participates in the dialectical thinking is not in fact an Other at all but "one's inner partner" the role of otherness in the construction of meaning is limited to the Self attempting to approximate what an Other might say or experience. There is no requirement in Arendt's approach to thinking that one actually exposes oneself to an Other, as Levinas does, for example.[10] For this reason, epistemologically speaking, the meaning that results can best be described as subject-centered.

Jean-Luc Nancy decenters the subject by focusing on listening. Though he utilizes a type of listening without a suitable English translation: *écouter*. Brian Kane notes that Nancy

> selects *écouter* as the axis for his interrogation of listening because of his sensitivity to the etymology and implications of the verb, *entendre*. Listening as *entendre* or as intention, preserves and prolongs the structure of a Cartesian epistemology: a subject possessing the capacity for attention, who wills its direction; and an intentional object towards which this attention is directed, and from which it attains its meaning.[11]

Conversely, *écouter* emphasizes observation and the concealment of the listener. It is "involved with situating sounds in the sonorous milieu, with grasping their distance and spatial location."[12] Nancy himself notes the use of *écouter* in espionage, in a way that is similar to eavesdrop or designates "a place where one could listen in secret."[13] The emphasis, thus, shifts from a listener acting with intention toward an object, to a listener who is tuned-in, attentive, and most importantly, receptive to the ways sound acts and reacts in a particular space. Nancy not only reserves a role for the Other in the construction of meaning, and places the construction of meaning itself in the in-between, but he silences the Self and relegates it to an observing posture.

Nancy, simultaneously, notes that philosophy has long associated itself with appearances and the visual.[14] Sight and the visual, however, tend toward objectification. To be seeing is to be turning a subject into an object. To be listening, on the other hand, "is to be straining toward a possible meaning . . . one that is not immediately accessible"[15] and as previously noted, neither meaning, nor sense can "take place for one alone."[16] Sound, thus, makes sense (i.e., acquires meaning) by reverberating and "resonating from self to self."[17] Reminiscent of Arendt's common sense, meaning is necessarily collective and need not require any specialized knowledge. It derives from the space in-between subjects. The listener is one who attends to and is receptive to the way sound reverberates between subjects; meaning is always reciprocal and always evolving. It does not take on a fixed, absolute or resolved quality. In short, for Nancy, both the act of listening and the meaning that derive from listening take the form of extending into an in-between, toward an Other, or a reaching outside of an internal construction of the Self in anticipation of "the resonance of a return [*renvoi*]."[18] The unique feature of listening is that the listening subject remains open to, anticipates any disclosure of the experience of Being that may occur in this space in-between; whereas the seeing subject projects his or her understanding or expectations onto a subject, who is then transformed into an object and in so doing transforms the Other into an object as well. In keeping with Nancy's ontological approach, the *Being-with* becomes, in fact, constitutive of meaning and sense, in short, of the world. The shift to the auditory sense as occupying a privileged position epistemologically, termed by Adrienne Janus the "antiocular turn,"[19] remedies several of the issues in Heidegger's fundamental ontology, perhaps most importantly, it opens up a space for reconsidering a provocative yet often overlooked element of *Being and Time*: "leaping-in" [*einspringen*] and "leaping-ahead" [*vorauspringen*].

LEAPING IN [*EINSPRINGEN*] AND LEAPING AHEAD [*VORAUSPRINGEN*]

Heidegger famously follows Husserl in the aim of offering a descriptive account of lived experience, but does so with an eye to the context in which such experience would occur. That is, Heidegger avoids the idealist worry faced by Husserl because Heidegger's notion of *Dasein* is essentially one of being-in-a-world.[20] Yet, even here, the notion of "world" is not directly understood relative to a political context, though that is not necessarily excluded, but rather "world" is relative to a hermeneutic context of meaning. For Heidegger, the "world" is best understood as a horizon of meaning internal to which meaning is then continually made. Accordingly, Heidegger's own account of "world" might be seen as all-too-worldless when one considers *Dasein* in its political existence. Indeed, Heidegger's own infamous political mistakes might be cited by some as evidence of this persistent occlusion of political realities in Heidegger's theory.[21] We might say, then, that there is a tension between Heidegger's descriptive phenomenology and his normative existentialism.[22] Unable, or unwilling, to decide in favor of the normative (as were later existential phenomenologists such as Sartre and de Beauvoir), Heidegger attempts to remain descriptive in his account of authentic selfhood without then advocating it as a better way of life than the average, everyday inauthentic existence in which *Dasein* so often finds itself. Ultimately, this tension in Heidegger's thought can lead to the worry that his ontological priorities led him to overlook the ontic realities in which *Dasein* is located, as Stern pointed out. Or, said slightly differently, the analytic of *Dasein* offered in *Being and Time* is only awkwardly applicable to the existential struggles of *this* particular individual in *this* particular context. *Dasein* might be ontically distinctive by being ontological, but *Dasein* is rarely directly considered as a woman, or a Jew.

Projectivity is the component of care which is futural in its orientation. Projectivity occurs when *Dasein*, from its state of fallenness, undertakes a forward motion toward "its ownmost potentiality-of-being."[23] Authentic *Dasein* acts with agency, if not necessarily planning or forethought, in an effort to transcend its own thrownness and overcome fallenness. Yet, this does not mean that one stops being thrown, or is not continually at risk of falling back into the mindset and mode of being characteristic of "the They." Instead, the futurally oriented motion associated with projection comprises "the very essence of freedom," authenticity and transcendence for Heidegger.[24] For Heidegger, this freedom is cashed out in two very general ways of being-with others. On the one hand, we can relate to others as singular individuals who project themselves into the future as a realization of their own possibilities and identities. Heidegger terms this way of relating others "leaping-ahead" [*vorausspringen*]. We leap-ahead and free others so that they can find themselves. Alternatively, we can relate to others as mere instances of our own freedom's working itself out. Accordingly, we don't free others to their own future, but instead eliminate the space in which their future would truly be their own. Heidegger terms this relationship "leaping-in" [*einspringen*]. Leaping-in takes over for others; leaping-ahead takes care of others but only by preserving and ensuring their agency in their own projection.[25] Heidegger's "leaping-ahead" has a resonating quality to it in the sense that the act of handing back one's possibilities necessarily decenters the subject.

Jean-Luc Nancy offers us a concrete way of understanding, first, what Heidegger might be getting at with the distinction between leaping-in and leaping ahead. Second, he suggests that this distinction, if taken seriously, further complicates our understanding of Heidegger since it lays the conceptual groundwork for an approach to identity politics that appears fundamentally inconsistent both with a conventional understanding of Heidegger's work, as well as his politics. Moreover, Nancy offers us one way of concretizing what Heidegger's notion of leaping ahead would require of us. Most important and most obviously, we must regard the Other, as well as our Self, not only as projecting but also as evolving. In guarding the Other's agency, Nancy would have us take up the position of listening (*écouter*), voiding my own claim to "know" or to ascribe meaning in favor of "straining toward a possible meaning . . . that is not immediately accessible" but rather results from the reverberations of sound in which I do not participate and to which I do not contribute except by observing and straining.

In terms of understanding Heidegger, the leaping-in and leaping-ahead distinction, particularly in conjunction with the revelations in the *Black Notebooks* problematize our interpretation of this already complex figure. It is now clear that Heidegger himself, not only fell victim to, but lent "height, weight and philosophical sophistication" to the demeaning stereotypes of his time[26] and suggested the optimal mode of care was that of taking care of others by preserving and ensuring their agency in their own projection. The question of how to understand Heidegger in light of these revelations is clearly one which will continue to be hashed out. The risk we run, however in dismissing Heidegger as morally bankrupt, is that despite his own shortcomings, he has important things to teach us, *especially* about identity. That Heidegger existed as thrown being in the world, both transcending and falling prey to his own thrownness seems on the face of it fairly straightforward. He fell prey, however, not simply to antisemitism but to the idle talk, mere talk and double talk of the Third Reich. In so doing, the philosopher who alerted us to the constitutive power of language succumbed to the power of Hitler's rhetoric: the quintessential critic of modernity came to be deceived by *the* most horrific manifestation of modernity.

If we are willing to allow that profound insight and epic failure can coexist, Heidegger's example has much to teach us, particularly about identity. Perhaps none of these lessons is more compelling than Nancy's cautionary note about the necessity of decentering the subject. I take decentering of the subject through listening (*écouter*) to be Nancy's most productive contribution. In decentering the subject, Nancy contributes to Heidegger's project of offering an alternative to metaphysics. Additionally, he advances Arendt's project of grounding the ontological in the world in a way that prioritizes *being-with*. In terms of democratic theory, Nancy pushes us to conceptualize listening as the cornerstone of democracy. If listening, rather than appearing or voting, was the primary responsibility of citizens, civic education could center around what it means to sit, hear and take-in the experiences or the perspective of someone else. If listening, rather than speaking or acting, was the primary responsibility of our elected representatives, members of congress could be evaluated based on their grasp of constituent issues.

JUDITH BUTLER'S PERFORMATIVITY

Following Arendt, Butler focuses our attention on the myriad of norms and social structures that press upon our existence. Arendt views these norms as pressing upon existential choices that individuals make, as individuals, and "innate" personalities that develop within a power structure or, perhaps more accurately, under conditions of powerlessness. Yet as the pariah/parvenu distinction illustrates, she views individuals as possessing agency. Like Butler, she celebrates those moments, rare though they may be, when an individual realizes the opportunity to contest or challenge a norm. Butler in many ways furthers this work by examining and emphasizing the significance of these norms and exploring the possibilities of creating an ethical standard or social responsibility out of the need to contest oppressive structures. In contrast to both Heidegger and Arendt, Butler does not associate stability with identity.[27] If Heidegger thinks about one's identity as having an essence that is rooted in a place, in the soil, and Arendt speaks about "the indisputable facts of [her] life"[28] and "belonging to a group [as] a natural condition,"[29] Butler takes issue with the presentation of identity as the *facts of one's life,* and particularly, with gender as a natural condition. Rather, "gender is an identity tenuously constituted in time, in an exterior space through a stylized repetition of acts."[30] She conceptualizes identity as performative, as distinct from performed. To say identity is performed is akin, for Butler, to saying that one is taking on a role, the implication being that the role precedes the actor's performance and is, at least to some degree, scripted but also that the actor makes to some degree a choice to take on this role,[31] when presumably another choice would be to take on a different role or to take up his or her actual Self. On the other hand, in saying that identity is performative, Butler posits, first, that gender is not a role from which one could simply walk away. For Butler, there is no distinction to be made between a role that one plays and the Being that one is. Rather, the iterative performance constitutes the Being that one is. The Self is constituted "through a stylized repetition of acts," which is to say, the feminine identity is constructed in the literally hundreds of decisions that individual women make daily to put on make-up, reign in anger and avoid taking up space. With each of these choices, I construct my Self as female. Secondly, "'performative' suggests a dramatic and contingent construction of meaning."[32] In other words, each performative act leaves something behind, an impression of what it is to be male, female or Jewish; this "contingent construction of meaning" is never owned or controlled by the subject.[33] Each time I present my Self in a skirt, in heels or offer a pre-emptive apology for blocking male space, I re-create femininity for others.

Thus, one way of characterizing the difference between Arendt and Butler on identity is that for Arendt, identity is constituted by a series of choices regarding self-understanding and self-presentation that may, in turn, affect one's self-understanding, self-presentation and the prospects of transcendence. Whereas for Butler identity is a continuous string of actions and appearances that "consolidate an impression of being a man or a woman."[34] Moreover, "it is always a reiteration of a norm or a set of norms."[35] Both Arendt and Butler regard identity as a process. In fact, Arendt approximates a performative theory of identity in her description of Benjamin Disraeli's use of his Jewishness to advance his career. She notes, not only, that he played a role, but that it was his "display of exoticism, strangeness, mysteriousness, magic and power drawn from secret societies" that gained him social acceptance. Arendt offers the portrait of Benjamin Disraeli, who "never thought seriously of anything except his career."[36] His Jewishness "was a fact of origin which he was at liberty to embellish." With social acceptance as his goal and astute powers of observation, yet "unhindered by actual knowledge" of Jewish history or Judaism, he adopted the persona of an exception Jew.[37] Arendt suggests that Disraeli's cheerful naiveté was both deliberately adopted and self-serving, "[h]is innocence made him recognize how foolish it would be to feel déclassé and how much more exciting it would be for himself and for others, how much more useful for his career, to accentuate the fact that he was a Jew 'by dressing differently, combing his hair oddly, and by queer manners of expression and verbiage.'"[38] Moreover, she includes the vignette of Disraeli, precisely because the performance of his Jewish identity left something in the world. In constructing his identity, Disraeli succeeded in creating a career that was "more exciting . . . for himself and for others" yet paradoxically, he also created a career in which he was "one of the last court Jews and one of the first victims of modern anti-Semitism."[39] He constituted the exception Jew as reality, as well as, a caricature. The long-term effect of Disraeli's "cheerful naiveté" is that he created a lasting impression that Jews were members of a secret society, aspiring to rule the world. His "contingent construction" of Jewishness reiterated and consolidated several anti-Semitic stereotypes, including those of naked ambition and opportunism. In this sense, Arendt's work on identity, not only foreshadows Butler's notion of performativity, Arendt's aims could be better understood, which is to say less readily misinterpreted, in the context of Butler's theoretical work.

Arendt's subject maintains its agency while simultaneously illustrating many of the limitations on agency; whereas Butler leaves us wondering whether agency is possible.[40] Lisa Disch, on the other hand, suggests that while Butler's account certainly renders autonomy impossible, agency and autonomy are not synonymous. According to Disch, Butler offers us an account of agency that "does not begin and end with the speaker . . . it is complicit with the forces it opposes, and . . . it is citational rather than original."[41] In other words, Butler's subject cannot control either the meaning or the outcome of his or her own speech. Perhaps most importantly, Butler's subject is complicit with the powers that create his or her own oppression, a series of observations with which Arendt would agree. Her vignettes of Disraeli, as well as Varnhagen, make it clear that they both made existential choices in a context they neither controlled, nor understood. Disraeli's presentation of Jewishness, for example, was hardly original. He wrote novels and created a variety of characters who conformed to anti-Jewish stereotypes, that he did not invent. He was fascinating as a Conservative, in part because he was Jewish, an apparent anomaly. He was a monarchist who sought to enfranchise the masses. As a political outsider, his allegiance to apparently contradictory causes rang true. Moreover, he became the Prime Minister of England, friend and confidante of the Queen, while cultivating an image of Jews conspiring to world domination, precisely the imagery that later stoked the fires of European antisemitism.

In this sense Disraeli beautifully illustrates what Butler means when she says "power is not simply what we oppose but also, in a strong sense, what we depend on for our existence and what we harbor and preserve in the beings that we are."[42] Moreover, it explains a common misunderstanding of Arendt's work. She is often accused of blaming the victim.[43] If we read her, on the other hand, as offering concrete examples of abstract concepts, as well as, seeking to reveal the role of power in existential choice, then one way of viewing Arendt's work is by providing concrete examples of the simultaneous phenomenon—of opposing and depending upon the power that oppresses us—for our identity. In the case of Disraeli, for example, his political power and his position was utterly dependent on gentile fascination with the exotic Jew. The public image he created clearly perpetuated that stereotype. Wealthy Jews are only exotic if that imagery contrasts with a negative stereotype of eastern Jews.

Following Arendt, one of Butler's aims is to approach ontological questions, mindful of the role of power. The vehicle that both imagine for reinserting social and political power into our understanding of the nature of Being, is the narrative. In telling the story of Rahel Varnhagen, Arendt stated that her aim was to tell Rahel's story, "as she herself might have told it."[44] Arendt, thus, uses her own perspective to tell Rahel's story "within the categories that were available to her and that she somehow accepted as valid."[45] In the process Arendt is also clearly coming to terms with her own identity, which is to say she is working through the question of whether or not one's existence, particularly in certain ontic categories, can be fated.[46] Thus, in constructing Rahel's narrative, Arendt attempts to give Rahel's account of herself, though she also contests it. As she explained to Jaspers, "[w]hat I meant to do was argue further with her, the way she argued with herself. . . . I tried to measure and correct the parvenu by constantly applying the standards of the pariah."[47] Butler's cautionary note is that even our self-narratives are not our own or at least not exclusively our own. Drawing on Foucault, she examines the task of self-creating in relation to a set of norms. The norms do not "produce the subject" nor "is the subject fully free to disregard the norm that inaugurates its reflexivity."[48] Thus, the "I" can provide neither a complete nor cohesive account of oneself. The self-narrative is never fully one's own because we appear in the world as thrown beings, like Disraeli, never fully cognizant of our own thrownness. One can never be fully aware of the material conditions that both create and are created by one's thrownness or the ways in which one's thrownness is perceived by and in turn presses upon one's listener. Butler refers to this as the "struggle with the unchosen conditions of one's life."[49] Her perhaps paradoxical claim is that agency becomes possible precisely because of the "the persistence of this primary condition."[50] It is after all the meaning associated with these norms that give meaning to insurrectionary acts. Rahel's salon was an exotic, intellectually vibrant space because of her Jewishness. Lacking in formal education, her curiosity and penchant for honest introspection was perceived as originality. The social norms associated with Jewishness made her exotic. The fact that her salon stood outside respectable society made it appealing. Her agency was possible precisely because of her "unchosen condition."

Further, Butler asserts that the demand to produce a cohesive account of oneself constitutes a form of ethical violence. What then are the prospects for identity politics? Given that identity is inextricably interconnected with power, identity is inherently political. What is the role for identity in the political sphere? One possible answer is that the aim of identity politics should be, following Heidegger, to create an ethical space within which to attempt to narrate the incomplete and, quite possibly, incoherent account of oneself. In other words, the aim of identity politics is not so much the enactment of a specific legislative agenda, as it is to "allow a wide errancy in which to feel at home."[51] This is an ethical space in which to grapple with the vacillation between separateness and relatedness, a way of further making sense of Heidegger's distinction between leaping-in and leaping-ahead. "Leaping-in" fails to recognize *Dasein*'s potential for selfhood and in so doing actually undermines that potential and impedes projection; whereas "leaping-ahead" recognizes the other's autonomous selfhood and thus, facilitates the development of an independent project. Lawrence Vogel suggests that the line between "leaping-in" and "leaping-ahead" may be determined by whether the Other ceases to be regarded as capable of caring for himself.[52] In view of this assertion, Vogel poses the query—what is it about authenticity that allows for liberating solicitude? He goes on to suggest that "leaping ahead" "involves three moments. First, one must appreciate what the other gets out of listening away and not owning up to anxiety."[53] In other words, one must understand why the Other would opt for inauthenticity. This awareness, in and of itself, likely presupposes a familiarity with authenticity. *Dasein* must also "appreciate the price" of opting for inauthenticity and finally the Self has an obligation to facilitate the Other's transition from the inauthentic to the authentic by helping the Other to see that the cost of fleeing this responsibility to his or her Self is simply too high.[54] Vogel's approach seems to presuppose a rather stark distinction between authentic and inauthentic. The obligation becomes still more daunting as we recall that authenticity is not a dichotomy. Even authentic individuals are always simultaneously falling prey.

Arendt's work does precisely these things in an attempt to hand back to both Jews and Germans their own possibilities. She illustrates through numerous vignettes the possible results of allowing one's Self to get lost in the "they." Benjamin Disraeli and Rahel Varnhagen opted for inauthenticity. Both allowed social acceptance to assume paramount importance in their lives in lieu of projection. Rahel lost herself in one romance after another; Disraeli carefully cultivated a cheerful eccentricity. Moreover, Arendt illustrates the price each paid for "fleeing from one's self responsibility."[55] Rahel lost herself in her own misery; Disraeli "played his part so well that he was convinced by his own make believe."[56] Finally, Arendt illustrates not only what can happen to the individual when "the benefits of fleeing are not worth the costs"[57] but also that the collective ramifications can be catastrophic. Rahel agonized over her own inauthenticity before realizing the costs of social acceptance. Disraeli never gained this self-awareness and inadvertently lays the groundwork for modern antisemitism in the midst of his own personal quest for a sense of belonging. In Vogel's words, Disraeli "compromised the very freedom that makes one human because [he found] his task too burdensome."[58] In her attempt to hand back possibilities, Arendt reveals the truly burdensome nature of this task and the devastating collective costs of shirking this responsibility.

Even with the examination of liberating solicitude, any reading of Heidegger that attempts to carve out a substantial role for the Other distorts his thought to some degree; whether it actually misrepresents or simply prioritizes a constitutive element of Being that Heidegger himself did not emphasize remains a question. My aim is not to resolve this matter but rather to suggest that this issue came to comprise the core of Arendt's project. Heidegger's penchant for abstraction, which includes the omission of ontic characteristics from his analysis, lies at the heart of fundamental ontology. It constitutes both Heidegger's brilliant contribution to philosophy and a trap from which he is never fully able to extricate himself. Blücher and Arendt had long considered Heidegger's concept of history (*Geschichtsbegriff*) to be the troublesome concept in Heidegger's fundamental ontology.[59] As such, Arendt's work can be read as attempting to right the flaws of fundamental ontology by grounding "liberating solicitude" in a continual reappraisal of key historical moments in light of an unfolding present.

Thus, taking Vogel and Butler together, we might understand the ethical obligation of identity politics to be a granting to each individual the liberating solicitude or "wide errancy" to construct and reconstruct a self-narrative that is both incoherent and incomplete, to struggle with the boundaries between and limits of one's Self and one's connectedness. At the same time, Butler, like Arendt, leaves us deeply ambivalent about the possibility of constructing a political agenda around identity, if the demand to produce a coherent account of one's Self constitutes a form of ethical violence and "an avowal of the limits of self-understanding" stands at the center of responsibility,[60] what are the implications for identity politics, for the creation of a political agenda? Does identity politics itself become an utter impossibility, as an ethical matter? Or alternatively, does the task of identity politics become to create a space and an ethical set of norms within which to attempt to narrate the incomplete and possibility incoherent account of one's Self? What are we to make of the attempt to narrate an account of a people? Must that narrative, in and of itself, constitute a form of ethical violence or could it be done in such a way as to hand back to others their own possibilities? Butler's admonishment may ultimately impose the most challenging expectations on members of one's own identity group. Her caution to Arendt might be that offering a narrative to a people that is simply contestable may not be enough to guard against the development of a coercive politics, a concern to which Arendt's own experience can certainly attest.

In carving out political action as the defining moment of selfhood, Arendt draws our attention back to Stern's observation. Moments of self-revelation are inherently alienating. It is not merely that in revealing the "who" as distinct from the "what" we run the risk of becoming alienated from the group that defines itself, according to ontic characteristics. Each act of revealing separates the Self from the group. Not all moments of revelation will be perceived as threatening by the group but alienation occurs nonetheless. Arendt, herself, experienced a rather extreme and public form of alienation. In her attempt to draw attention to the myriad of structures that pressed upon Jewish victims of the German Holocaust, she did not confine herself to structures that were unambiguously Nazi. She drew attention to structures that were ambiguously Jewish as well. Certainly not all attempts at self-revelation yield such extreme results. Still, the challenge that Heidegger and Arendt point us toward represents an existential dilemma with profound political implications. Without a sense of group identity in the act of projecting, individuals run the risk of seeking acceptance of the dominant group, as Benjamin Disraeli illustrates, in ways inadvertently detrimental to the "what." With a sense of group identity, the task of projecting necessarily creates a fissure with the group. Thus, Arendt resigns herself to the life of the conscious "pariah." In elevating the ontological status of things, Heidegger inadvertently lays the groundwork for the dehumanization of *Dasein*. He admonishes us to "listen to" and "thank" things and leave our responsibility to the human Other underdeveloped. Moreover, as his own experience makes clear, in the failure to recognize the Other as *Dasein*, one's quest for Selfhood is thwarted since the failure to acknowledge another's potential project always reverberates back, limiting one's own self-concept. Collectively speaking, the devaluation of Other lays the groundwork for oppression and ultimately genocide; since in devaluing one, all are devalued. Therein lies the existential lesson of genocide and the potential consequence of engaging the other in a mode of *besorgen*, rather than *fürsorge*.

Chapter 9
ADRIANA CAVARERO'S RELATIONAL ONTOLOGY

Cavarero's existent is described as an "exposable and narratable" Self, not narrated, since the recognition of one's uniqueness does not require either knowledge of his or her story, or a conscious memory.[61] The essential aspect of narratability lies in a "familiar sense [of] a story without text; that is, in a narrative attitude of memory which does not cease."[62] In other words, even if my life story has never been told, I remain aware that I have a story, and that I in some way "consist in this story"; therein lie the essential features of narratability. The transcendent self, for Cavarero, has a somewhat vague and general sense of itself as having a story that is unique, an "unrepeatable uniqueness" as well as a sense that selfhood is to be found in this story. Reminiscent of Heidegger, it is the episodic act of remembering that alerts one to one's own narratability. The Self "makes her home, so to speak in the narrating memory" which she refers to as the "inalienable dwelling."[63] Thus, like Heidegger, Cavarero grants memory an important role in transcendence though its role is an ambiguous one. It is the existence of sporadic memories that makes us aware that we have a uniqueness, though personal memories are notoriously inaccurate in Cavarero's mind. For this reason, the self-narrative does not result from one's personal memories. Moreover, in contrast to Heidegger, for Cavarero, one's narratability derives from exposability, which is to say, it derives from encounters with others in the world. The unique life story, in other words, must necessarily result from coming into contact with the world; in this sense the world becomes constitutive of *Being*. Unlike Butler, Cavarero does not locate the construction of Self in the text of the narrative, but rather in "the familiar sense [*sapore familiare*] of every self, in the temporal extension of a life story that is this and not another."[64] Transcendence is to be found in an awareness of one's own unique story, as an "embodied and unrepeatable uniqueness" among others. Thus, transcendence requires not only a recognition of one's own uniqueness but also a recognition of the uniqueness of others.

If Cavarero is extremely skeptical of the accuracy of personal memories, she places a great deal of stock in the "familiar sense [*sapore familiare*] of every self."[65] Memories may mislead but the *sapore familiare*, perhaps intuition, is a reliable guide to one's true story. This sense of familiarity is innate in every existent and it seems to be the thing that triggers the emotional response upon hearing one's story narrated. Moreover, if she trusts in this familiar sense, she "becomes through the story, that which she already was. The self is thus also able to recuperate the constitutive worldly and relational identity from which the story itself resulted."[66] As with Heidegger, the process of arriving at one's story, in other words, actualization has a circular quality to it and returns to or *recuperates* an innate and pre-existing essence. For Cavarero, however, that essence is constituted through a relation, not only to the Other who narrates the story, but also to the world; whereas for Heidegger that return to one's essence is constituted through a reconnection with or rediscovery of one's roots, the soil or landscape, culture and tradition.

For Cavarero, the pivotal moment of actualization derives from hearing one's story narrated by another. She relays the tale of Oedipus to illustrate the flaw in self-narratives, their innate unreliability. Oedipus's autobiographical tale, "concealed rather than revealed who he is."[67] Cavarero views his autobiography as inherently unreliable. In contrast to Heidegger, Cavarero simultaneously grants memory a significant place in transcendence and grapples with the limitations of memory as a constitutive feature of Being. Cavarero's existent must necessarily constitute itself in relation to another. One can only discover who one is by discovering who or what one is not. One's own personal memory, in isolation, fails in this regard for a number of reasons. First, there are simply things one cannot remember, such as the facts of one's birth. Oedipus serves as the case and point. He remains ignorant of his story less through his own failing than because we are always dependent on others to reveal certain aspects of our stories, the facts of birth, for example. Second, metaphysically speaking, memory fails because in memories the Self serves as "both the actor and the spectator, the narrator and the listener." The Self, thus achieves unity in the story at the expense of truth since there is no opportunity to interrogate or question the story; it "is rather the irreflexive object of the desire for the unity of the self in the form of story."[68] In arriving at a narrative, the narratable self must contend with innate and competing desires: unity and accuracy. Given the episodic nature of personal memories, unity or cohesion is unlikely in a narrative that relies exclusively on memory. Moreover, accuracy with regard to the facts of one's own life is impossible for the Self to achieve based on memories alone. Additionally, any interpretation of the meaning of the facts of one's life will necessarily be inaccurate because the existent lacks the necessary perspective or distance to understand and articulate the meaning of its existence, let alone to place that meaning in a context. Like a *daimon*, the meaning of one's own existence is clearly visible only to others.[69]

Cavarero, thus, gives us another way of conceptualizing what it would mean for *Being-with* to be constitutive of *Being*. I am dependent on an Other to construct the story of my life because first, I cannot possibly remember or reconstruct even the basic facts. Second, even the memories I can recount are likely to be inaccurate, and finally, if I have some assistance putting together the basic facts and the sporadic memories I recall are factually accurate, the absence of perspective makes it impossible for me to construct and express the meaning of my own story. The interpretation of my story must necessarily come from an Other. Ulysses reacts to hearing his story told with such strong emotion because he has never before understood the importance of his actions for others and he was unaware of his desire to hear his story told by another. In other cases, the emotional response, as well as the transformative moment, lies in recognizing the desire for and importance of relationality. One can only achieve transcendence through a process of relating to others, since transcendence requires recognizing the Other's uniqueness, the Other's insight into my own life story, as well as my desire to know and be understood by an Other.

Thus, Cavarero provides an alternative interpretation of the trap of which Arendt writes. Heidegger creates a conception of transcendence in which the roles of both memory and rootedness are almost entirely self-referential. In keeping with the title of Arendt's piece, he opts for unity and cohesion, a grand vision, at the expense of accuracy. Like Berlin's hedgehog, he sought to "relate everything to a single vision, one system more or less coherent," to focus on big questions and "a single universal, organizing principle."[70] His view of philosophy is as a discipline that seeks universalizing principles. The trap, which obviously extends beyond Heidegger himself and in fact indicts most of philosophy, is the quest for Man as a universal, at the expense of an understanding of her uniqueness. In contrast to Oedipus's tragic tale, Ulysses wept at hearing his own story narrated by an Other. But why exactly is Ulysses moved to tears and what is the actualizing moment in his story? Cavarero tells us that "when he had lived them directly he had not understood their meaning"[71] a statement that could also apply to Heidegger. Self-awareness and understanding, thus, depend on the Other. Transcendence becomes impossible without an Other's perspective on one's life. As such, *being-with* is constitutive of *Being*.

Cavarero also makes space for emotion in transcendence. The transcendent moment for both Oedipus and Ulysses is the moment of hearing their stories narrated by an Other. In both cases, the experience of hearing one's story told by an Other is transformative and in both cases one of the indications of the transformative nature of this experience is the protagonist's emotional response. While the reason for the strong emotion remains ambiguous, Cavarero recognizes emotion as communicating ontological significance. Placing emotion alongside reason or the intellectual in her discussion of transcendence undermines the age-old reason-emotion dichotomy that has plagued women and been used to discredit women and people of color from occupying positions of political power. If tears or other displays of emotion indicate that I am experiencing a moment of authentic revelation, rather than that I am weak or unable to control my physiological responses to stress, then public displays of emotion could be embraced by voters rather than serving as a virtual disqualifier for public office.

If Butler cautions us against relying on the self-narrative, that is to say she points out the pitfalls of narrating one's own story, Cavarero offers an alternative conception, not only of the Self, namely the narratable Self, but also of authenticity. Butler's authenticity is to be found in the fleeting act of rejecting social expectations and charting one's own path, whereas for Cavarero the authentic moment is the moment of hearing one's story told by an Other. In listening to the telling of his story, incognito, Ulysses must remain open and attentive to an Other's interpretation of his actions and their meaning. His disguise makes it impossible for him to interject, correct the details or substitute his understanding of events for that of the Other. He is not free to question or second guess the Other's judgment. Rather, he must take in the version of his life offered by the Other. Like Nancy, who positions listening as the cornerstone of the citizenship, Cavarero also reserves for listening a crucial role, yet she focuses on a moment in which the listener cannot, without revealing himself, interrupt, interject, correct or augment the Other's tale. In other words, authenticity is contingent upon silence, receptivity and the vulnerability that comes with turning the interpretation of one's life story over to the care of an Other.

What does this receptivity require? What is required of me, if I am to remain open to the Other's narrative of my life story? First, I must be willing to grant that the Other is capable of insight and, specifically, capable of insight about my existence. Second, I must be willing to live with my own vulnerability and relinquish exclusive rights to my story. There may be alternative perspectives on the story of my life that are worthy of consideration. Each Other brings a unique voice (or perspective) to the tale, receptivity requires acknowledging or accepting the legitimacy of each unique voice. In Heideggerian terminology, *Dasein* must be willing to accept the insights of the Other's "leaping-ahead" [*vorauspringen*] for the purpose of handing back the possibility of freeing itself: at the same time in the act of handing back, the Other must be willing to release the narrative. One cannot hand back an Other's possibilities while attempting to control the meaning of the narrative. Heidegger never fully explores the leaping-in/leaping-ahead distinction or its implications, yet he certainly suggests that leaping-in is ethically problematic.

In the case of Ulysses, this receptivity may not be difficult to achieve, given that the story that is being recounted is one of heroism. We should, however, not naively embrace Cavarero; the request that we remain open to an Other's interpretation of our actions is neither a simple nor benign undertaking, as the Oedipus tale illustrates. Cavarero requires nothing less than the public exposure and vulnerability of each individual Self. In the context of contemporary identity politics, she offers us a way forward though it would require a profound courage, in light of BlackLivesMatter and #MeToo, to listen and to grant to the Other, the authority to tell *my* story. Some of us will discover that we are Harvey Weinstein and that we have done more harm than we realized. While this experience would undoubtedly be enlightening, recall that Cavarero expects us to receive the narrative without contradicting, explaining or interjecting: we may neither offer not request clarification.

Cavarero exposes the risks of pursuing the universal as the aim of philosophy while simultaneously proscribing her own version of the universal, namely that actualization lies in hearing one's story told by an Other. Ulysses may be moved to tears by hearing his story told by an Other, but what if transcendence is also to be found in the act of narrating? Put another way, is it Alice or Gertrude who finds actualization in *The Autobiography of Alice Toklas*? Transcendence would, thus, lie in the reciprocity, would also be found in the act of giving to an Other one's own interpretation of her life story. What exactly does narrating the life of an Other require? In this version of Cavarero's thesis, listening remains the cornerstone of citizenship, yet it is a listening *with the aim of re-telling*. Transcendence thus requires attentiveness, taking on the perspective of an Other and thinking from the standpoint of someone else. Moreover, reciprocity takes on a practical importance as one of my obligations becomes to accept my own vulnerability, as I remain silent and open to an Other's telling of my story, I must similarly expect to assume the responsibility of telling an Other's tale. If democratic theory were to be grounded in the reciprocal nature of this responsibility then Cavarero's relational ontology could assume its place as the cornerstone of the political; in that sense, Cavarero furthers Arendt's project of creating a democratic ontology.

In terms of democratic theory, Cavarero pushes us to imagine the reciprocity of narrating the life of an Other as the cornerstone of democracy. What if my responsibility as a citizen was two-fold: rather than voting or declaring allegiance to a political party, my primary responsibility as a citizen could be to receive and re-tell an Other's life story and to receive an Other's narrative of my own story. Civic education could center around what it means to sit, and engage with curious empathy the experiences or the perspective of someone else. What if, narrating the life of an Other, rather than speaking or acting, was the primary responsibility of our representatives? Members of congress could be evaluated based on their ability to tell an Other's story. What if receiving an Other's interpretation of one's own story, rather than declaring or obfuscating, was an important component of leadership? Democracy would not only cease to be individualistic, but the political could be grounded in empathy, or at the very least, a genuinely curious engagement.

CONCLUSION

It is easy as well as valuable to read both Arendt and Heidegger with an eye to illuminating their shortcomings. Both are often read as, at best, indifferent to, or at worst, hostile to, identity politics. Feminists have certainly found much with which to quibble in Arendt's work and Heidegger's insensitivity approaches legendary status. Moreover, it is certainly tempting to conclude that one whose philosophy led to such a dark place should be dismissed out of hand, as incapable of offering anything useful. Yet I have suggested precisely the opposite course. It is because of, rather than in spite of, his disastrous foray into the public sphere that we must re-examine Heidegger's work, as well as the efforts of his students to make sense of his calamitous error. Hannah Arendt not only grappled with Heidegger's error; reconstructing fundamental ontology for responsible, which is to say prescriptive, use in the public realm became her project. Gender was not the most politically salient feature of her identity during her lifetime. Nonetheless, her critique of, as well as, modifications of Heidegger have proven fertile ground for consideration of contemporary identity politics in continental philosophy, feminist theory, as well as, political theory. Jean-Luc Nancy, Judith Butler and Adriana Cavarero are but three illustrations of the contemporary relevance, as well as the considerable potential, of building on Arendt and Heidegger to create new approaches to democratic theory, identity politics and forge productive pathways between continental philosophy and political theory.

NOTES

1. Günther Stern, "On the Pseudo-Concreteness of Heidegger's Philosophy," *Philosophy and Phenomenological Research* 8 (1947): 337–71; Sandra L. Bartky, "Originative Thinking in the Later Philosophy of Heidegger," *Philosophy and Phenomenological Research* 30 (1970): 368–81; Jacques Derrida, "*Geschecht*: Sexual Difference, Ontological Difference," in *Feminist Interpretations of Martin Heidegger*, eds. Nancy J. Holland and Patricia Huntington (University Park, PA: Pennsylvania State University Press, 2001), 53–72.

2. Sandra L. Bartky, "Shame and Gender," in *Femininity and Domination: Studies in the Phenomenology of Oppression* (New York: Routledge, 1990), 83–98; Nancy J. Holland, "The Universe Is Made of Stories, Not of Atoms: Heidegger and the Feminine They-Self," in *Feminist Interpretations of Martin Heidegger*, eds. Nancy J. Holland and Patricia Huntington (University Park, PA: Pennsylvania State University Press, 2001), 128–48; Tina Chanter, "The Problematic Normative Assumptions of Heidegger's Ontology," in *Feminist Interpretations of Martin Heidegger*, eds. Nancy J. Holland and Patricia Huntington (University Park, PA: Pennsylvania State University Press, 2001), 73–108.

3. Judith Butler, *Gender Trouble: Feminism and the Subversion of Identity* (New York: Routledge, 1990); Judith Butler, *Giving an Account of Oneself* (New York: Fordham University Press, 2005).

4. Jean-Luc Nancy, *Being Singular Plural*, trans. Robert D. Richardson and Anne E. O'Byrne (Stanford, CA: Stanford University Press, 2000).

5. It is worth noting that I use the term "identity politics" broadly such that it comprises a matter of self-constitution in political contexts. As such identity politics comprises more than simply a focus on gender, race, group dynamics or political issues that are thought to pertain particularly to people of color or women. Rather identity politics requires us to consider how one constructs and presents oneself authentically internal to the markers of political discourse.

6. Stern, "On the Pseudo-Concreteness of Heidegger's Philosophy," 346.

7. Butler, *Giving an Account of Oneself.*

8. Martin Heidegger, "Conversations on a Country Path About Thinking," in *Discourse on Thinking*, trans. John M. Anderson and E. Hans Freud (New York: Harper and Row, 1966), 68.

9. Hannah Arendt, *Life of the Mind: Thinking* (New York: Harcourt Brace, 1978), 188.

10. Emmanuel Levinas, *Totality and Infinity: An Essay on Exteriority*, trans. Alphonso Lingus (Pittsburgh: Duquesne University Press, 1969).

11. Brian Kane, "Jean-Luc Nancy and the Listening Subject," *Contemporary Music Review* 5–6 (2012): 443.

12. Ibid., 440.

13. Jean-Luc Nancy, *Listening*, trans. Charlotte Mandell (New York: Fordham University Press, 2007), 4.

14. Nancy is not alone, nor indeed the first, to make this observation. See also, Jay Martin, *Downcast Eyes: The Denigration of Vision in Twentieth Century Thought* (Berkeley: University of California Press, 1993); Adrienne Janus, "Jean-Luc Nancy and the 'Anti-Ocular' Turn in Continental Philosophy and Critical Theory," *Comparative Literature* 63 (2011): 182–202.

15. Nancy, *Listening*, 6.

16. Jean-Luc Nancy, *The Sense of the World*, trans. Jeffrey Librett (Minneapolis: University of Minnesota Press, 1997), 88.

17. Nancy, *Listening*, 9.

18. Ibid., 12.

19. Janus, "Jean-Luc Nancy and the 'Anti-Ocular' Turn."

20. Largely this is Heidegger's improvement over Husserl in *Being and Time*. However, given Husserl's notion of the "lifeword" that is developed in *The Crisis* (during the period of 1934–1937), there is certainly room to question whether the notion of "world" in Heidegger is really going beyond Husserl or just an anticipation of where Husserl himself was already going. See Edmund Husserl, *The Crisis of European Sciences and Transcendental Phenomenology*, trans. David Carr (Evanston, IL: Northwestern University Press, 1970). For more on Heidegger's notion of being-in-the-world, see Stephen Mulhall, *On Being in the World: Wittgenstein and Heidegger on Seeing Aspects* (New York: Routledge, 1990).

21. See Richard Wolin, *The Politics of Being*; Victor Farias, *Heidegger and Nazism*, eds. Joseph Margolis and Tom Rockmore (Philadelphia, PA: Temple University Press, 1989).

22. See Pierre Bourdieu, *The Political Ontology of Martin Heidegger*, trans. Peter Collier (Stanford, CA: Stanford University Press, 1991); Philippe Lacoue-Labarthe, *Heidegger, Art and Politics*, trans. Chris Turner (Oxford: Basil Blackwell, 1990).

23. Heidegger, *Being and Time*, 203–4.

24. Simon Critchley, "Originary Inauthenticity—on Heidegger's *Sein und Zeit*," in *On Heidegger's Being and Time*, ed. Steven Levine (London: Routledge, 2008), 142.

25. Heidegger, *Being and Time*, 114–15.

26. Eduardo Mendieta, "Metaphysical Anti-Semitism and Worldlessness: On World Poorness, World Forming, and World Destroying," in *Heidegger's Black Notebooks: Responses to Anti-Semitism*, eds. Andrew J. Mitchell and Peter Trawny (New York: Columbia University Press, 2017), 41.

27. Butler, *Gender Trouble*, 191.

28. Hannah Arendt, "The Eichmann Controversy: A Letter to Gershom Scholem," in *The Jewish Writings*, eds. Jerome Kohn and Ron H. Feldman (New York: Schocken Books, 2007), 466.

29. Hannah Arendt, "What Remains? The Language Remains: Interview with Günter Gaus," in *The Portable Hannah Arendt*, ed. Peter Baehr (New York: Penguin Putnam, 2000), 16.

30. Butler, *Gender Trouble*, 191.

31. Ibid.

32. Ibid., 190.

33. Judith Butler, *Big Think*, Feb. 19, 2013.

34. Ibid.

35. Judith Butler, *Bodies that Matter: On the Discursive Limits of "Sex"* (New York: Routledge, 1993), 12.

36. Hannah Arendt, *The Origins of Totalitarianism* (New York: Harcourt Brace, 1958), 68.

37. Ibid., 69.

38. Ibid., 68.

39. David Cesarani, *Disraeli: The Novel Politician* (New Haven, CT: Yale University Press, 2016), 236.

40. Martha Nussbaum, "The Professor of Parody: The Hip Defeatism of Judith Butler," *New Republic* 22 (1999): 37–45; Alison Weir, *Identities and Freedom: Feminist Theories Between Power and Connection* (Oxford: Oxford University Press, 2013).

41. Lisa Disch, "Judith Butler and the Politics of the Performative," *Political Theory* 27 (1999): 556.

42. Judith Butler, *The Psychic Life of Power: Theories in Subjection* (Stanford, CA: Stanford University Press, 1997), 2.

43. Norman Podhoretz finds her discussion of the Jewish leadership "wholly unwarranted" ("Hannah Arendt on Eichmann: A Study in the Perversity of Brilliance," *Commentary* (September 1, 1963): 204); Bernard Wasserstein accuses her of "delineating the main characteristics of what she called the 'Jewish type' [a term she] *plainly reified*" (emphasis added) ("Blame the Victim," *Times Literary Supplement* (October 9, 2009), 14).

44. Hannah Arendt, *Rahel Varnhagen: The Life of a Jewess*, ed. Liliane Weissberg (Baltimore, MD: Johns Hopkins University Press, 1997), 81.

45. Hannah Arendt to Karl Jaspers, September 7, 1952, in *Hannah Arendt to Karls Jaspers Correspondence, 1926–1969*, eds. Lotte Kohler and Hans Saner, trans. Robert and Rita Kimber (New York: Harcourt Brace Jovanovich, 1992), 200.

46. Arendt to Jaspers, March 24, 1930, in *Hannah Arendt to Karl Jaspers Correspondence*, 11.

47. Arendt to Jaspers, September 7, 1952 in *Hannah Arendt to Karl Jaspers Correspondence*, 200.

48. Butler, *Giving an Account of Oneself*, 19.

49. Ibid.

50. Ibid.

51. Martin Heidegger, *Ponderings VII-XI: Black Notebooks 1938–1939*, trans. Richard Rojcewicz (Bloomington: Indiana University Press, 2017), 35.

52. Lawrence Vogel, *The Fragile "We": Ethical Implications of Heidegger's Being and Time* (Evanston, IL: Northwestern University Press, 1994), 90–91.

53. Ibid., 76.

54. Ibid., 76–77.

55. Ibid., 76.

56. Arendt, *Origins of Totalitarianism*, 68.

57. Vogel, *The Fragile "We,"* 76.

58. Ibid., 77.

59. Heinrich Blücher to Hannah Arendt, June 7, 21, 1952, and Hannah Arendt to Heinrich Blücher, June 21, 1952. In *Within Four Walls: The Correspondence between Hannah Arendt and Heinrich Blücher, 1936–1968*, ed. Lotte Kohler (New York: Harcourt & Brace, 1992), 186, 193, 195.

60. Christa Hodapp, "Giving an Account of Oneself: Review," *Pluralist* 8 (1): 117.

61. Adriana Cavarero, *Relating Narratives: Storytelling and Selfhood*, trans. and intro. Paul A. Kottman (London: Routledge, 2000), 34.

62. Ibid., 35.

63. Ibid., 34.

64. Ibid.

65. Ibid.

66. Ibid., 36.

67. Ibid., 14.

68. Ibid., 40.

69. Ibid., 27.

70. Isaiah Berlin, *The Hedgehog and the Fox: An Essay on Tolstoy's View of History* (New York: Simon & Schuster, 1953), 1–2.

71. Cavarero, *Relating Narratives*, 18.

Chapter Ten

Theorizing #MeToo

#MeToo represents one of the most important recent developments in the women's movement. At this stage, the connection between #MeToo as a political movement and feminist theory remains ambiguous, as does the future of the movement. Despite intergenerational and intersectional criticisms, #MeToo has succeeded in demonstrating the ongoing relevance of feminism, as well as mobilizing a new generation. The work of #MeToo, however, is far from complete and it runs the risk of slipping into irrelevance if we don't take this opportunity to think through its importance in terms of democratic theory. Namely, we must take up the question—how should #MeToo transform our politics? In what follows, I propose that #MeToo provides an opportunity to make good on the premise of the previous chapter, namely that thinking Arendt through Heidegger, positions us to view them both as productive resources for identity politics. Moreover, their contributions, flawed though they may be, laid the groundwork for thinkers like Jean-Luc Nancy, Judith Butler and Adriana Caverero to take up the critical question—how can *Being-with* become genuinely constitutive of *Being*. My contention is that doing so, not only, provides us with a way of understanding #MeToo, but it also demonstrates the value and contemporary relevance of Arendt's *experiential ontology*. Most importantly, #MeToo provides us with an opportunity to move toward a democratic theory that values the role of the Other as something other than object.

On October 5th, 2017, the *New York Times* published an article by Jodi Kantor and Megan Twohey in which Ashley Judd accused Harvey Weinstein of sexual harassment. Moreover, they claimed Weinstein had been paying off women with similar claims for over three decades.[1] Immediately thereafter, Ronan Farrow detailed the accounts of eight of Weinstein's accusers, demonstrating that Weinstein stood accused of not just harassment but also assault.[2]

Ten days later, Alyssa Milano tweeted that anyone who had experienced sexual harassment should use the #MeToo and share the story. Within 24 hours, the hashtag was used almost a half a million times on Twitter alone, leading Alexandra Schwarz to ponder whether there were any women who hadn't been sexually harassed.[3] In early March, Chana Joffe-Walt produced a program for This American Life in which she interviewed five of the Alternet employees who accused Don Hazen of sexual harassment. To Joffe-Walt's surprise, each employee placed her experience of sexual harassment in the context of her emerging understanding of power and gendered relationships. Vivian, Hazen's partner, recalls watching his attention make women uncomfortable. Deanna describes expecting that she would be responsible for the emotional labor in any romantic relationship; Tana's parents led her to believe that sexual harassment is part and parcel of being female in any workplace. It is Kristen, the youngest of the five, who labels Hazen's behavior as harassment and encourages the others to view their experiences through that lens; all the others ultimately come to understand their relationship to Hazen differently in light of Kristen's labeling of the workplace dynamic as one of sexual harassment.[4]

In the nearly two years since Kantor and Twohey's groundbreaking piece, the list of powerful men implicated in workplace sexual harassment reaches across partisan lines, across industries as well as international borders. It has forced into early retirement figures like Charlie Rose, Al Franken, and Garrison Keillor, as well as revealed the horrific abuse of Larry Nassar. Yet the future direction of the movement appears ambiguous. Despite Catharine MacKinnon's claim that social media has taken us where legal actions could not, the question of whether sexual harassment law needs revisiting remains, as does the question of due process in the #MeToo era.[5] But if these revelations are to have more than a fleeting impact, they must invite us to reconsider the very essence of political obligation. In the spirit of Sheldon Wolin's entreaty to view political philosophy as uniquely positioned to assist us in "accommodating new political experiences," I explore the ways in which political theory could facilitate our political transformation post- #MeToo.[6] Specifically, I examine the ways in which Jean-Luc Nancy, Judith Butler and Adriana Cavarero attempt to move beyond the Self-Other dichotomy by taking seriously the notion of *Being-with* as a constitutive feature of *Being*. In so doing they provide us with the opportunity to think through the potential of #MeToo to re-imagine democratic theory. Moreover, in bringing Nancy, Butler and Cavarero to bear on this moment of political transformation, we must also consider the challenges that they leave with us.

JEAN-LUC NANCY AND THE INTIMACY OF STRANGENESS

With their innovations as well as their shortcomings, Arendt and Heidegger lay the groundwork for a political philosophy that is mindful of and sensitive to difference. Thus, perhaps paradoxically, they pave the way for advances in contemporary philosophy and political theory in the area of identity politics. Building on the work of Martin Heidegger, Jean-Luc Nancy attempts to move beyond the Self-Other dichotomy by taking seriously the notion of *Being-with* as a constitutive feature of *Being*. Nancy posits that *Being-with* is equiprimordial with *Being*. However, unlike Heidegger, Nancy attends to what this would require. In order for this assertion to take on concrete value, otherness must be part and parcel of the experience of Self. Jean-Luc Nancy and Judith Butler hash this out in different ways. Butler, following Adorno, examines the role of other in creating a notion of morality which then presses upon the Self.[7] Conversely, Nancy uses Heidegger explicitly to develop an approach to ontology that privileges plurality. Moreover, he uses Arendt, implicitly, to hash out what it would require to elevate *Being-with* to a genuinely constitutive role in the nature of Being. In the process he shifts us away from a Cartesian epistemology, challenges the privilege of ocularity in western philosophy in favor of an auditory approach and explores ways in which otherness is central to the experience of ipseity. For one thing, he posits that the Other is part and parcel of the Self.

Building on the age-old analogy of the body politic, Nancy uses his own heart transplant, as a metaphor for the Other, as well as a way to rethink strangeness or foreignness. The heart, the most intimate of organs "[u]ntil now it was foreign by virtue of its being insensible, not even present." An organ absolutely crucial to life but, in its proper functioning, also unknown and virtually unknowable. "But now it falters, and this very strangeness refers me back to myself."[8] Did the heart become strange (or foreign) in the process of its removal, in being transplanted or in its failure? With this question, Nancy draws attention to the ambiguity of otherness, which will be picked up by both Butler and Cavarero. The Other is unknown to me, but to what degree is it possible to know my Self? The Other (transplanted heart) was both necessary to life and also resulted in a suppressed immune system. In the process it revealed the intruder(s) within, his own immune system. Identity he suggests, "is equivalent to immunity, the one identifying itself with the other. To reduce the one is to reduce the other. Strangeness and strangerness become ordinary, everyday occurrences. This is expressed through a constant self-exteriorization. I must be monitored, tested . . . the most vigorous enemies are inside."[9] Contra Heidegger who identified foreignness as a threat to the national essence, Nancy would have us consider two possibilities. First, accommodation of foreignness may be necessary to survival itself. And second, the most profound threats to our existence may be internal. This strangeness, this foreignness that destabilizes and threatens in fundamental ways may be part of my (either physical or emotional) Self. Alternatively, it may come from something very close to me, perhaps intimately connected, a life partner for example.

Nancy's shift toward *écouter* provides us with a conceptual tool for understanding not only why some responses to sexual harassment allegations seem to miss the mark, but also with a way to re-imagine how we engage with others in the wake of the, not entirely earthshattering, realization that even well-intentioned actions sometimes cause harm, and sexual harassment is one example. In other words, Nancy's focus on *écouter* helps us understand why "leaping-in" [*einspringen*] not only falls short of our aspirations by taking over for others, but it harms by eliminating the space in which the future could become the Other's own. *Écouter* places the subject in a primarily silent and observational posture. This posture preserves the Other's space in which to take him or her Self up as a futurally oriented Being; in other words, it preserves the Other's Selfhood. Nancy describes observation as developing an awareness of the reverberation which is the way others react to a sound, in a particular space. *Écouter* encourages us to be attentive both to the reactions of the Other and also to the way sound itself responds in a milieu. An attentive and observing subject would, for example, be aware of whether a comment or a touch was solicited or unsolicited. In the context of #MeToo, a listening subject would attend to different reactions, would attend to the difference in the way a fellow employee responded, for example, to an unsolicited touch or comment. Was there a disconnect, for example, between the physical and verbal reactions? Meaning derives from the reverberations, which is to say truth or meaning emanates neither from the intent of the toucher, nor from the response of the recipient, in isolation. Rather, meaning derives from the reverberations, which is to say the way these two experiences interact in a context.

For Nancy it is crucial that neither the accuser nor the accused is transformed into an object, that neither the accuser nor the accused project his or her understanding onto the Other. Rather, they must both remain open to the disclosure that occurs in the in-between. As such Nancy would caution us that in asserting a claim to female agency, we must guard against the powerful tendency to simply replace female objectification with perpetrator objectification. In this way, he would join with those who worry not only that due process, as a legal construct, is at risk in the modern context of indictment via social media, but even more importantly Nancy's approach does not allow the accuser's version of events to replace the alleged perpetrator's version, as the authoritative account. Thus, in taking up the position of listening (*écouter*), Nancy is, in effect, guarding the Other's agency. The listening role voids my own claim to "know" or ascribe meaning, independently. Instead, the listening role gives us the responsibility of "straining toward a possible meaning . . . that is not immediately accessible" and results from the reverberations of sound in which I do not participate and to which I do not contribute except by observing and straining.[10]

In his critique of liberalism, Jean-Luc Nancy aspires to an unsentimental, which is to say non-romanticized, way of arriving at a notion of *Being-with*, a manner of being in the world in which "the plurality of beings is at the foundation of Being."[11] In the process of moving us towards a way of being in the world that more fully appreciates the Other as part and parcel of our own existence, Nancy transforms two concepts that will help us understand our experiences with #MeToo: strangeness and compassion. For Nancy "'strangeness' refers to the fact that each singularity is another access to the world."[12] Moreover, it is access to the world beyond our own singularity that we all crave. Herein lies, according to Nancy, the reason literature and the arts "interests us or touches us."[13] Each novel, each photograph or painting provides an other point of access to the world. In other words, each work of art, each story provides us with the opportunity to encounter the world anew. It may also explain our fascination with that which we perceive as exotic. He also offers us compassion as, "the contact of being with one another in this turmoil . . . [in this] disturbance of violent relatedness."[14] He does not view compassion as an act or feeling of either pity or charity as both are based on the "more or less hidden axiom of condescension."[15] The relationship must, therefore, be asymmetrical, with an event or a disturbance affecting one Being or group adversely while the other more fortunate Being or group responds with benevolence to that misfortune.[16] Both pity and charity can be understood as manifestations of Heidegger's "leaping-in" [*einspringen*]. They preserve an asymmetrical relationship, which is to say that they give rise to a future in which the existing power relationships are not only preserved, but also protected.

In terms of #MeToo, each story, whether it comes from an alleged perpetrator or someone bringing allegations, provides us with the opportunity to encounter the world anew. Yet strangeness for Nancy is also paradoxical in so far as it simultaneously reveals and conceals. "At the point where we would expect 'something,' a substance or a procedure, a principle or an end, a signification, there is nothing but the manner, the turn of the other access, which conceals itself in the very gesture wherein it offers itself to us—and whose concealing is the turn itself."[17] Thus, each encounter necessarily results in ambivalence. If we understand each story as both a revealing and a concealing, the ambivalence in our own reaction derives perhaps from the combination of familiarity and alienation. Certain aspects of the story make sense, which is to say, feel familiar, resonate with our own experiences; whereas other aspects of the story are more jarring, they constitute a disturbance of *violent relatedness*. Yet Nancy cautions "[t]he movement of violence is entirely contrary to the movement of sense." Instead of opening an interaction, an engagement, the search for commonality and understanding, violence denies commonality and shuts down the search for commonality, seeking instead "to appropriate everything that is not itself into itself."[18] Thus, in listening to the story of the other, I simultaneously experience the movement of sense and the movement of violence. I desire both an opening to the world as experienced by the other and as such I take up the posture of receiving the story, while straining towards understanding. At the same time, I seek a closing down and I may attempt to take over the other's tale for the purpose of subsuming this story into my own. In *Five Women*, Kristen's story elicits this duality perhaps more clearly than any of the others.

In listening to Kristen's perspective, Tana experiences the movement toward violence, repeating her parents' perspective, "this isn't news that this happens . . . what do you expect?" In this reaction, we can see Tana attempting to subsume Kristen's story into her own, to impose her own understanding of Hazen's behavior onto Kristen. Whereas Deanna exhibits the value of *écouter*, as she quite literally watches, in silence, as Hazen picks Kristen out of the crowd, approaches her and offers to publish her work, exactly as he once approached Deanna.[19] Her receptive posture is indicative of the movement toward sense. In learning of Kristen's allegation of sexual harassment, Deanna receives the story, experiences familiarity and allows this experience to inform her understanding of her own relationship with Don. Ultimately she comes to view her experience with Don, less as their story (characterized by mutual agency and reciprocity) and more as a pattern of Hazen's behavior in which she figured as an object (one of many), rather than co-creator. Deanna takes up the position of *écouter*, "straining toward a possible meaning . . . that is not immediately accessible"[20]; she remains open to a commonality with Kristen's unconcealment. We see the same impulses in Vice President Biden's response to allegation that he made women uncomfortable with his displays of affection.

Biden's initial statement in the wake of these allegations, like Tana's, exemplifies the movement toward violence, as he draws attention to his reputation, "I'm not sorry for anything that I have ever done. I've never been disrespectful intentionally to a man or a woman."[21] Biden followed this categorical rejection of any and all alternative perspectives or interpretations with several highly questionable jokes. In delivering the keynote address to International Brotherhood of Electrical Workers after Lucy Flores's allegations, Biden greeted union President Lonnie Stephenson with a one-armed embrace and then quipped, "I just want you to know, I had permission to hug Lonnie."[22] As Nancy suggests the movement toward violence shuts down the search for commonality and instead seeks "to appropriate everything that is not itself into itself."[23] His second statement continues to focus on *his* understanding and *his* intention, but it also opens up the possibility of a movement towards sense. "In my many years on the campaign trail and in public life, I have offered countless handshakes, hugs, expressions of affection, support and comfort," Biden said in a statement. "And not once—never—did I believe I acted inappropriately. If it is suggested I did so, I will listen respectfully. But it was never my intention. I may not recall these moments the same way, and I may be surprised at what I hear," Mr. Biden said. "But we have arrived at an important time when women feel they can and should relate their experiences, and men should pay attention. And I will."[24] Though Biden indicates a willingness to listen, rather than a categorical denial of any and all wrongdoing, this response was unsurprisingly received as inadequate, lacking in self-reflection.

It is with his third statement that Biden begins to self-reveal, though he may not yet be straining towards meaning. In explaining that he may not have fully understood the impact of his own tendency to invade the personal space of others, he offered "I've always tried to make a human connection. I shake hands, I hug people, I grab men and women by the shoulders, and say, 'you can do this'. . . . It's the way I've tried to show I care about them and I'm listening."[25] Biden's own personal tragedies have long been part of his story. His ability to grow from tragedy and empathize with others is rooted in an impoverished childhood, the tragic loss of his first wife and his daughter, his struggle to single-parent his young sons amidst unimaginable tragedy and a hectic career. Biden is doubtless providing us with an insight into the behavior of many when he said he sought to "make a human connection." In a subject centered epistemology, that goal, that intention would indeed assume a privileged position. Herein lies the importance of Nancy's decentering. Biden's intention matters, but it cannot be afforded a central position; it is merely one of countless reverberations. Truth emerges from the reverberations of Biden's intention and Lucy Flores's discomfort. The challenge Nancy sets for us "is to account for the intrusion at the heart of intimacy."[26] If we accept Nancy's approach as a critical component of citizenship then our civic education would have to prioritize the skills of listening in a receptive mode to the discomfort of the Other. Again, for Nancy, it is crucial to understand that both the accuser and the accused occupy a position that requires straining toward meaning.

Nancy, thus, offers us an approach to epistemology or citizenship in which no voice, no perspective enjoys privilege over any other. This radical approach while crucial in decentering both the subject and white-male privilege, is also concerning, as it not only reserves a place in the dialogue for the illegal, unethical and degrading voice but that voice must also be preserved, protected *and* valued. The evolving *truth* about sexual harassment, thus, includes the infamous voice of Donald Trump, proudly claiming his ability to grab whoever he wants, as a function of his wealth and status. Nancy's approach would not only require us to protect this voice, but to "strain toward understanding" as we listen from a position of concealment. While this radical inclusion is certainly deeply disconcerting and it may be hard to imagine valuing Trump's perspective, epistemologically speaking, our understanding of sexual harassment does indeed owe a debt to Donald Trump and to the unabashed and violent nature of his claim of unfettered access to the female body.

BUTLER'S STYLIZED REPETITION OF ACTS

Judith Butler continues the work of clarifying Heidegger's notion of a throw and elaborating on the structures that press upon us and our existential choices. In terms of sexual harassment, she would direct our attention to sexual harassment as a stylized repetition of acts, on the part of both the perpetrator, as well as, the recipient. For women in the workplace, "as a strategy of survival, gender is a performance with clearly punitive consequences."[27] It is a repeated set of behaviors that likely originate before any specific work experience and come to constitute who we are. In a work environment, like Alternet, Don Hazen and the female employees who ultimately accused him of sexual harassment engaged in a repetition of stylized acts based on expected gender roles. Joffe-Walt's interviews with Alternet employees highlights the contiguity in their previous experiences with men and their experiences with Hazen. These interviews also draw attention to the survival strategies that lead to different coping mechanisms, as well as, the punitive consequences and social sanctions that attach. Finally, Butler suggests, as we have previously seen with Benjamin Disraeli, that the task of crafting an identity is, in part, strategic. Power is not, in Butler's words, "simply what we oppose but also in a strong sense what we depend on for our existence and what we harbor and preserve in the being that we are."[28] In other words, Joffe-Walt's interviews provide us with an opportunity to see Butler's notion of stylized acts, as well as, her take on power and complicity at work in the thought processes of five women coping with sexual harassment.

Masculinity as a social construct requires pursuit and sexual assertion, noticing and commenting on women's appearance, women's bodies. Men are expected to initiate, to appreciate and to notice. Femininity is receptive, passive, alluring. Women are expected to receive appreciation. These expectations derive from a particular historical moment, but as constitutive behaviors they also leave something behind in the world. Both masculinity and femininity derive from a historical moment in which women had few options for self-support. The dominant survival strategy was to make the best marriage possible. In keeping with that goal, a series of rules for courting developed. Among these rules, women never discouraged or rebuffed male attention, no matter how uninterested she might be in a particular suitor; the dominant strategy was to attract as many potential suitors as possible, so that one could choose. The feminine behavior that resulted was an openness to male attention and a pleasing personality. Despite the evolution of what Butler has called the "exterior space," remnants of these stylized acts remain very much intact, buffeted by the punitive costs of failing to perform one's expected gender roles. In keeping with the way Arendt directed our attention to the stylized performance of Jewishness that Disraeli used to create a career that was "much more exciting . . . for himself and for others," Butler would have us attune ourselves to the various performative acts that make up sexual harassment. Moreover, like Disraeli, who paradoxically, created a career in which he was "one of the last court Jews and one of the first victims of modern anti-Semitism,"[29] women often find that playing into expected gender roles involves a certain complicity with oppressive patriarchal structures.

Recruitment of new employees is undoubtedly part of the boss' role. Identifying, seeking out, assessing qualifications and potential is a formal job requirement and there are many performative acts that comprise this responsibility. Several Alternet employees noted Hazen's tendency to approach young, attractive women at rallies or protests and use his position to strike up and continue a conversation with them. He approached Kristen, who appeared to be taking notes for a story, with an offer to read and perhaps publish what she had written. He approached Deanna, a campaign staffer for Howard Dean, with a request to interview her after the rally. In both cases, the interaction began as a professional interaction and at some point once the young, either unemployed or underemployed, woman was made aware of Hazen's power, the flirtation began.[30] Much like the Victorian woman in need of a good marriage, calling out inappropriate comments at this stage could prove disadvantageous and so instead the recipient avoids a confrontation, focuses on the professional opportunity and either ignores or laughs off the inappropriate comments. Both Deanna and Kristen performed the role of female, receptive to male attention. As Butler and Arendt both suggest, these performative acts leave something in the world. In the case of Alternet, the stage was set for sexualized commentary to be accepted and expected as an ongoing feature of workplace interactions with Hazen. In the case of Tana, Hazen followed up the interview (she had not yet been offered a job) by commenting "so I hear you and your roommates have pretty wild and crazy sex lives." She laughed off the comment, explicitly willing to trade her retail job for a professional opportunity that included sexual harassment.[31] The pattern of their interaction was thus established in "an exterior space" in which Hazen was making a decision about whether or not to extend a job offer and Tana understood that the fact that Hazen found her attractive created for her an opportunity. The trade off, more or less explicitly, required her to accept his comments about her sex life and her body. Hazen's pattern was to identify women in need of a job, make them aware of his power, offer assistance and then engage in sexually assertive behavior that was unlikely to be rebuffed. Like Disraeli, Tana and Deanna engaged in a stylized repetition of acts designed to create an opportunity.

Toxic masculinity usually does not go unnoticed.[32] Many bystanders are aware of this behavior. Hazen's partner, Vivian, grapples with her role in the interview; she acknowledged thinking Don's behavior made women uncomfortable. She explained it as a simple failure on his part to pick up on cues of discomfort, rather than an intentionally, exploitative strategy to surround himself with young, attractive women who needed his approval for their livelihoods. Vivian's way of performing her gender, at least as she recounts it, consisted in two different responses or stylized acts. With the other women, she would make eye contact and they usually shared an eye roll, a shared sign of exasperation with a masculine abuse of power.[33] In other words, women, both enablers and victims, silently join together in a protest of sorts that establishes a common understanding between them. With Don, she occasionally objected and let the matter drop when he responded that she was either overreacting or she couldn't appreciate the humor in the situation, although the other woman did. Sexual harassment often features at least one enabler who is aware of the problematic pattern of behavior and explains it away with some kind of claim to understand the truly benevolent person behind a series of awkward or misunderstood social behaviors. It is only in retrospect that Vivian describes her relationship to Don's harassing tendencies as one of complicity.

More than any other Alternet employee, Tana was aware from the first interview that she was entering into a reciprocal relationship with Hazen. The fact that he found her attractive meant that she would have an opportunity to situate herself close to his power. She could occupy this position and benefit from her proximity to him as long as she could "handle" the mercurial behavior and the undesired attention.[34] Access to power would require toughness on her part and she also minimized concerns raised by her colleagues about his behavior. Tana was also quick to point out Hazen's contributions to female empowerment. He supported and featured many female writers, assigned them serious stories and prominently featured their work. Moreover, Alternet is a left leaning publication; presumably most of its employees bring progressive political goals. It certainly has a reputation for challenging traditional power structures. Thus, not only as individuals operating in a workplace dominated by Hazen but also as a group, it could be said of the women working at Alternet that "power is not simply what we oppose but also in a strong sense what we depend on for our existence and what we harbor and preserve in the being that we are."[35]

Finally, the examination of Alternet provides us with an opportunity to reexamine the question of agency in the context of Butler's work on performativity. As previously stated one of the main differences between Arendt and Butler on the question of identity is that Arendt leaves the subject's agency intact; whereas agency remains an intriguing question in the context of performativity.[36] Once we take into account the role of power and the compulsory nature of social sanctions, what are the prospects of agency? Under what conditions can the subject take her Self up as a projecting *Being*? Recalling Disch's distinction between autonomy and agency, original and citational,[37] the answer might be that in isolation, neither Tana, Deanna nor Vivian would likely have realized the full impact of Don's behavior and none of the three might have taken the necessary steps to address sexual harassment at Alternet. Yet prompted to some degree by Kristen and supported by a historical moment increasingly sensitive to sexual harassment, they joined together and as a collective they assumed agency. The Alternet example, thus, helps us answer both a question regarding Butler's performativity and Stern's question from 1947. Autonomy is likely impossible; yet agency becomes increasingly feasible in conjunction with others. Thus, to Stern's question regarding whether self-revealing is "inherently alienating,"[38] it is, unless *Being-with-others* is genuinely constitutive of *Being* and humility, which is to say a recognition of the limits of our own agency, is part and parcel of our comportment.

The notion of performativity quite likely renders autonomy an impossibility and agency a mere fleeting possibility. Butler cautions that identity politics should "center perhaps on a . . . willingness to acknowledge the limits of acknowledgement itself." My experience is only one manifestation of what it is to be female and may well be at least in part a product of my stylized performance. The interpretation that I offer should, thus, be tentative since "when we claim to know and present ourselves, we will fail in some ways that are nevertheless essential to who we are." Moreover, we "cannot expect anything different from others."[39] Thus, in joining with others agency becomes plausible, yet my willingness to recognize the limits of my own experience and understanding are crucial if I am to avoid rendering the Other's self-revealing, the alienating experience of which Stern writes.

One of the final caveats for feminism and for identity politics at this critical juncture is that the demand to produce a cohesive account of oneself is a form of ethical violence, which clearly renders cohesion in some kind of collective impossible (as well as unethnical) way. Despite the fascinating questions this admonishment raises for identity politics, the cautionary note for feminism is relatively clear: there is an exceedingly thin line that we must tread in drawing strength and support from the collectivity while simultaneously guarding against the temptation to impose cohesion on any one, including my Self, and in the case of #MeToo, the perpetrator. Herein lies the danger of Heidegger's "leaping-in" [*einspringen*], that it may fail to respect the Other's authentic self, and in so doing undermine the other, while rendering the self-reveal "inherently alienating." Taking Vogel and Butler together, we can find a common ethical ground in "liberating solictude"[40] or in an identity politics that creates a "wide errancy" to construct and reconstruct a self-narrative that is incoherent and incomplete. Where does that leave us in the quest for a legal approach to either sexual harassment or sexual assault? Philosophically, the goal of creating a "wide errancy" seems a tenable position, whereas, legally speaking, it is far less so.

In terms of the trap, a Butler-esque approach might suggest that Heidegger is trapped in the notion of a core essence. In grounding identity in the core essence, particularly one that relies so heavily on tradition and the past, he fails to recognize that identity itself is a project, futural in its orientation. He casts identities themselves as static and fails to "acknowledge the limits of acknowledgement itself." Given that identity itself is a project, granting "a wide errancy" may require relinquishing the metaphorical notion of a home altogether. In other words, it may require *becoming at home* not being at home or "learning to live in the anxiety." In terms #MeToo, this approach might add to the importance of listening, the need to moderate our own expectations as we listen. "[A]s we ask to know the other . . . it will be important that we do not expect an answer that will ever satisfy. And by not pursuing satisfaction, we let the other live."[41]

ADRIANA CAVARERO'S EXPOSABLE SELF

Stories lie at the heart of the #MeToo movement. Feminism has always relied on stories and storytelling as a methodology.[42] Harriet Taylor Mill told the stories of Mary Ann Parsons and Susan Moir in her attempt to combat domestic violence.[43] Victoria Woodhull used a similarly tragic story to illustrate the injustice of laws that restrict abortion.[44] Andrea Dworkin returned to the issue of domestic violence by focusing on Nicole Brown Simpson's futile attempts to separate from O. J. Simpson.[45] The importance of stories clearly persists as the premise behind #MeToo is that sexual harassment is such a pervasive feature of life as a woman that we *all* have stories to tell. And the systemic nature of patriarchal oppression only becomes readily apparent (or inescapable) once we share those stories. Though the telling of the tragic tale certainly has its place in feminism, these examples do not meet the criterion of Adriana Cavarero's relational ontology since for Cavarero the transcendent moment exists in hearing one's story told by an Other, since one of the limitations of attempting to tell one's own story is that nearly impossible to understand the significance as you are living it. Both Butler and Cavarero shift away from appearance as the crucial component of transcendence in favor of, exposure. With this shift, Butler and Cavarero acknowledge the vulnerability inherent in the *Being-with*. The Self can find support and sustenance in the *Being-with-others* though she also becomes vulnerable to violence, very much a concern of Arendt, Butler and Cavarero.[46] Both Arendt and Cavavero discuss the impact of ontological violence, for Arendt it is totalitarianism[47]; Cavarero uses the term: horrorism.[48] In both cases, the result is a profound severing of ties to the world. Thus, Cavarero's contribution to our understanding of #MeToo lies in the notion of an exposable Self.

Cavarero's existent "from its birth, is exposed; that is brought into appearance as someone who is abandoned."[49] Though she shares Arendt's interest in natality, the enduring ontological condition is the sense of the Self as moving through the world alone. "Existence as exposure becomes, in this case, the perceptible truth of every existent, made more acute by the immediate loss of one's own origin."[50] The Self cannot remember and cannot recount the story of its arrival. One component of this sense of abandonment is the ontological condition of not knowing who she is. "With all the inimitable wisdom of a familiar feeling [*sapore*], she knows that she is an unrepeatable uniqueness, but she does not know who she is."[51] That knowledge can only come from encounters with the world, from the experience of *Being-with* since "the existent always constitutes herself in relation to an other."[52] Neither transcendence nor the formation of identity are possible in isolation, thus for Cavarero *being-with* is constitutive of *Being* in several different ways. "Birth, action and narration become the scenes of an identity that always postulates the presence of an other."[53] I can only work out who I am as I encounter the world, which is to say as I bump up against beings who I am not. In Caverero's words, it is as if the Self has an identity, "who is his distinct identity, but appears and is visible only to others."[54] My awareness of my own identity presupposes an Other. The importance of narration emerges as well since my distinctiveness is visible only to exogenous beings who can with certain a distance and perspective discern the patterns and the uniqueness of my story. My understanding of my own identity or my own story, thus, necessarily comes from an Other.

The moments that the Alternet employees recount for Joffe-Walt are the moments of constituting themselves "in relation to an other,"[55] of trying to make sense of their encounters with the world. Tana and Kristen clearly describe their evolving understanding of who they are through their experiences with sexual harassment. Tana begins her story with a memory of being asked to have an opinion about Anita Hill; she was eight years old. As a nineteen-year-old, she recalls telling her parents that she was being sexually harassed at work. Expecting them to be upset, her understanding of her Self evolves when her parents, far from being horrified at the thought of their daughter experiencing sexual harassment, instead respond with "you're nineteen-years-old, of course you're being sexually harassed." She recalls thinking, "okay, this is just a thing that happens."[56] As Cavarero suggests, Tana can tell the story of her experience with sexual harassment in the workplace, but she looks to an Other for help in understanding what the experience means. She can describe the what, but the significance escapes her. She needs assistance in this case from her parents in deciding what to think about the experience, how to feel about it and therefore, what to do about it. With the perspective offered by her parents, she is somewhat reassured that it is not necessary for her to feel particularly upset since "this is just a thing that happens," a function of her throw, her female body at the age of nineteen. Kristen, on the other hand, has a different experience of encountering the world. As a middle school student, she receives a note from some boys in her class that says, "you have nice boobs; you should use them." In Kristen's case, a guidance counselor informs her that this is a form of sexual harassment, and positions her as a victim of male aggression. Again, it is an Other that helps Kristen to name and understand the significance of this particular event in her story. Though she does not entirely embrace this understanding of her experience, at the time, it does inform her understanding of a sexual assault later in life. Drawing on both those events, Kristen is quick to name the experience with Hazen as sexual harassment and encourages the others to view Hazen's behavior as inappropriate and in need of change.

As exposed beings both Tana and Kristen lack the necessary perspective to make sense of their experiences in isolation. The exposure of the existent creates a sense of vulnerability for Tana in the encounter of her nineteen-year-old self. Kristen does not seem to feel particularly vulnerable in her middle school encounter with boys who want her to "use" her boobs. Though she might describe her Self feeling exposed in the sense that others, first, drew attention to her body, and, second, offered authoritative accounts of how she should feel and think about her experience. Rather it is her subsequent experience with date rape that acquaints Kristen with the experience of being exposed and vulnerable. The point that she highlights in telling her story is the process of coming to label the experience "rape." She grapples with a variety of ways of applying words to the experience such that they reflect her feelings of betrayal and exposure, including he had "taken advantage" of her. Since for Cavarero, we are all exposed and vulnerable, "it is important to analyze what happens . . . when this exposure, this vulnerability is exploited."[57] In other words, #MeToo calls out for an ontology of sexual harassment. Perpetrators select targets based on their perceived vulnerability but there is vulnerability in the perpetrator as well. The perpetrator needs to touch, or to comment because he needs to connect; there is a profound isolation in that need. A phenomenological account of sexual harassment must explore both.

In their examinations of the harm of physical violence Arendt, Cavarero and Lafford all call attention to way that totalitarianism, horrorism or sexual violence eliminate individuality itself by reducing the Self to a mere body, to an object at hand. Sexual harassment does not eliminate individuality; rather it calls it out, highlights it, puts it on public display in a manner not of one's own choosing. In so doing, the perpetrator "disregards the victim's intentionality" in a way that undermines *being-in-the-world* by creating a "rupture between one's intentionality and one's physical activity."[58] A phenomenological account of sexual harassment would then explore how to rejoin the world. Part of the challenge from Cavarero's perspective is that actualization lies in hearing one's story told. For the victim of sexual assault or sexual harassment, the perpetrator becomes an unreliable narrator. The perpetrator cannot retell the victim's story because his experience of the encounter is that of an event; whereas the victim continues to relive the experience through her lack of confidence in *being-in-the-world*. Sexual assault or sexual harassment violates Cavarero's three stages of identity (birth, action and narration) by truncating narration. Sexual harassment also clarifies Cavarero's interpretation of the trap. If Cavarero would caution, as I have suggested, that Heidegger is trapped in the search for a universal, in the quest for unity at the expense of accuracy. If he tends toward a transcendence that could be found in isolation. In his interpretation the quest of philosophy is an understanding of man as a universal and that quest comes at the expense of an understanding of her experiences in all of their uniqueness. Heidegger's approach, thus, leaves us with no way of understanding (or seeking transcendence for) the exposed and vulnerable Self.

In terms of democratic theory, a phenomenological account of sexual harassment has the potential to fundamentally alter our understanding of *Being-with*. It allows us to re-imagine citizenship as an obligation to a collective, to listen from a place of concealment, to strain toward meaning without imposing expectations of unity or coherence, to prioritize observation and receptivity over speech and re-presentation. Civic education might focus less on the memorization of names, dates and procedures and reserve some time for developing the ability to listen to an Other. What if civic education focused on exploring, not only the importance of the Other and listening, but emphasized that listening necessarily requires wanting to hear? Civic education could help us develop the skill of straining toward understanding, which again requires decentering the Self. This approach might steer us away from sexual harassment trainings that impose a legal doctrine, in favor of exercises in telling the story of an Other. How can we tell an Other's story without imposing coherence or unity? Can I tell my own story without imposing coherence? Finally, allowing #MeToo to transform democratic theory, the objective of identity politics becomes granting to both the Other and my Self "a wide errancy" to learn to "live in the anxiety"[59] of understanding that identity is never something stable that can be "handed back" but rather identity is itself a project.

NOTES

1. Jodi Kantor and Megan Twohey, "Harvey Weinstein Paid Off Sexual Harassment Accusers for Decades," *The New York Times*, October 5, 2017.

2. Farrow's article appeared in print on October 23rd, but it was published online on October 10th (Ronan Farrow, "From Aggressive Overtures to Sexual Assault: Harvey Weinstein's accusers tell their Stories," *The New Yorker*, October 23, 2017).

3. Alexandra Schwartz, "#MeToo, #Itwasme, and the Post-Weinstein Megaphone of Social Media," *The New Yorker*, October 19, 2017.

4. Chana Joffe-Walt. "Five Women," This American Life. Podcast Audio, March 2, 2018. https://www.thisamericanlife.org/640/five-women .

5. Catharine A. MacKinnon, "#MeToo Has Done What the Law Could Not," *New York Times*, February 4, 2018; Kristen Renwick Monroe, "Harassment Charges: Metoo but Due Process," *Science* 361 (2018): 656; Ramit Mizrahi, "Sexual Harassment Law After #MeToo: Looking to California as a Model," *The Yale Law Journal*, June 18, 2018.

6. Sheldon Wolin, *Politics and Vision: Continuity and Innovation in Western Political Thought*, expanded edition (Princeton, NJ: Princeton University Press, 2004), 22.

7. Judith Butler, *Giving an Account of Oneself* (New York: Fordham University Press, 2005).

8. Jean-Luc Nancy, "L'Intrus," trans. Susan Hanson, *CR: The New Centennial Review* 2 (2002): 4.

9. Ibid., 9.

10. Jean-Luc Nancy, *Listening*, trans. Charlotte Mandell (New York: Fordham University Press), 6.

11. Jean-Luc Nancy, *Being Singular Plural*, trans. Robert D. Richardson and Anne E. O'Byrne (Stanford, CA: Stanford University Press, 2000), 12.

12. Ibid., 14.

13. Ibid.

14. Ibid., xiii.

15. Jean Luc Nancy, "On Human Rights: Two Simple Remarks," trans. Gilbert Leung in *The Meaning of Rights: The Philosophy and Social Theory of Human Rights*, eds. Costas Douzinas and Conor Gearty (Cambridge: Cambridge University Press, 2014), 15.

16. Ibid.

17. Nancy, *Being Singular Plural*, 14.

18. Miranda Pilipchuk, "Artemisia's Revenge: Rape and Art in the Work of Jean-Luc Nancy," *Concept* 37 (2014): 3.

19. Joffe-Walt, "Five Women."

20. Nancy, *Listening*, 6.

21. Lisa Lerer, "Joe Biden Jokes About Hugging in a Speech, Then Offers a Mixed Apology," *New York Times*, April 5, 2019.

22. Karl Baker, "In First Remarks since 'Creepy Uncle Joe' Claims, Biden Shifts Conversation to Worker Rights," *Delaware News Journal*, April 5, 2019.

23. Pilipchuk, "Artemisia's Revenge," 3.

24. Matt Stevens and Sydney Ember, "Joe Biden Says He Did Not Act Inappropriately With Lucy Flores," *New York Times*, March 30, 2019.

25. Sydney Ember and Jonathan Martin, "Joe Biden in Video, Says He Will be 'More Mindful' of Personal Space," *New York Times*, April 3, 2019.

26. Philip M. Adamek, "The Intimacy of Jean-Luc Nancy's 'L'Intrus,'" *CR: The New Centennial Review* 2 (2002): 191.

27. Judith Butler, "Performative Acts and Gender Constitution: An Essay in Phenomenology and Feminist Theory," *Theatre Journal* 40 (1988): 522.

28. Judith Butler, *The Psychic Life of Power: Theories in Subjection* (Stanford, CA: Stanford University Press, 1997), 2.

29. David Cesarani, *Disraeli: The Novel Politician* (New Haven, CT: Yale University Press, 2016), 236.

30. Joffe-Walt, "Five Women."

31. Ibid.

32. Ryan Douglass argues that toxic masculinity is differentiated from masculinity in that it relies on sexual conquest and violence ("More Men Should Learn the Difference Between Masculinity and Toxic Masculinity," *The Huffington Post*, August 4, 2017). Maya Salam adds to that definition the suppression of emotions or masking of distress ("What Is Toxic Masculinity?," *New York Times*, January 22, 2019).

33. Ibid.

34. Joffe-Walt, "Five Women."

35. Butler, *The Psychic Life of Power*, 2.

36. Martha Nussbaum, "The Professor of Parody: The Hip Defeatism of Judith Butler," *New Republic* 22 (1999): 37–45.

37. Lisa Disch, "Judith Butler and the Politics of the Performative," *Political Theory* 27 (1999): 556.

38. Günther Stern, "On the Pseudo-Concreteness of Heidegger's Philosophy," *Philosophy and Phenomenological Research* 8 (1947): 337–71.

39. Judith Butler, *Giving an Account of Oneself* (New York: Fordham University Press, 2005), 42.

40. Lawrence Vogel, *The Fragile "We": Ethical Implications of Heidegger's Being and Time* (Evanston, IL: Northwestern University Press, 1994), 90–91.

41. Judith Butler and William E. Connolly, "Politics, Power and Ethics: A Discussion Between Judith Butler and William Connolly," *Theory & Event* 4, no. 2 (2000).

42. Catharine MacKinnon, *Toward a Feminist Theory of the State* (Cambridge, MA: Harvard University Press, 1989), 83–105.

43. Harriet Taylor Mill and John Stuart Mill, "The Case of Mary Ann Parsons [1]," *Daily News*, February 5, 1850, in *The Complete Works of Harriet Taylor Mill*, ed. Jo Ellen Jacobs (Bloomington: Indiana University Press, 1997), 98–100; Harriet Taylor Mill and John Stuart Mill, "The Case of Mary Ann Parsons [2]," *Morning Chronical*, March 26, 1850, in *The Complete Works of Harriet Taylor Mill*, ed. Jo Ellen Jacobs (Bloomington: Indiana University Press, 1997), 104–8; Harriet Taylor Mill and John Stuart Mill, "On Susan Moir," *Morning Chronical*, March 29, 1850, in *The Complete Works of Harriet Taylor Mill*, ed. Jo Ellen Jacobs, (Bloomington: Indiana University Press, 1997), 108–11.

44. Victoria Woodhull, "The Social Volcano," *Woodhull and Claflin's Weekly*, September 16, 1871.

45. Andrea Dworkin, *Life and Death: Unapologetic Writings on the Continued War against Women* (New York: Little, Brown, 1997), 41–49.

46. Sarah Lafford, "Natality and Exposure: A Philosophical Account of the Harm of Sexual Violence," *The Philosophical Journal of Conflict and Violence* 2 (2018), 68.

47. Hannah Arendt, "Ideology and Terror: A Novel Form of Government," *Review of Politics* 15 (1953): 303–27.

48. Adriana Cavarero, *Horrorism: Naming Contemporary Violence*, trans. William McCuaig (New York: Columbia University Press, 2009).

49. Adriana Cavarero, *Relating Narratives: Storytelling and Selfhood*, trans. and intro. Paul A. Kottman (London: Routledge, 2000), 19.

50. Ibid.

51. Ibid., 40.

52. Ibid.

53. Ibid., 28.

54. Ibid., 27.

55. Ibid., 40.

56. Joffe-Walt, "Five Women."

57. Lafford, "Natality and Exposure," 69.

58. Ibid., 73.

59. Martin Heidegger, *Ponderings VII-XI: Black Notebooks 1938–1939*, trans. Richard Rojcewicz (Bloomington: Indiana University Press, 2017), 35; Butler and Connolly, "Politics, Power and Ethics."

Conclusion

Elzbieta Ettinger's 1995 exposé suggested that far from a mere youthful fling, Hannah Arendt and Martin Heidegger shared a deeply passionate, lifelong, devoted relationship.[1] Moreover, Ettinger implied it was also a profoundly exploitative relationship in which Heidegger pulled the strings and Arendt never grew beyond the role of enthralled and devoted student. This revelation might have remained a topic of tangential academic interest, except that it also called Arendt's professional judgment into question, a damning charge to level against a political philosopher interested in judgment. In this project I argue that Arendt not only grew beyond the role of naïve and beguiled student, she became one of Heidegger's most astute critics. Well acquainted with and deeply respectful of his contributions to philosophy, she viewed his work as both profoundly insightful and extraordinarily myopic. Additionally, not contented to simply offer a critique of her mentor's work, Arendt engaged in a lifelong struggle to come to terms with the political implications of fundamental ontology. She shifts to political philosophy, less to escape her personal disappointment, than to right the collective flaws of fundamental ontology. Moreover, I argue that Arendt's purpose, far from rejecting philosophy, is to offer a politically responsible, modification. In other words, she suggests that Heidegger's insight into the nature of being is necessarily incomplete, and potentially irresponsible, unless it is undertaken in a manner which is mindful of the collective implications.

Martin Heidegger elucidates highly abstract, descriptive concepts, primarily aimed at exploring the individual experience of being as *Being*. For example, he considers the challenges of thrownness without offering a single example. He claims that his concepts are non-normative, which is to say that he merely describes deficient and proficient forms of care, rather than attaching value judgments to either. Moreover, his focus is on the experience of

Being, as an individual. He leaves questions related to the *being-with* of Being to the side. For example, can *being-with* ever facilitate projectivity? Arendt, on the other hand, employs Heideggerian concepts in a political context. She utilizes Heideggerian concepts in a manner that is attentive to the collective implications of the manner of being of *Being*, mindful of the imperative that political engagement must be a widespread, as well as authentic, endeavor. She grounds the political, ontologically and illustrates that the manner of being of *Being* is inherently political. Moreover, she advocates an approach to the study of Being that derives guideposts or cautionary tales from the lived experiences of real people.

Hannah Arendt had an ambivalent relationship with feminism. As a German-Jewish political thinker, indebted in many ways to Martin Heidegger, gender was never the most salient marker of political identity for her. In thinking back over her relationship with Arendt, Elizabeth Minnich reveals, "I think Hannah Arendt did not want to be bothered much with 'the woman question.' Being a Jew pressed much harder on her."[2] Arendt was mindful of the degree to which her Jewishness limited her ability to choose. I have suggested that Arendt can be read as less opposed to identity politics than is often thought if we understand her *oeuvre* to center around the project of taking up ontological questions through the ontic. As we have seen, in this way, Arendt continues an important Heideggerian philosophical strategy but toward a different end. For Arendt the ultimate goal was a collective one, that of learning to share the earth. With this interpretation in mind, Heidegger and Arendt can be viewed as important resources for contemporary debates concerning identity politics occurring within the frame of continental philosophy and political theory. While Heidegger rarely addresses otherness, Arendt routinely deals with otherness, albeit in ways that at times appear contradictory. None of her voluminous writings deal specifically with gender, though some of her work certainly deals with notable women. She both smoked cigars with the men and suggested that certain occupations were not very becoming to women. Moreover, she warned of potential danger in any political movement based only on shared victim status and touted the importance of finding political solutions to political problems. Yet both Heidegger and Arendt contribute in important ways to contemporary debates in identity politics by providing a framework within which the challenge of identity can be constructed, as well as, deconstructed.

They both understand, anticipating someone like Judith Butler,[3] that taking seriously concrete political identities requires constructing and listening to historical narratives of such identities. Moreover, in ways that will be picked up and expanded by thinkers such as Jean-Luc Nancy, they both attend to the ontological stakes of such identity.[4] Namely, thrownness and the goal of projecting oneself into the future are neither the results of history nor should they be undertaken in the absence of some form of connectedness to or rootedness in self-understanding. Rather, thrownness and projection illustrate that historicity is the ontological condition for the ontic practice of history itself. As such, like Adriana Cavarero, Arendt and Heidegger allow us to attend to the specifics of historical existence without being tempted to reduce existence to history.[5]

Further, the leaping-in/leaping-ahead distinction could be an important supplement to contemporary debates in identity politics.[6] In particular, this distinction allows us to remain sensitive to the complicated ways in which identity is never something stable such that it could be taken over and handed back to a person or group, even with the best of intentions. Instead, identity is itself a project that allows a person or group to find their own possibilities, at least in part, in the task of taking themselves up as projected into the future in particular ways. These projects are shaped by, though never owned by, group affiliation. Relating to others by "leaping-ahead," allows us to take seriously the potential importance of interventionist political strategies, while attending to concrete ways that "handing back" could manifest itself. This approach requires us to always remain vigilant not to regard such intervention as a terminus (*telos*), but instead as an opening up for others to a future in which they have the necessary ontological, as well as, political tools (status and power) to be able to activate their own identity as a matter of their own project.

Thus, an examination of Arendt's own project, particularly when juxtaposed with her concern regarding political movements based on "shared victim status" and her attention to otherness suggests another possible interpretation of the metaphorical trap. Certainly one of Heidegger's main contributions to philosophy is the gender neutral, ontological concept: *Dasein*. As "that being for whom its being is a question,"[7] neither gender nor race nor socio-economic status are relevant to *Dasein*'s ability to take up questions of *Being*. As an ontic matter, *Dasein* is, of course, gendered. Ontologically, *Dasein* is not. In other words, for Heidegger, questions of being are not matters of gender, ethnicity nor socio-economic status. The neutrality of Dasein, though ontologically defensible, may also constitute a trap from which Heidegger cannot escape in so far as it leads him to undervalue certain questions and devote little attention to the nature of *being-with-others*. Without taking into consideration the concrete, ontic concerns which comprise the world in which *Dasein* finds herself, *being-with-others* is merely labeled a constitutive feature of Dasein without that proposition itself meriting sustained attention. Thus, both philosophically and perhaps personally, Heidegger's *being-with-others* is deficient. In an attempt either conscious or unconscious to remedy this flaw of fundamental ontology, Arendt approaches the ontological through the ontic by first situating herself in the world as a German Jewess and offering up her experiences as a way of reclaiming *being-with-others* as constitutive of *Existenz* and illustrating the concrete ways that *being-with-others* was a genuinely constitutive component of her authentic political existence.

In her 1960 address to the American Political Science Association, Arendt offered a justification of political philosophy as an undertaking.

> Thought itself . . . arises out of the actuality of incidents, and incidents of living experience must remain [the] guideposts by which it takes its bearings, if it is not to lose itself in the heights to which thinking soars, or in the depths to which it must descend. In other words, the curve which the activity of thought describes must remain bound to incident as the circle remains bound to its focus.[8]

In other words, since thought requires isolation, any responsible philosophizing must necessarily remain "bound to incident." As such identity politics should be undertaken mindful, at least, of several admonishments that can be drawn from the conjoined work of Hannah Arendt and Martin Heidegger. First, Vogel suggests that we must, at the very least, regard the Other as a projecting being and pose the following question: can we facilitate the Other's transition to authenticity?[9] In keeping with the rest of Arendt's work, this proposition sets a standard for authentic political engagement that may be nearly impossible to attain. Yet it is not an elitist conception. Authenticity in the public realm, though possibly rare, is a viable option for us all—indeed, this is one of the important results of Heidegger's conception of authenticity, as an ontological possibility, and not merely an ontic accomplishment. It does not require one to be conversant in Greek philosophy nor trained in legal precedents. In fact, extensive training in a particular system of thought may prove more of a distraction or even a trap. The most useful insight may derive from those who are quite simply willing to offer up their own experiences for interpretation. Herein lies the importance of a moment like #MeToo, which originates quite simply with individuals' willingness to share their own experiences for reflection, interpretation and re-interpretation.

Second, Arendt illustrates both personally and philosophically, the continued relevance of Stern's insight. Moments of self-revelation are inherently alienating. In other words, even if one approaches the ontological through the ontic, with an awareness of one's throw, a sense of rootedness in a time and place, the individual's act of projecting sets her apart from the group. The act of self-revelation, in and of itself, creates a separation from the group, if not necessarily a fissure within the group. Herein lies the paradox of *being-with-others* in the world, particularly as a political phenomenon. The political goal of a cohesive group or a stable agenda is antithetical to the individual's project of self-revealing. Moreover, in trying to act on a political agenda, the group presses upon and constricts, if not constructs, the individual's self-concept. The myriad of ways in which a group can press upon an individual may either undermine the individual's awareness of his or her thrownness (as in the case of Benjamin Disraeli) or ostracizes the individual who does not conform to the group's definition of itself (as in the case of the pariah). Either one threatens the authenticity of the individual's project and undermines one of the primary goals of identity politics: facilitating the individual's transition to authenticity. As such the challenge of arriving at a legal definition or set of procedures may, in and of itself, undermine the project of identity.

In this text, I have tried simply to open the space for beginning to think about such contributions. I hope that in light of my arguments, the suggestion that Arendt and Heidegger are the wrong places to look for positive conceptions of identity theory within contemporary philosophy is problematized. Though neither thinker offers a fully formed theory,[10] as we might have wished, each provides a way of thinking through the stakes of what such a theory might involve. The experiential ontology of Arendt—as a critical response to and appropriation of Heidegger's phenomenological approach to human existence—is a productive place to look as one continues to think through the critical questions in identity politics. Who is it that "one" is in the context of a "we"? Who do "we" understand ourselves to be and how do we arrive at that understanding?

NOTES

1. Elzbieta Ettinger, *Hannah Arendt/Martin Heidegger* (New Haven, CT: Yale University Press, 1997).

2. Elizabeth K. Minnich, "Hannah Arendt: Thinking As We Are," in *Between Women: Biographers, Novelists, Critics, Teachers and Artists Write About Their Work on Women*, eds. C. Ascher, L. De Salvo, and S. Ruddick (Boston: Beacon Press, 1984), 179.

3. Judith Butler, *Giving an Account of Oneself* (New York: Fordham University Press, 2005).

4. Jean-Luc Nancy, *Being Singular Plural*, trans. Robert D. Richardson and Anne E. O'Byrne (Stanford, CA: Stanford University Press, 2000).

5. Adriana Cavarero, *Relating Narratives: Storytelling and Selfhood*, trans. and introduced by Paul A. Kottman (London: Routledge, 2000).

6. J. Aaron Simmons, "Finding Uses for Used-Up Words: Thinking *Weltanschauung* After Heidegger," *Philosophy Today* 50 (2006): 156–70.

7. Clark, Kelly James, Richard Lints, and James K. A. Smith, *101 Key Terms in Philosophy and Their Importance for Theology* (Louisville, KY: Westminster John Knox Press, 2004), 36.

8. Hannah Arendt, "Action and the Pursuit of Happiness," Hannah Arendt Manuscripts Collection, Library of Congress, 1960, 1.

9. Lawrence Vogel, *The Fragile "We": Ethical Implications of Heidegger's Being and Time* (Evanston, IL: Northwestern University Press, 1994).

10. In fact, Arendt would view a fully formed theory itself as problematic (Arendt, "Action and the Pursuit of Happiness," 1).

Bibliography

Abel, Lionel. "The Aesthetics of Evil: Hannah Arendt on Eichmann and the Jews." *Partisan Review* 30 (1963): 226–28.
Adamek, Philip M. "The Intimacy of Jean-Luc Nancy's 'L'Intrus.'" *CR: The New Centennial Review* 2 (2002): 189–201.
Anderson-Gold, Sharon. "Kant, Radical Evil and Crimes Against Humanity." In *Kant's Anatomy of Evil*, edited by S. Anderson-Gold and P. Muchnik, 195–214. Cambridge: Cambridge University Press, 2010.
Arendt, Hannah. "On the Emancipation of Women." In *Essays in Understanding*, edited by Jerome Kohn, 66–68. New York: Harcourt Brace, 1994 [1933].
———. "Anti-Semitism." In *The Jewish Writings*, edited by Jerome Kohn and Ron H. Feldman, 46–121. New York: Schocken Books, 2007 [1938/1939].
———. "We Refugees." *The Menorah Journal* 31 (1943): 69–77.
———. "What Is Existenz Philosophy?" *Partisan Review* 13 (1946): 34–56.
———. "The Image of Hell." *Commentary* 2 (1946): 291–95.
———. "The Great Tradition and the Nature of Totalitarianism." Lecture presented at the New School for Social Research, New York. Hannah Arendt Papers, Manuscript Division, Library of Congress, Container #74, 1953.
———. "Ideology and Terror: A Novel Form of Government." *Review of Politics* 15 (1953): 303–27.
———. "Understanding and Politics." *Partisan Review* 20 (1953): 377–92.
———. "Understanding and Politics." In *Essays in Understanding, 1930–1954*, edited by Jerome Kohn, xx–xx. New York: Schocken Books, 1994.
———. "Heidegger the Fox." In *The Portable Hannah Arendt*, edited by Peter Baehr, 543–44. New York: Penguin Putnam, 2000 [1953].
———. "The Difficulties of Understanding." Hannah Arendt Papers, Manuscript Division, Library of Congress, Container #73, 1953.
———. "The Assets of Personality: A Review of Chaim Weizmann: Statesman, Scientist, Builder of the Jewish Commonwealth." In *The Jewish Writings*, edited by Jerome Kohn and Ron H. Feldman, 402–4. New York: Schocken Books, 2007 [1944].
———. *Rahel Varnhagen: The Life of a Jewess*, edited by Liliane Weissberg. Baltimore, MD: Johns Hopkins University Press, 1997 [1957].
———. *The Origins of Totalitarianism*, 2nd ed. New York: Harcourt Brace, 1958.
———. *The Human Condition*. New York: Harcourt Brace, 1958.
———. "Reflections on Little Rock." *Dissent* 6 (1959): 47–58.
———. "Action and the Pursuit of Happiness." Hannah Arendt Manuscripts Collection, Library of Congress, 1960.

———. "Outline of 'Elements of Shame: Anti-Semitism, Imperialism and Racism.'" Hannah Arendt Manuscripts Collection, Library of Congress.
———. *Eichmann in Jerusalem: A Report on the Banality of Evil*. New York: Harcourt Brace, 1963.
———. "Martin Heidegger at Eighty." *The New York Review*, October, 21, 1971.
———. "'What Remains? The Language Remains': A Conversation with Günter Gaus." In *The Portable Hannah Arendt*, edited by Peter Baehr, 3–22. New York: Penguin Putnam, 2000 [1964].
———. "Some Questions of Moral Philosophy." In *Responsibility and Judgment*, edited by Jerome Kohn, 49–146. New York: Schoken Books, 2003 [1965].
———. "Thinking and Moral Considerations." In *Responsibility and Judgment*, edited by Jerome Kohn, 159–89. New York: Schoken Books, 2003 [1971].
———. "The Concept of History." In *Between Past and Future*. New York: Viking Press, 1968.
———. *Men in Dark Times*. New York: Harcourt Brace, 1968.
———. *Life of the Mind: Thinking*. New York: Harcourt Brace, 1978.
———. *Life of the Mind: Willing*. New York: Harcourt Brace, 1978.
———. *The Jew as Pariah: Jewish Identity and Politics in the Modern Age*. New York: Grove Press, 1978.
———. *Lectures on Kant's Political Philosophy*. Chicago: University of Chicago Press, 1982.
———. "Original Assimilation: An Epilogue to the One Hundredth Anniversary of Rahel Varnhagen's Death." In *The Jewish Writings*, edited by Jerome Kohn and Ron H. Feldman, 22–28. New York: Schocken Books, 2007 [1933].
———. "Creating a Cultural Atmosphere." In *The Jewish Writings*, edited by Jerome Kohn and Ron H. Feldman, 298–302. New York: Schocken Books, 2007 [1947].
———. "The Eichmann Controversy: A Letter to Gershom Scholem." In *The Jewish Writings*, edited by Jerome Kohn and Ron H. Feldman, 465–71. New York: Schocken Books, 2007 [1963].
———. "For the Honor and Glory of the Jewish People." In *The Jewish Writings*, edited by Jerome Kohn and Ron H. Feldman, 199–201. New York: Schocken Books, 2007 [1944].
———. "Jewish Chances: Sparse Prospects, Divided Representation." In *The Jewish Writings*, edited by Jerome Kohn and Ron H. Feldman, 238–40. New York: Schocken Books, 2007 [1945].
———. "Zionism Reconsidered." In *The Jewish Writings*, edited by Jerome Kohn and Ron H. Feldman, 343–74. New York: Schocken Books, 2007 [1944].
———. "The Concept of History: Ancient and Modern." In *Between Past and Future: Eight Exercises in Political Thought*, 41–90. New York: Penguin Books, 1968.
Ascheim, Steven. "Archetypes and the German-Jewish Dialogue: Reflections Occasioned by the Goldhagen Affair." *German History* 15 (1997): 140–50.
Badiou, Alain. *Meta-Politics*. Translated by Jason Barker. New York: Verso, 2005.
Baehr, Peter. "Debating Totalitarianism: An Exchange of Letters Between Hannah Arendt and Eric Voegelin." *History and Theory* 51 (2012): 364–80.
Bakan, Mildred. "Arendt and Heidegger: The Episodic Intertwining of Life and Work." *Philosophy & Social Criticism* 12 (1987): 71–98.
Baker, Karl. "In First Remarks Since 'Creepy Uncle Joe' Claims, Biden Shifts Conversation to Worker Rights." *Delaware News Journal*, April 5, 2019.
Bambach, Charles. *Heidegger's Roots: Nietzsche, National Socialism and the Greeks*. Ithaca, NY: Cornell University Press, 2005.
Bartky, Sandra L. "Originative Thinking in the Later Philosophy of Heidegger." *Philosophy and Phenomenological Research* 30 (1970): 368–81.
———. "Shame and Gender." In *Femininity and Domination: Studies in the Phenomenology of Oppression*, 83–98. New York: Routledge, 1990.
Barnouw, Dagmar. *Visible Spaces: Hannah Arendt and the German-Jewish Experience*. Baltimore: Johns Hopkins University Press, 1990.
Bedford, Sybille. "Emancipation and Destiny." *Reconstructionist*, December 12, 1958.

Benhabib, Seyla. "Feminist Theory and Hannah Arendt's Concept of Public Space." *History of the Human Sciences* 6 (1993): 97–114.

———. "Hannah Arendt and the Redemptive Power of Narrative." In *Hannah Arendt: Critical Essays*, edited by Lewis P. and Sandra K. Hinchman, 111–38. Albany: State University of New York Press, 1994.

———. *The Reluctant Modernism of Hannah Arendt*. New York: Rowman & Littlefield, 2000.

———. "The Pariah and Her Shadow: Hannah Arendt's Biography of Rahel Varnhagen." *Political Theory* 23 (1995): 5–24.

———. "Who's Trial? Adolph Eichmann's or Hannah Arendt's: The Eichmann Controversy Revisited." In *The Trial That Never Ends: Hannah Arendt's Eichmann in Jerusalem in Retrospect*, edited by Richard J. Golsan and Sarah M. Misemer, 209–28. Toronto: University of Toronto Press, 2019.

Berlin, Isiah. *The Hedgehog and the Fox: An Essay on Tolstoy's View of History*. New York: Simon & Schuster, 1953.

Bernstein, Richard J. *Hannah Arendt and the Jewish Question*. Cambridge, MA: MIT Press, 1996.

———. "Did Hannah Arendt Change Her Mind? From Radical Evil to the Banality of Evil." In *Hannah Arendt: Twenty Years Later*, edited by Larry May and Jerome Kohn, 127–46. Cambridge, MA: MIT Press, 1996.

———. *Radical Evil: A Philosophical Interrogation*. Oxford: Blackwell Publishers, 2002.

Bittman, Michael. "Totalitarianism: The Career of a Concept." In *Hannah Arendt: Thinking, Judging, Freedom*, edited by G. T. Kaplan and C. S. Kessler, 56–68. Sydney: Allen and Unwin, 1989.

Borren, Marieke. "'A Sense of the World': Hannah Arendt's Hermeneutic Phenomenology of Common Sense." *International Journal of Philosophical Studies* 21 (2013): 225–55.

Bourdieu, Pierre. *The Political Ontology of Martin Heidegger*. Translated by Peter Collier. Stanford, CA: Stanford University Press, 1988.

Brightman, Carol, ed. *Between Friends: The Correspondence of Hannah Arendt and Mary McCarthy, 1949–1975*. New York: Harcourt Brace, 1995.

Butler, Judith. *Giving an Account of Oneself*. New York: Fordham University Press, 2005.

———. *The Psychic Life of Power: Theories in Subjection*. Stanford, CA: Stanford University Press, 1997.

———. *Bodies that Matter: On the Discursive Limits of "Sex."* New York: Routledge, 1993.

———. *Big Think*. February 19, 2013.

———. *Gender Trouble: Feminism and the Subversion of Identity*. New York: Routledge, 1990.

———. "Performative Acts and Gender Constitution: An Essay in Phenomenology and Feminist Theory." *Theatre Journal* 40 (1988): 519–31.

Butler, Judith, and William E. Connolly. "Politics, Power and Ethics: A Discussion Between Judith Butler and William Connolly." *Theory & Event* 4, no. 2 (2000).

Canovan, Margaret. *Hannah Arendt: A Re-interpretation of Her Political Thought*. New York: Cambridge University Press, 1992.

Card, Claudia. *The Atrocity Paradigm: A Theory of Evil*. New York: Oxford University Press, 2002.

———. "Kant's Moral Excluded Middle." In *Kant's Anatomy of Evil*, edited by Sharon Anderson-Gold and Pablo Muchnik, 74–92. Cambridge: Cambridge University Press, 2010.

Cavarero, Adriana. *Relating Narratives: Storytelling and Selfhood*. Translated and introduced by Paul A. Kottman. London: Routledge, 2000.

———. *Horrorism: Naming Contemporary Violence*. Translated by William McCuaig. New York: Columbia University Press, 2009.

Cesarani, David. *Disraeli: The Novel Politician*. New Haven, CT: Yale University Press, 2016.

Chanter, Tina. "The Problematic Normative Assumptions of Heidegger's Ontology." In *Feminist Interpretations of Martin Heidegger*, edited by Nancy J. Holland and Patricia Huntington, 73–108. University Park, PA: Pennsylvania State University Press, 2001.

Clark, Kelly James, Richard Lints, and James K. A. Smith. *101 Key Terms in Philosophy and Their Importance for Theology*. Louisville, KY: Westminster John Knox Press, 2004.

Cohen, Richard. "A Generation's Response to *Eichmann in Jerusalem*." In *Hannah Arendt in Jerusalem*, edited by Steven Ascheim, 253–77. Berkeley: University of California Press, 2001.

Crick, Bernard. "Arendt and *The Origins of Totalitarianism*: An Anglo-Centric View." In *Hannah Arendt in Jerusalem*, edited by Steven E. Ascheim, 93–104. Berkeley: University of California Press, 1999.

Critchley, Simon. "Originary Inauthenticity—on Heidegger's *Sein und Zeit*." In *On Heidegger's Being and Time*, edited by Steven Levine, 132–51. London: Routledge, 2008.

Cutting-Gray, Joanne. "Hannah Arendt's *Rahel Varnhagen*." *Philosophy and Literature* 15 (1991): 229–45.

———. "Hannah Arendt, Feminism, and the Politics of Alterity: 'What Will We Lose If We Win?'" *Hypatia* 8 (1993): 35–54.

Dallmayr, Fred. "Heidegger and Politics: Some Lessons." In *The Heidegger Case: On Philosophy and Politics*, edited by Tom Rockmore and Joseph Margolis, 282–312. Philadelphia: Temple University Press, 1992.

Derrida, Jacques. "Geschecht: Sexual Difference, Ontological Difference." In *Feminist Interpretations of Martin Heidegger*, edited by Nancy J. Holland and Patricia Huntington, 53–72. University Park, PA: Pennsylvannia State University Press, 2001.

———. *Heidegger: The Question of Being and History*. Edited by Thomas DuToit and Marguerite Derrida. Translated by Geoffrey Bennington. Chicago: University of Chicago Press, 2016.

Des Forges, Alison. *Leave None to Tell the Story: Genocide in Rwanda*. New York: Human Rights Watch, 1999.

Deutscher, Isaac. *Stalin: A Political Biography*. New York: Vintage, 1960.

Di Cesare, Donatella. "Heidegger's Metaphysical Anti-Semitism." In *Reading Heidegger's Black Notebooks, 1931–1941*, edited by Ingo Farin and Jeff Malpas, 181–94. Cambridge, MA: MIT Press, 2016.

Disch, Lisa J. "More Truth than Fact: Storytelling as Critical Understanding in the Writings of Hannah Arendt." *Political Theory* 21 (1993): 665–94.

———. "Please Sit Down but Don't Make Yourself at Home: 'Visiting' and the Prefigurative Politics of Consciousness-Raising." In *Hannah Arendt and the Meaning of Politics*, edited by Craig Calhoun and John McGowan, 132–65. Minneapolis: University of Minnesota Press, 1997.

———. "Judith Butler and the Politics of the Performative." *Political Theory* 27 (1999): 545–59.

Dreyfus, Hubert. *Being-in-the-World: A Commentary on Heidegger's Being and Time, Division I*. Cambridge, MA: MIT Press, 1991.

Douglass, Ryan. "More Men Should Learn the Difference Between Masculinity and Toxic Masculinity." *The Huffington Post*, August 4, 2017.

Dumm, Thomas. *Loneliness as a Way of Life*. Cambridge, MA: Harvard University Press, 2008.

Dworkin, Andrea. *Life and Death: Unapologetic Writings on the Continued War against Women*. New York: Little, Brown, 1997.

Ember, Sydney, and Jonathan Martin. "Joe Biden in Video, Says He Will be 'More Mindful' of Personal Space." *New York Times*, April 3, 2019.

Erza, Michael. "The Eichmann Polemics: Hannah Arendt and Her Critics." *Democratiya* 9 (2007): 141–65.

Escudero, Jesús Adrián. "Heidegger on Discourse and Idle Talk: The Role of Aristotelian Rhetoric." *Gatherings* 3 (2013): 1–17.

Ettinger, Elzbieta. *Hannah Arendt/Martin Heidegger*. New Haven, CT: Yale University Press, 1997.

Ewegen, S. Montgomery. "Being Just? Just Being: Heidegger's Just Thinking." *Philosophy Today* 56 (2012): 285–94.

Farias, Victor. *Heidegger and Nazism*. Edited by Joseph Margolis and Tom Rockmore. Philadelphia, PA: Temple University Press, 1989.

Bibliography 195

Farrow, Ronan. "From Aggressive Overtures to Sexual Assault: Harvey Weinstein's Accusers Tell Their Stories." *The New Yorker*, October 23, 2017.
Farwell, Paul. "Can Heidegger's Craftsman be Authentic?" *International Philosophical Quarterly* 29 (1989): 77–90.
Feldman, Ron H. "The Jew as Pariah: The Case of Hannah Arendt (1906–1975)." In *The Jewish Writings*, edited by Jerome Kohn and Ron H. Feldman, xli-lxxvi. New York: Schocken Books, 2007.
Fleishman, Avrom. *Conrad's Politics*. Baltimore, MD: Johns Hopkins University Press, 1967.
Freeman, Lauren. "Recognition Reconsidered: A Re-reading of Heidegger's *Being and Time* §26." *Philosophy Today* 53 (2009): 85–99.
Fried, Gregory. "The King Is Dead: Martin Heidegger after the Black Notebooks." In *Reading Heidegger's Black Notebooks, 1931–1941*, edited by Ingo Farin and Jeff Malpas, 45–58. Cambridge, MA: MIT Press, 2016.
Friedan, Betty. 1963. *The Feminine Mystique*. New York: Norton.
Gadamer, Hans-Georg. "The Political Incompetence of Philosophy." In *The Heidegger Case: On Philosophy and Politics*, edited by Tom Rockmore and Joseph Margolis, 364–72. Philadelphia: Temple University Press, 1992.
Gilman, Sander L. "Cosmopolitan Jews v. Jewish Nomads: Sources of a Trope in Heidegger's *Black Notebooks*." In *Heidegger's Black Notebooks: Responses to Anti-Semitism*, edited by Andrew J. Mitchell and Peter Trawny, 18–35. New York: Columbia University Press, 2017.
Glassman, Peter J. *Language and Being: Joseph Conrad and the Literature of Personality*. New York: Columbia University Press, 1976.
Gornick, Vivian. "Outsideness Personified," *The Village Voice*, January 6, 1975.
Graves R., and R. Patai. *Hebrew Myths: The Book of Genesis*. New York: Doubleday, 1964.
Guignon, Charles. "The History of Being." In *A Companion to Heidegger*, edited by Hubert L. Dreyfus and Mark A. Wrathall, 392–406. Oxford: Blackwell Publishing, 2005.
Gurko, Leo. *Joseph Conrad: Giant in Exile*. New York: Macmillan, 1962.
Habermas, Jürgen. "Martin Heidegger: On the Publication of the Lectures of 1935." In *The Heidegger Controversy: A Critical Reader*, edited by Richard Wolin, 186–97. New York: Columbia University Press, 1991.
———. *The Philosophical Discourse of Modernity: Twelve Lectures*. Translated by F. Lawrence. Cambridge, MA: MIT Press, 1987.
Harries, Karsten. "Nostalgia, Spite, and the Truth of Being." In *Reading Heidegger's Black Notebooks, 1931–1941*, edited by Ingo Farin and Jeff Malpas, 207–22. Cambridge, MA: MIT Press, 2016.
Hartsock, Nancy. C. M. *Money, Sex and Power: Toward a Feminist Historical Materialism*. New York: Longman, 1983.
Harzfeld, Jean. *The Antelope's Strategy: Living in Rwanda after the Genocide*. New York: Picador, 2010.
Hatton, Denys Finch. "Lions at their Ease: Stalking by Car." *The Times*, January 21, 1928.
———. "Stalking with a Camera: The New African Sport." *The Times*, June 29, 1929.
———. "Hunting from Motorcars." *The Times*, July 3, 1929.
———. "Hunting from Motorcars: The Affected Area." *The Times*, July 10, 1929.
Heidegger, Martin. *Being and Time*. Translated by Joan Stambaugh. Albany, NY: SUNY Press, 1997.
———. "On the Essence of Ground." In *Pathmarks*, translated and edited by William O'Neill, 97–135. Cambridge: Cambridge University Press, 1998 [1928].
———. "What Is Called, What Calls for, Thinking." In *Martin Heidegger: Philosophical and Political Writings*, edited by Manfred Stassen, 80–86. New York: Continuum, 2003.
———. "Why Do I Stay in the Provinces?" In *Martin Heidegger: Philosophical and Political Writings*, edited by Manfred Stassen, 16–18. New York: Continuum, 2003.
———. "Memorial Address." In *Discourse on Thinking*, translated by John M. Anderson and E. Hans Freud, 43–57. New York: Harper and Row, 1966.
———. "Conversations on a Country Path About Thinking." In *Discourse on Thinking*, translated by John M. Anderson and E. Hans Freud, 58–90. New York: Harper and Row, 1966.

———. "The Origin of the Work of Art." In *Off the Beaten Path*, edited and translated by Julian Young and Kenneth Hayes, 1–56. Cambridge: Cambridge University Press, 2002.

———. *Ponderings VII-XI: Black Notebooks 1938–1939*. Translated by Richard Rojcewicz. Bloomington: Indiana University Press, 2017.

———. *Ponderings XII-XV: Black Notebooks 1939–1941*. Translated by Richard Rojcewicz. Bloomington: Indiana University Press, 2017.

Hertz, Deborah. "Hannah Arendt's Rahel Varnhagen." In *German Women in the Nineteenth Century: A Social History*, edited by J. C. Fout, 73–87. New York: Holmes and Meier, 1984.

Hinchman, Lewis P., and Sandra K. Hinchman. "In Heidegger's Shadow: Hannah Arendt's Phenomenological Humanism." *The Review of Politics* 46 (1984): 183–211.

Hinchman, Sandra K. "Common Sense & Political Barbarism in the Theory of Hannah Arendt." *Polity* 17 (1984): 317–39.

Hodapp, Christa. "Giving an Account of Oneself: Review." *Pluralist* 8 (1) 2013: 115–18.

Holland, Nancy J. "The Universe Is Made of Stories, Not of Atoms: Heidegger and the Feminine They-Self." In *Feminist Interpretations of Martin Heidegger*, edited by Nancy J. Holland and Patricia Huntington, 128–48. University Park, PA: Pennsylvania State University Press, 2001.

Hoy, David Couzens. "History, Historicity and Historiography in *Being and Time*." In *Heidegger and Modern Philosophy*, edited by Michael Murray, 329–53. New Haven, CT: Yale University Press, 1978.

Husserl, Edmund. *The Crisis of European Sciences and Transcendental Phenomenology*. Translated by David Carr. Evanston, IL: Northwestern University Press, 1970.

Isaac, Jeffrey C. *Arendt, Camus and Modern Rebellion*. New Haven, CT: Yale University Press, 1992.

Janus, Adrienne. "Jean-Luc Nancy and the 'Anti-Ocular' Turn in Continental Philosophy and Critical Theory." *Comparative Literature* 63 (2011): 182–202.

Jardine, Douglas. "Hunting from Motorcars: The Law and Public Opinion." *The Times*, July 8, 1929.

———. "Hunting from Cars." *The Times*, July 18, 1929.

Joffe-Walt, Chana. "Five Women." *This American Life*. Podcast audio. March 2, 2018. https://www.thisamericanlife.org/640/five-women.

Johnson, Bruce. *Conrad's Models of Mind*. Minneapolis: University of Minnesota Press, 1971.

Jones, Michael T. "Heidegger the Fox: Hannah Arendt's Hidden Dialogue." *New German Critique* 73 (1998): 164–91.

Kane, Brian. "Jean-Luc Nancy and the Listening Subject." *Contemporary Music Review* 5–6 (2012): 439–47.

Kant, Immanuel. *Religion Within the Limits of Reason Alone*. Translated by T. M. Greene and H. H. Hudson. New York: Harper & Row, 1960 [1793].

Kantor, Jodi, and Megan Twohey. "Harvey Weinstein Paid Off Sexual Harassment Accusers for Decades." *New York Times*, October 5, 2017.

Kateb, George. *Hannah Arendt: Conscience, Evil and Politics*. Totowa, NJ: Rowman & Littlefield Publishers, 1984.

———. "Ideology and Storytelling." *Social Research* 69 (2002): 321–58.

———. *Patriotism and Other Mistakes*. New Haven, CT: Yale University Press, 2006.

King, Magda. *A Guide to Heidegger's Being and Time*. Edited by John Llewelyn. Albany: State University of New York Press, 2001.

Kipling, Rudyard. *Kim*. Introduction by Edward Said. New York: Penguin Classics, 1987.

Kirsch, Adam. "Beware of Pity." *The New Yorker*, January 12, 2009.

Kohler, Lotte, ed. *Within Four Walls: The Correspondence between Hannah Arendt and Heinrich Blücher, 1936–1968*. New York: Harcourt, 2000.

Kohler, Lotte, and Hans Saner, eds. *Hannah Arendt—Karl Jaspers Correspondence, 1926–1969*. Translated by Robert and Rita Kimber. New York: Harcourt, 1992.

Kohn, Jerome. "Arendt's Concept and Description of Totalitarianism." *Social Research* 69 (2002): 621–56.

———. "A Jewish Life: 1906–1975." In *The Jewish Writings*, edited by Jerome Kohn and Ron H. Feldman, ix–xxxi. New York: Schocken Books, 2007.

Kristeva, Julia. *Hannah Arendt*. New York: Columbia University Press, 2001.
Lacoue-Labarthe, Phillipe. *Heidegger, Art and Politics*. Oxford: Basil Blackwell, 1990.
Lafford, Sarah. "Natality and Exposure: A Philosophical Account of the Harm of Sexual Violence." *The Philosophical Journal of Conflict and Violence* 2 (2018): 64–77.
Lane, Anne M. "The Feminism of Hannah Arendt." *Democracy* 3 (1983): 101–17.
Lawrence, T. E. *Seven Pillars of Wisdom: A Triumph*. Blacksburg, VA: Wilder Publications, 2011.
———. *Lawrence of Arabia: The Selected Letters*. Edited by Malcolm Brown. London: Little Books, 2007.
LeBon, Gustave. *The Crowd: A Study of the Popular Mind*. New York: Viking Press, 1960.
Leibovici, Martine. "Arendt's *Rahel Varnhagen*: A New Kind of Narration in the Impasses of German-Jewish Assimilation and *Existenzphilosophie*." *Social Research* 74 (2007): 903–22.
Lerer, Lisa. "Joe Biden Jokes About Hugging in a Speech, Then Offers a Mixed Apology." *New York Times*, April 5, 2019.
Levinas, Emmanuel. *Totality and Infinity: An Essay on Exteriority*. Translated by Alphonso Lingus. Pittsburgh, PA: Duquesne University Press, 1969.
Lipstadt, Deborah. *The Eichmann Trial*. New York: Schocken Books, 2011.
Longman, Timothy. "Genocide and Socio-Political Change: Massacres in Two Rwandan Villages." *Issue: A Journal of Opinion* 23 (1995): 18–21.
———. *Christianity and Genocide in Rwanda*. Cambridge: Cambridge University Press, 2009.
Löwith, Karl. "My Last Meeting with Heidegger in Rome." In *The Heidegger Controversy: A Critical Reader*, edited by Richard Wolin, 140–43. New York: Columbia University Press, 1991.
———. "The Political Implications of Heidegger's Existentialism." *New German Critique* 45 (1988): 117–34.
Luban, David. "Explaining Dark Times: Hannah Arendt's Theory of Theory." *Social Research* 50 (1983): 215–47.
Ludz, Ursula, ed. *Letters: 1925–1975, Hannah Arendt and Martin Heidegger*. New York: Harcourt Brace, 2004.
Lustiger, Arno. "Feldwebel Anton Schmid." In *Retter in Uniform*, edited by Wolfram Wette, 45–67. Frankfurt: Frankfurt Main, 2002.
MacKinnon, Catharine. *Toward a Feminist Theory of the State*. Cambridge, MA: Harvard University Press, 1989.
———. "#MeToo Has Done What the Law Could Not." *New York Times*, February 4, 2018.
Mamdani, Manhood. *When Victims Become Killers: Colonialism, Nativism, and the Genocide in Rwanda*. Princeton, NJ: Princeton University Press, 2001.
Markus, Maria. "The Anti-Feminism of Hannah Arendt." In *Hannah Arendt: Thinking, Judging, Freedom*, edited by Gisela Kaplan and Clive Kessler, 119–29. Sydney: Allen and Unwin, 1989.
Martin, Jay. *Downcast Eyes: The Denigration of Vision in Twentieth Century Thought*. Berkeley: University of California Press, 1993.
Medvedev, Roy A. *Let History Judge: The Origins and Consequences of Stalinism*. New York: Vintage, 1974.
Melvern, Linda. *Conspiracy to Murder: The Rwandan Genocide*. New York: Verso, 2004.
Mendieta, Eduardo. "Metaphysical Anti-Semitism and Worldlessness: On World Poorness, World Forming, and World Destroying." In *Heidegger's Black Notebooks: Responses to Anti-Semitism*, edited by Andrew J. Mitchell and Peter Trawny, 36–51. New York: Columbia University Press, 2017.
Midlarsky, Manus I. *The Killing Trap: Genocide in the Twentieth Century*. Cambridge: Cambridge University Press, 2005.
Mill, Harriet Taylor, and John Stuart Mill. "The Case of Mary Ann Parsons [1]." In *The Complete Works of Harriet Taylor Mill*, edited by Jo Ellen Jacobs, 98–100. Bloomington: Indiana University Press, 1997.
Mill, Harriet Taylor, and John Stuart Mill. "The Case of Mary Ann Parsons [2]." In *The Complete Works of Harriet Taylor Mill*, edited by Jo Ellen Jacobs, 104–8. Bloomington: Indiana University Press, 1997.

Mill, Harriet Taylor, and John Stuart Mill. "The Case of Susan Moir." In *The Complete Works of Harriet Taylor Mill*, edited by Jo Ellen Jacobs, 108–11. Bloomington: Indiana University Press, 1997.

Minnich, Elizabeth K. "Hannah Arendt: Thinking as We Are." In *Between Women: Biographers, Novelists, Critics, Teachers and Artists Write about Their Work on Women*, edited by Carol Ascher, Louise De Salvo, and Sara Ruddick, 171–85. Boston: Beacon Press, 1984.

Mitchell, Andrew J., and Peter Trawny, eds. *Heidegger's Black Notebooks: Responses to Anti-Semitism*. New York: Columbia University Press, 2017.

Mizrahi, Ramit. "Sexual Harassment Law After #MeToo: Looking to California as a Model." *The Yale Law Journal*, June 18, 2018.

Monroe, Kristen Renwick. "Harassment Charges: Metoo but Due Process." *Science*, August 18, 2018.

Moruzzi, Norma Claire. *Speaking Through the Mask: Hannah Arendt and the Politics of Social Identity*. Ithaca, NY: Cornell University Press, 2000.

Mouffe, Chantal. *On the Political*. New York: Routledge, 2005.

Mulhall, Stephen. *On Being in the World: Wittgenstein and Heidegger on Seeing Aspects*. New York: Routledge, 1990.

Nagel, Mechthild. "Thrownness, Playing-in-the-World, and the Question of Authenticity." In *Feminist Interpretations of Martin Heidegger*, edited by Nancy J. Holland and Patricia Huntington, 289–308. University Park, PA: Pennsylvania State University Press, 2001.

Najder, Zdzislaw. "The Personal Voice in Conrad's Fiction." In *Joseph Conrad: Voice, Sequence, History, Genre*, edited by Jakob Lothe, Jeremy Hawthorn, and James Phelan, 23–40. Columbus: The Ohio State University Press, 2008.

Nancy, Jean-Luc. *Being Singular Plural*. Translated by Robert D. Richardson and Anne E. O'Byrne. Stanford, CA: Stanford University Press, 2000.

———. *The Banality of Heidegger*. Minneapolis: University of Minnesota Press, 1991.

———. *The Sense of the World*. Translated by Jeffrey Librett. Minneapolis: University of Minnesota Press, 1997.

———. *Listening*. Translated by Charlotte Mandell. New York: Fordham University Press, 2007.

———. "On Human Rights: Two Simple Remarks." Translated by Gilbert Leung. In *The Meaning of Rights: The Philosophy and Social Theory of Human Rights*, edited by Costas Douzinas and Conor Gearty, 15–20. Cambridge: Cambridge University Press, 2014.

———. "L'intrus." Translated by Susan Hanson. *CR: The New Centennial Review* 2 (2002): 1–14.

Neiman, Susan. *Evil in Modern Thought: An Alternative History of Philosophy*. Princeton, NJ: Princeton University Press, 2002.

———. "Theodicy in Jerusalem." In *Hannah Arendt in Jerusalem*, edited by Steven Ascheim, 65–90. Berkeley, CA: University of California Press, 2001.

Nussbaum, Martha. "The Professor of Parody: The Hip Defeatism of Judith Butler." *New Republic* 22 (1999): 37–45.

Passerin D'Entreves, Maurizio. *The Political Philosophy of Hannah Arendt*. London: Routledge, 1994.

Pilipchuk, Miranda. "Artemisia's Revenge: Rape and Art in the Work of Jean-Luc Nancy." *Concept* 37 (2014): 1–10.

Podhoretz, Norman. "Hannah Arendt on Eichmann: A Study in the Perversity of Brilliance." *Commentary* 36 (1963): 201–8.

Pöggeler, Otto. *The Paths of Heidegger's Life and Though*. Translated by John Bailiff. Atlantic Highlands, NJ: Humanities Press, 1997.

Richards, Kevin. "The Origins of Totalitarianism Part I—Anti-Semitism." May 3, 2018. https://u.osu.edu/richards.113/2018/05/03/the-origins-of-totalitarianism-part-i-anti-semitism-hannah-arendt.

Rickey, Christopher. *Revolutionary Saints: Heidegger, National Socialism, and Antinomian Politics*. University Park, PA: Penn State University Press, 2001.

Ring, Jennifer. "The Pariah as Hero: Hannah Arendt's Political Actor." *Political Theory* 19 (1991): 433–52.

---. *The Political Consequences of Thinking: Gender and Judaism in the Work of Hannah Arendt*. Albany: State University of New York Press, 1997.
Salam, Maya. "What Is Toxic Masculinity?" *New York Times*, January 22, 2019.
Schürmann, Reiner. "Heidegger's *Being and Time*." In *On Heidegger's Being and Time*, edited by Steven Levine, 56–131. London: Routledge, 2008.
Schwartz, Alexandra. "#MeToo, #Itwasme, and the Post-Weinstein Megaphone of Social Media." *The New Yorker*, October 19, 2017.
Shapiro, Leonard. *Totalitarianism*. New York: Praeger, 1972.
Shapiro, Meyer. "The Still Life as a Personal Object—A Note on Heidegger and Van Gogh." In *Theory and Philosophy of Art: Style, Artist and Society*, 135–49. New York: George Braziller, 1994.
Sherratt, Yvonne. *Hitler's Philosophers*. New Haven, CT: Yale University Press, 2013.
Shklar, Judith N. "Hannah Arendt as Pariah." *Partisan Review* 50 (1983): 64–77.
Simmons, J. Aaron. "Finding Uses for Used-Up Words: Thinking *Weltanschauung* After Heidegger." *Philosophy Today* 50 (2006): 156–70.
Stambaugh, Joan. "Translator's Preface." In Martin Heidegger, *Being and Time*, translated by Joan Stambaugh, xiii–xvi. Albany, NY: SUNY Press, 1997.
Staub, Ervin. *The Roots of Evil: The Origins of Genocide and Other Group Violence*. Cambridge: Cambridge University Press, 1989.
Stern, Günther. "On the Pseudo-Concreteness of Heidegger's Philosophy." *Philosophy and Phenomenological Research* 8 (1947): 337–71.
Stevens, Matt, and Sydney Ember. "Joe Biden Says He Did Not Act Inappropriately With Lucy Flores." *New York Times*, March 30, 2019.
Straus, Scott. *The Order of Genocide: Race, Power and War in Rwanda*. Ithaca, NY: Cornell University Press, 2006.
Syrkin, Marie. "Miss Arendt Surveys the Holocaust." *Jewish Frontier* 30 (1963): 6–14.
---. "Setting the Record Straight." *Midstream* 12 (1966): 67–70.
Taminiaux, Jacques. *The Thracian Maid and the Professional Thinker: Arendt and Heidegger*. Translated and edited by Michael Gendre. Albany, NY: SUNY Press, 1997.
---. "The Philosophical Stakes in Arendt's Genealogy of Totalitarianism." *Social Research* 69 (2002): 423–69.
---. *Poetics, Speculation and Judgment: The Shadow of the Work of Art from Kant to Phenomenology*. Translated and edited by Michael Gendre. Albany: State University of New York Press, 1993.
Thompson, Iain. "Thinking Love: Heidegger and Arendt." *Continental Philosophy Review* 50 (2017): 453–78.
Trawny, Peter. "Heidegger, "World Judaism, and Modernity." Translated by Christopher Merwin. *Gatherings: The Heidegger Circle Annual* 5 (2015): 1–20.
---. *Heidegger and the Myth of a Jewish World Conspiracy*. Translated by Andrew J. Mitchell. Chicago: University of Chicago Press, 2016.
---. "The Universal and Annihilation: Heidegger's Being Historical Anti-Semitism." In *Heidegger's Black Notebooks: Responses to Anti-Semitism*, edited by Andrew J. Mitchell and Peter Trawny, 1–17. New York: Columbia University Press, 2017.
Tsao, Roy. "The Evolution and Structure of Arendt's Theory of Totalitarianism." *Social Research* 69 (2002): 579–619.
Tucker, Robert C. "The Dictator and Totalitarianism." *World Politics* 17 (1965): 555–83.
Uvin, Peter. *Aiding Violence: The Development Enterprise in Rwanda*. West Hartford, CT: Kumarian Press, 1998.
Verwimp, Philip. "Development Ideology, the Peasantry and Genocide: Rwanda Represented in Habyarimana's Speeches (1973–1994)." *Journal for Genocide Research* 2 (2000): 325–61.
---. "An Economic Profile of Peasant Perpetrators of Genocide: Micro-Level Evidence from Rwanda." *Journal of Development Economics* 77 (2005): 297–323.
Villa, Dana. *Arendt and Heidegger: The Fate of the Political*. Princeton, NJ: Princeton University Press, 1996.

———. *Politics, Philosophy and Terror: Essays on the Thought of Hannah Arendt*. Princeton, NJ: Princeton University Press, 1999.

———. "Arendt, Heidegger and the Tradition." *Social Research* 74 (2007): 983–1002.

———. "*Eichmann in Jerusalem*: Conscience, Normality, and the 'Rule of Narrative.'" In *The Trial That Never Ends: Hannah Arendt's Eichmann in Jerusalem in Retrospect*, edited by Richard J. Golsan and Sarah M. Misemer, 43–66. Toronto: University of Toronto Press, 2019.

Voegelin, Eric. "The Origins of Totalitarianism." *Review of Politics* 15 (1953): 68–76.

Vogel, Lawrence. *The Fragile "We": Ethical Implications of Heidegger's Being and Time*. Evanston, IL: Northwestern University Press, 1994.

Vollrath, Ernst. "Hannah Arendt and the Method of Political Thinking." *Social Research* 44 (1977): 160–82.

Walzer, Michael. *Spheres of Justice*. New York: Basic Books, 1983.

Wasserstein, Bernard. "Blame the Victim." *Times Literary Supplement*, October 9, 2009, 14.

Weinreich, Max. *Hitler's Professors: The Part of Scholarship in Germany's Crimes Against the Jewish People*. New Haven, CT: Yale University Press, 1946 [1999].

Weir, Alison. *Identities and Freedom: Feminist Theories Between Power and Connection*. Oxford: Oxford University Press, 2013.

Weissberg, Liliane. "Hannah Arendt, Rahel Varnhagen and Writing of (Auto)biography." In *Rahel Varnhagen: The Life of a Jewess*, edited by Liliane Weissberg, 3–69. Baltimore, MD: Johns Hopkins University Press, 1997.

Wheeler, Sara. *Too Close to the Sun*. New York: Random House, 2006.

Whitfield, Stephen. *Into the Dark: Hannah Arendt and Totalitarianism*. Philadelphia: Temple University Press, 1980.

Wilkens, Carl. *I'm Not Leaving*. Spokane, WA: World Outside My Shoes, 2011.

Wolin, Richard. *The Politics of Being: The Political Thought of Martin Heidegger*. New York: Columbia University Press, 1990.

———. "An Affair to Remember: Hannah and the Magician." *The New Republic*, October 9, 1995.

Wolin, Sheldon. *The Presence of the Past*. Baltimore, MD: Johns Hopkins University Press, 1989.

———. *Politics and Vision: Continuity and Innovation in Western Political Thought*, expanded edition. Princeton, NJ: Princeton University Press, 2004.

Wood, Allen W. "Kant and the Intelligibility of Evil." In *Kant's Anatomy of Evil*, edited by Sharon Anderson-Gold and Pablo Muchnik, 144–72. Cambridge: Cambridge University Press, 2010.

Woodhull, Victoria. "The Social Volcano." *Woodhull and Claflin's Weekly*, September 16, 1871.

Young-Bruehl, Elisabeth. "Hannah Arendt's Storytelling." *Social Research* 44 (1977): 183–90.

———. *Hannah Arendt: For Love of the World*. New Haven, CT: Yale University Press, 1982.

Index

absence of continuity, 101
absolute evil, 120
action, 134, 139, 140; loneliness and, 141; selfhood and, 157
actualization, 26–27
Adorno, Theodor, 147, 169
adventurers, 87
Africa, 86, 87, 104
agency, 151, 153, 170
Alternet, 174, 175, 176, 179
American Political Science Association, 188
Anderson-Gold, Sharon, 119
antisemitism, 1, 2, 61, 62, 81; assimilation and, 51; Clemenceau condemning, 71; colonialism and, 85; Disraeli and, 67, 69; Dreyfus Affair and, 69; European, 154; Heidegger and, 18, 34, 53, 64, 65; imperialism and, 85, 96; internalizing, 88; modern, 31; philosophical, 64, 65; transition in, 72
Anti-Semitism (Arendt), 60, 62, 64, 66, 68, 88; historicity and, 76, 77; ontic structures and, 93; *Origins of Totalitarianism* and, 75; publication of, 72; revisions of, 63
Arab National Movement, 85
Arendt, Hannah, 3, 11, 40; assimilation and, 59; attempting to humanize Heidegger, 44–45; authenticity and, 93, 127; *Being-with* and, 14; Butler and, 151, 152; calculation and, 66; classless society and, 99; Clemenceau and, 71; democratic ontology and, 142; on Disraeli, 66, 153; Eichmann and, 25, 116; on essence, 28–29; evil, ways talked and thought about, 115, 120, 123; existential philosophy and, 2; fundamental ontology and, 7; Gaus and, 94; "The Great Tradition and the Nature of Totalitarianism", 13; *Heart of Darkness* and, 87; Heidegger devoted relationship to, 185; Heidegger tumultuous relationship with, 5; identity politics and, 145, 146; ideology and, 80, 81; Jewish history and, 69; Jewishness and, 46, 59, 60, 65; Kant and, 117, 119; Kimball O'Hara and, 83; lack of thinking and, 139; Lessing Prize and, 52; loneliness and, 131; "Martin Heidegger at Eighty", 8, 9; meditative thinking and, 26; metaphysical roots and, 18; on mobs, 69; modernity and, 33; ontic characteristic and, 17; ontic structures, focus on, 76, 93; Other and, 148; on personification of diabolical evil, 122; political philosophy and, 1; rootlessness and, 24, 29–30, 32, 34, 53; roots and, 20, 31; on *schuld* (guilty), 12; secularization and, 67; solitude and, 9; storytelling and, 21; thinking and, 9, 10, 128; vignettes and, 39; Zionism and,

32. *See also specific works*
art, 28–29
assimilation, 51, 53; Arendt and, 59; *being-in-the-world* and, 62; insane optimism and, 137; of Jews, 28, 67, 68, 88
at home in the world, 9
Auschwitz, 125
authenticity, 22, 23, 26, 44, 84, 131; Arendt and, 93, 127; Butler and, 161; as ontological possibility, 188; public revealing and, 142; pursuit of, 62; search for, 33; transcendence and, 150; uniqueness and, 137
authentic Self, 68, 85
authentic selfhood, 11
authentic thinking, 26
authentic work, 20
autocracy, 131
autonomy, 153

Bagatelles pour un Massacre (Celine), 102
Bambach, Charles, 27
Barayagwiza, 106
Barnouw, Dagmar, 59
Bartky, Sandra Lee, 147
Bedford, Sybille, 41
Being, 6, 7, 16n46; nature of, 8, 10, 23; politically engaged, 59; rootedness and, 20
Being, 18; *Being-with* constitutive of, 159, 160, 167, 169, 177, 179; *Being-with* equiprimordial with, 147; experience of being as, 185; rootedness and, 27; roots and, 18; unable to be self-aware, 28
Being and Time (Heidegger), 116; *Dasein* and, 150; overlooked element of, 149
being-in-the-world, 7, 30; being-with and, 47
being-in-the-world, 17, 60, 181; assimilation and, 62; loneliness and, 142; Self and, 131
Being-in-the-world, 23
being-in-world, 116
being-toward-death, 62
being-with, 63; being-in-the-world and, 47; manner of, 11
being-with, 9, 19, 22, 88; normalizing for political purposes, 116; projectivity and, 186; questions of, 14, 40; transcendence and, 28
Being-with, 4
Being-with, 7, 31, 77, 181; constitutive of *Being*, 159, 160, 167, 169, 177, 179; construction of, 146; deficiencies of, 14; deficiency of, 8; equiprimordial with *Being*, 147; meaning and, 149; modes of, 125; racism and, 79; shared story and, 76; vulnerability and, 178
being-with-others, 187–188
Being-with-others, 146; Self and, 178–179
Benhabib, Seyla, 21, 42, 75, 95, 111n21; Canovan and, 97; on loneliness and ideology, 132; on *Origins of Totalitarianism*, 96
Berlin, Isaiah, 5–6, 6, 14, 160
Bernstein, Richard J., 59, 119, 120
besorgen, 116, 125, 128, 157
Best, Werner, 39
Biden, Joe, 172–173
Biguhu, 108
Black Forest, 8, 27
BlackLivesMatter, 161
Black Notebooks (Heidegger), 1, 17, 18, 19, 24, 63, 64, 150–151
Le Blanc Est Arrive, Le Roi Est Parti (Nahimana), 106
Blücher, Heinrich, 120
body politic, 169
Boers, 30, 79
Bolsheviks, 18
bourgeoisie, 102
Brecht, Bertolt, 102
Broch, Herman, 52
Bugesera, 106
Burundi, 104, 107
Butler, Judith, 4, 146, 147, 153, 154, 163, 186; Adorno and, 169; Arendt and, 151, 152; authenticity and, 161; Disraeli and, 154, 174–175; ethical violence and, 155; gender and, 152; identity politics and, 177; self-narrative and, 160; Self-Other dichotomy and, 168; sexual harassment and, 174

calculation, 23–24, 25, 66, 78
Canovan, Margaret, 95, 96, 97, 133
capitalism, 69, 97, 146
Card, Claudia, 118

Index

Cartesian epistemology, 169
categorical phenomena, 135
Caucasians, 105
causality, 94
Cavarero, Adriana, 4, 146, 147, 158, 159, 162, 163, 179; on emotion in transcendence, 160; Lafford and, 180; relational ontology and, 178; Self-Other dichotomy and, 168
CDR. *See* Coalition for the Defense of the Republic
Celine, Louis-Ferdinand, 102
charity, 171
Charles Marlow (fictional character), 86
Chelmo, 124
classless society, 99
class structure, 47
clearing (*Lichtung*), 23, 27
Clemenceau, Georges, 39, 71
Coalition for the Defense of the Republic (CDR), 107
collective choices, 77
collectivity, 177
colonial era, 105
colonialism, 78, 88, 101; adventurers and, 87; antisemitism and, 85; imperialism and, 79; superfluousness and, 79
colonial powers, 105
commonality, 172
common sense, 148
communication, 140
comparative genocide literature, 96
compassion, 171
concentration camps, 95, 103
connectedness, 78, 131, 134, 138, 156, 186
Conrad, Joseph, 86, 87, 88
conscience, 139
consciousness, 9, 121
conscious pariahs, 115
continental philosophy, 146, 163, 186
controlling maxims, 123
core essence, 178
Court Jews, 67, 105
"Creating a Cultural Atmosphere" (Arendt), 33
Crick, Bernard, 75, 76
Cutting-Gray, Joanne, 41

Danish dockworkers, 126

dark times, 20
Darwinism, 22, 105
Dasein, 43–44; constitutive structures of, 127; inherent duality in, 47, 49
Dasein, 7, 8, 11, 33; *Being and Time* and, 150; being-toward-death and, 62; constitutive structure of, 18–19, 22; constitutive structures of, 76; gender and, 187; inauthenticity and, 155; inherent nullity of, 12–13; mode of care and, 109; political existence of, 149
Dean, Howard, 175
de-distancing, 10
deductive reasoning, 25, 121
deep thinking, 22
dehumanization, 103, 109
democracy, 131
democratic ontology, 142
democratic theory, 147, 151, 162, 163, 168, 181
D'Entrèves, Maurizio Passerin, 132
deportation, 126
diabolical evil, 122
Dinesen, Isak, 39
Disch, Lisa, 21, 153
Discourse on Thinking (Heidegger), 9
Disraeli, Benjamin, 39, 63–64, 64, 152; antisemitism and, 67, 69; Arendt on, 66, 153; Butler and, 154, 174–175; inauthenticity and, 156; Jewishness and, 65, 68; political power of, 154
distancing, 10
domestic violence, 178
Douglass, Ryan, 183n32
Dreigroschenoper (Brecht), 102
Dreyfus Affair, 63, 64; antisemitism and, 69; Clemenceau and, 71; mob as agitators of violence during, 97; mob-elite alliance and, 70–71
due process, 168
Dumm, Thomas, 134
Dworkin, Andrea, 178

écouter, 148, 170, 172
Eichmann, Adolph, 3, 24, 32, 81; Arendt and, 25; crimes of, 123; deficient mode of care and, 115; evil and, 121, 122; Final Solution and, 124; Schmidt and, 124; Storfer and, 117, 125; trial of, 81;

uncritical in accepting orders, 131
Eichmann in Jerusalem (Arendt), 39, 61, 110, 128; *being-with* and, 116; criticism of, 115
einspringen (leaping-in), 149, 150, 155, 161, 187
elites, 69–70, 101; intellectual, 77, 99, 108; intellectual, race and, 82; mobs alliance with, 70–71, 77, 88, 97; mobs resemblance to, 98; political, 77, 88, 99, 108
elitism, 131
Enlightenment, 42, 49
Escudero, Jesús Adrián, 12
essence, 28–29, 158, 178
ethical standards, 126
ethical violence, 155, 156
Ethiopia, 104
Ettinger, Elzbieta, 185
evil, 3, 139; absolute, 120; banality of, 117, 120; egregious forms of, 120; Eichmann and, 121, 122; extreme, 120; gratuitous, 119; Kant on, 118, 123; at ontological level, 122; personification of diabolical evil, 122; radical, 117, 118, 119, 120, 129n19; ways Arendt talks and thinks about, 115, 120, 123
exceptionalism, 67
existant loneliness, 140
existence, 44
existential choice: ontic structures interaction with, 3; ontological condition and, 62, 84
existential guilt, 12
existentialism, 46; political, 136; Varnhagen, R., and, 47
existential loneliness, 122
existential phenomena, 135
existential philosophy, 1, 2
existentials, 8, 40, 134; non-normative, 14; validity and significance of, 115
Existenz, 6, 11, 43, 53; *being-with-others* and, 187; social relations in, 147
experiential ontology, 14, 40, 45, 53, 189; contemporary relevance of, 167; normative, 115
extraordinary adaptability, 101
extreme evil, 120

fallenness, 3, 45, 47, 52
falling prey, 44
familiarity, 158
familiar sense (*sapore familiare*), 158
fantasy, 102, 112n61
Farrow, Ronan, 167
fear, 140, 141
Feldman, Ron H., 59
femininity, 174
feminism, 135, 146, 163, 167, 177
Final Solution, 77, 81, 105, 124
Finch-Hatton, Denys, 87, 90n60
First World War, 101
"Five Women" (Joffe-Walt), 172
Fleishman, Avrom, 87
Flores, Lucy, 172, 173
foreign adventures, 78, 79, 98, 101
foreignness, 147
Foucault, Michel, 154
Franken, Al, 168
Freidan, Betty, 140
French Revolution, 42
Friedan, Betty, 143n36
fundamental ontology, 2, 7, 40, 45, 60, 126; collective flaws of, 185; elitism and, 131; flaw of, 187; implications of, 14
fürsorge, 116, 117, 124, 125, 127, 128, 157

Gaus, Günter, 94, 140
gender, 67, 94, 186; Butler and, 152; *Dasein* and, 187; Heidegger and, 145; Jewishness and, 45–46, 48, 50
genocide, 80, 103; academics justification of, 108; comparative genocide literature, 96; Darwinism and, 105; emergence of, 96, 99; ideology and, 80; necessary condition for, 97; ontological underpinnings of, 94; perpetrators of, 126; research, 104; temporary legitimization of, 109; victims of, 88; violence of, 70
gerede (idle talk), 12, 148
German Holocaust, 157
German Jews, 49, 52, 54
German philosophy, 11, 31
German Youth Movement, 27
Geschichtsbegriff (history), 156
ghettoization, 103

Giti, 107, 128
Glassman, Peter, 87
gratuitous evil, 119
gratuitous suffering, 119
Great Game, 84
"The Great Tradition and the Nature of Totalitarianism" (Arendt), 13
Greek philosophy, 188
Grynszpan, Zindel, 39
Guignon, Charles, 62
guilty (*schuld*), 12
Gurko, Leo, 87

Habyarimana regime, 104, 106
Hamitic hypothesis, 104, 105
Hamitic myth, 105
Harries, Karsten, 27
Hazen, Don, 168, 174, 175, 176
Heart of Darkness (Conrad), 86, 87, 88
"The Hedgehog and the Fox" (Berlin), 5–6
Heidegger, Martin, 3, 17, 149; antisemitism and, 18, 34, 53, 64, 65; Arendt attempting to humanize, 44–45; Arendt devoted relationship to, 185; Arendt tumultuous relationship with, 5; being-in-world and, 116; in Black Forest, 8; core essence and, 178; *Dasein* and, 11; *Dasein* and *Being and Time*, 150; on essence, 28–29; fundamental ontology of, 2, 7, 40, 60; gender and, 145; historicity and, 18–19, 21; historiography and, 62; Hitler and, 126; human existence and, 43; identity politics and, 145, 146; idle talk and, 12; insensitivity of, 163; Jaspers and, 133; meditative thinking and, 24, 26; *Mitdasein* and, 18; modernity and, 33; Nahimana and, 106; National Socialism and, 1, 10, 63, 81, 99; ontological questions and, 93; on return to an origin, 28; rootlessness and, 12, 29–30, 53; Self and, 13; stillness, 10; theology and mysticism and, 7; on thinking, 9; Third Reich and, 14; track of being and, 19–20; understanding, 150–151; uprootedness and, 32
"Heidegger the Fox" (Arendt), 53
Hertz, Deborah, 41
Hill, Anita, 179

Hinchman, Lewis P., 134
Hinchman, Sandra K., 134
historical narrative, 82
historical scapegoating, 80
historicity, 18–19, 21, 60, 63; appeal to, 61; awareness of, 62; causality and, 94; as feature of lived existence, 146; *Imperialism* and, 76, 77; ontological condition and, 146, 187; transcendence and, 88
historiography, 62, 93–94
history (*Geschichtsbegriff*), 156
Hitler, Adolf, 8, 12, 14, 94; Heidegger and, 126; Peace Speech, 11; rhetoric of, 151; rootlessness and, 12
Holzweg (path), 27
homelessness, 102
Hoy, David Couzens, 63
The Human Condition (Arendt), 2, 3, 4, 54, 135, 137, 146; isolation and, 132; Jaspers and, 133; utter loneliness and, 140
human frailty, 117, 118
human nature, 109–110
human plurality, 133
human rights, 103
Huntington, Patricia, 147
Husserl, Edmund, 149, 164n20
Hutu Power, 109
Hutus, 104, 106, 108

identity politics, 3, 145, 146, 155, 163n5, 167; Butler and, 177; contemporary, 163; contemporary debates in, 186; critical questions in, 189; ethical obligation of, 156; leaping-ahead and, 147; political theory and, 169; task of, 157
ideological thinking, 77, 81, 88
ideology: Arendt and, 80, 81; cornerstones of, 121; genocide and, 80; logical simplicity of, 102; loneliness and, 132; mass mobilization and, 100; political elite and, 88; racism and, 87; Social Darwinism and, 82
"Ideology and Terror" (Arendt), 93, 109
idle chatter, 47
idle talk (*gerede*), 12, 148

imperialism, 2, 78, 101; antisemitism and, 85, 96; colonialism and, 79; Conrad and, 87; existential struggles of those caught in, 82; "innate" imperialistic personality, 76; innate imperialist personality, 84; pan-, 78, 80; superfluousness and, 77, 78; totalitarianism and, 76
Imperialism (Arendt), 75; alliance between mob and elite in, 88; existential choice and ontological condition and, 84; historicity and, 76, 77; lasting importance of, 95; ontic structures and, 93
impurity, 118
impurity of maxims, 117
impuzamugambi, 107
inauthenticity, 155, 156
innate personality, 63, 67, 68, 76, 84, 85, 110
insane optimism, 137
intellectual elites, 77, 82, 99, 108
intelligensia, 108
interahamwe, 107, 108
intermarriage, 71
International Brotherhood of Electrical Workers, 172
inversion of maxims, 120
ipseity, 147
isolation, 132, 135, 140; labor and, 139; memory and, 159; radical, 133; work and, 139, 141

Janus, Adrienne, 149
Jaspers, Karl, 41, 54, 63, 116, 120, 121; Heidegger and, 133
Jewish councils (*Judenrate*), 125–126
Jewish history, 69, 72
Jewishness, 17, 28, 152; Arendt and, 46, 59, 60, 65; Disraeli and, 65, 68; gender and, 45–46, 48, 50; rootlessness and, 29; secularization and, 67; social norms associated with, 155; Varnhagen, R., and, 50, 51
Jewish personality, 85
Jews, 18, 24, 124; assimilated, 28, 67, 68, 88; Court, 67, 105; German, 49, 52, 54; harm suffered by, 121; intermarriage and, 71; stereotypes about, 154

Joffe-Walt, Chana, 168, 172, 174, 179
Johnson, Bruce, 87
Judd, Ashley, 167
Judenrate (Jewish councils), 125–126
Judeo-Christian myths, 105
judgment, 13–14

Kane, Brian, 148
Kant, Immanuel, 3, 41, 53, 120; Arendt and, 117, 119; on evil, 118, 123; on personification of diabolical evil, 122
Kantor, Jodi, 167, 168
Kateb, George, 76, 85, 95, 96, 97, 134
Kayibanda regime, 104
Keillor, Garrison, 168
Kidston, G. J., 85
Kim (Kipling), 82
Kimball O'Hara (fictional character), 83, 85, 88
Kipling, Rudyard, 82, 83, 84
Kirinda, 108
Kohn, Jerome, 59, 66, 95
Kristeva, Julia, 41–42, 75

labor, 20, 134, 139, 140
Lafford, Sarah, 180
law of nature, 81
Lawrence, T. E., 84, 85, 86, 87, 88
Lawrence of Arabia (fictional character), 84, 85
League of Nations, 11
leaping-ahead (*vorausspringen*), 147, 149, 150, 155, 161, 187
leaping-in (*einspringen*), 149, 150, 155, 161, 187
Leibovici, Martine, 41, 42
Lessing, G. E., 52
Lessing Prize, 52
liberalism, 171
Lichtung (clearing), 23, 27
Life of the Mind (Arendt), 2, 146
Lipstadt, Deborah, 123
listening, 148, 149, 151
Lithuania, 123
logical thinking, 25, 121
loneliness, 3, 13, 122, 133, 135; action and, 141; alleviation of, 135; Arendt and, 131; *being-in-the-world* and, 142; collective outcomes associated with,

135; *existant*, 140; exploration of, 136; ideology and, 132; inescapable nature of, 134; labor and, 140; ontological condition and, 136, 140; radical isolation and, 133; utter, 133, 140
Longman, Timothy, 108
Luxembourg, Rosa, 39

machination, 18, 63, 64, 65
MacKinnon, Catherine, 168
Mamdani, Manhood, 104
marginalization, 52
marriage, 137
"Martin Heidegger at Eighty" (Arendt), 8, 9, 53
Marxism, 22, 94, 104, 111n21
masculinity, 174, 176, 183n32
masses, 70; mobs and, 100; propaganda and, 96; thinking and, 128
mass manipulation, 132
mass mentality, 94
mass mobilization, 100
mass murder, 124
maxims: controlling, 123; impurity of, 117; inversion of, 120; moral, 118; non-moral, 118; reversal of, 117; self love as, 119
McCarthy, Mary, 81, 121
meaning, 148; listening and, 149; straining toward, 173
meditative thinking, 22, 24, 26
Melvern, Linda, 107
Memorial Address (Heidegger), 24
memory, 127, 158, 159
mere talk, 11, 12, 40, 151
metaphysical roots, 18
metaphysics, 53
#MeToo, 4, 161, 177, 180; democratic theory and, 181; feminism and, 167; listening and, 170; strangeness and compassion and, 171; use of hashtag, 168
Midlarsky, Manus, 109
Milano, Alyssa, 167
Mill, Harriet Taylor, 178
Minnich, Elizabeth, 186
Mr. Kurtz (fictional character), 86, 87, 88
mitdasein, 8, 22, 61, 94
Mitdasein, 18, 23, 116

mitsein, 9
mobs, 69, 70, 107, 128; as agitators of violence during Dreyfus Affair, 97; capitalism and, 97; elites alliance with, 70–71, 77, 88, 97; elites resemblance to, 98; masses and, 100; rootlessness and, 97–98; totalitarianism and, 98
mode of care, 109, 115
modernity, 2, 33, 110; conditions of, 24; horrific manifestations of, 151; moral standards broken down under, 126; nihilism and, 12
Moir, Susan, 178
moral maxims, 118
moral standards, 126
Moruzzi, Norma Claire, 66
motherhood, 138
MRND. *See* National Republican Movement for Development and Democracy
Mugesera, 108
mysticism, 7

Nahimana, 108
Nahimana, Ferdinand, 106
Nairobi, 106
Nancy, Jean-Luc, 4, 146, 147, 150, 163, 186; de-centering, 173; democratic theory and, 151; *écouter* and, 148, 170; liberalism and, 171; Self-Other dichotomy and, 168, 169
Nassar, Larry, 168
natality, 179
National Republican Movement for Development and Democracy (MRND), 107, 108
National Socialism, 1, 10, 63, 64, 81; genuine commitment to, 99; structure of, 122
Nazi commanders, 126
Nazi personnel, 123
Nazi regime, 95, 96
negation, 137
nihilism, 12
non-moral maxims, 118
non-normative ontological categories, 115
non-normativity, 145
non-totalitarian world, 102

objective reality, 103
occurrence-with, 61
Oedipus, 159, 161
ontic characteristic, 17
ontic reality, 133, 136
ontic structures, 77, 88; Arendt focus on, 76, 93; existential choice interaction with, 3
ontic traits, 17
ontological condition, 3, 26, 93, 122, 126, 142; existential choice and, 62, 84; historicity and, 146, 187; ideological thinking and, 77, 88; loneliness and, 136, 140; natality and, 179; ontic reality and, 133; ontic traits and, 17; political implications of, 14
ontological questions, 93
"The Origin of the Work of Art" (Heidegger), 23, 28
Origins of Totalitarianism (Arendt), 3, 32, 39, 61, 62, 72; *Being-with-others* and, 146; Benhabib on, 96; crisis of our time and, 131; difficulty to categorize, 75; evolving nature of Arendt's thought around, 110n6; historiography and, 93–94; on ideology and genocide, 80; incoherent nature of, 76; isolation and, 132, 135; perplexing nature of, 77; provisional nature of, 94; revisions of, 63; subterranean streams and, 95; Taminiaux and, 133
ORINFO. *See* Rwandan Bureau of Information
Other, 10, 20, 26, 79, 161; ambiguity of, 169; Arendt and, 148; exploitation of, 82; helping, 155; responsibility to, 157; scapegoating, 101; story of, 162

pan-imperialism, 78, 80
pariah/parvenu, 41, 42, 49, 151
Parsons, Mary Ann, 178
passionate thinking, 10
path (*Holzweg*), 27
Peace Speech, 11
performativity, 152, 176–177
pity, 171
Plato, 27
Pöggeler, Otto, 11
Poland, 124

political action, 157
political autonomy, 79
political elites, 77, 88, 99, 108
political existentialism, 136
political ontology, 4
political philosophy, 1
political rights, 103
political strategy, 66
political theory, 146, 169
powerlessness, 151
project, 44
projection, 52
projectivity, 3, 45, 49–50, 150; *being-with* and, 186; thrownness and, 145
projectivity, 44
propaganda, 96
public revealing, 142
public sphere, 76, 142

quietness, 22

race, 82
race thinking, 80, 82
racism, 79, 86; *Being-with* and, 79; ideology and, 87
radical evil, 117, 118, 119, 120, 129n19
radical isolation, 133
Radio Télévision Libre des Mille Collines (RTLM), 106, 107
Rahel Varnhagen (Arendt), 3, 39, 41–42, 61, 84; *Being-with-others* and, 146; isolation and, 132
reality, 112n61; objective, 103; ontic, 133
receptivity, 161
refugees, 131, 137–138, 138
relational ontology, 178
Reluctant Modernism of Hannah Arendt (Benhabib), 132
remembering, 22, 76
re-presentation, 141
resoluteness, 50
resolute will, 64–65
respectable society, 99
Responsibility and Judgment (Arendt), 146
reversal of maxims, 117
Richards, Vyvyan, 85
Rights of Englishmen, 75
Rights of Man, 75
Romanticism, 42, 46

Index

rootedness, 21; Being and, 20; *Being* and, 27; lack of, 26, 122; metaphysical, 31
rootlessness, 12, 17, 18; Arendt and, 24, 29–30, 32, 34, 53; Heidegger and, 29–30, 45, 53; Jewishness and, 29; Kimball O'Hara and, 83; metaphysical, 30; mobs and, 97–98; negative effects of, 24; territorial, 30; of thinking, 23; thrownness and fallenness and, 52
roots, 18, 20, 26, 31
Rose, Charlie, 168
RPF. *See* Rwandan Patriotic Front
RTLM. *See* Radio Télévision Libre des Mille Collines
Rwanda, 103, 104
Rwandan Bureau of Information (ORINFO), 106
Rwandan Patriotic Front (RPF), 105, 128

sapore familiare (familiar sense), 158
scapegoating, 101
Schmidt, Anton, 39, 110, 117, 123, 124
schuld (guilty), 12
Schwarz, Alexandra, 168
secrecy, 101
secularization, 67
Self, 11, 13, 148, 156, 169; authentic, 68, 85; *being-in-the-world* and, 131; *Being-with-others* and, 178–179; uniqueness and, 137
self-awareness, 84
self-desertion, 135, 136
self-disclosure, 52, 54
self-governance, 140, 141
selfhood, 157
self-interest, 119
self-loathing, 134
self love, 119
self-narrative, 154, 158, 160
self-negation, 51
Self-Other dichotomy, 147, 168, 169
self-reflection, 25, 122, 127, 136
self-revealing, 28, 177
self-revelation, 157, 188
Seven Pillars of Wisdom (Lawrence), 86
sexual harassment, 167–168, 170, 174, 178; Butler and, 174; enablers of, 176; evolving truth about, 173; ontology of, 180; phenomenological account of, 180–181; workplace, 168
shadows governments, 101
shared history, 21
shared story, 76
shared victim status, 145
Shklar, Judith, 42
silence, 161
Simpson, Nicole Brown, 178
Simpson, O. J., 178
social connectedness, 94
Social Darwinism, 82
social media, 168
solicitude, 155
solitude, 9, 10, 134
Somalia, 104
"Some Questions of Moral Philosophy" (Arendt), 136
Sorge, 44
South Africa, 78
spatiality, 147
spontaneity, 100, 110
Stalin, Joseph, 94, 96, 101
statelessness, 107
stateless persons, 131
Stephenson, Lonnie, 172
Stern, Günther, 149, 177
stillness, 10
Storfer, Bertold, 117, 123, 125
storytelling, 20, 21, 25, 178
strangeness, 171
Straus, Scott, 107, 108
subjects, 148
subterranean streams, 82, 95
Suez Canal, 78
superfluidity, 77, 82
superfluousness: colonialism and, 79; imperialism and, 77, 78; Kipling and, 83
Symposium (Plato), 27

Taminiaux, Jacques, 53, 133
terminus (*telos*), 187
territory, 31
theology, 7
thinking, 9; Arendt and, 128; authentic, 26; calculative, 78; deep, 22; ideological, 77, 81, 88; lack of, 139; logical, 25, 121; masses and, 128; meditative, 22, 24, 26; passionate, 10; race thinking,

80, 82; remembering and, 76; rootlessness of, 23; self-reflection and, 127. *See also* ideological thinking

Third Reich, 11, 12, 14, 151

This American Life (podcast), 168

thoughtfulness, 84, 138

thoughtlessness, 129n34

thrownness, 3, 19, 44, 45, 46, 54, 186, 189; awareness of, 61; challenges of, 185; experience of, 45; never fully cognizant of our own, 154; projectivity and, 145; rootlessness and fallenness and, 52

Tolstoy, Leo, 6, 14

totalitarianism, 70, 76, 80, 94, 111n21, 180; appeal of, 122; conceptual value of, 103; emergence of totalitarian man, 132; ideology and, 80; Kateb on, 134; legitimizing, 99; literature on, 96; as manifestation of crisis of our time, 131; mobs and, 98; nature of, 95; ontological core of, 93; personality, 103, 109; preconditions of, 135; redefining, 96; secrecy and, 101; victims of, 120

"Totalitarianism in Power" (Arendt), 110

toxic masculinity, 176, 183n32

track of being, 19–20

transcendence, 11, 19, 22, 28, 44, 162, 179; authenticity and, 150; *being-with* and, 28; emotion in, 160; historicity and, 88; ontic barriers to, 147; preconditions for, 127

Treaty of Versailles, 11, 12

Trump, Donald, 173, 174

Tsao, Roy, 95, 96

Tutsi migration hypothesis, 104, 105

Tutsis, 103, 104, 106, 128

Twohey, Megan, 167, 168

two-in-one, 10, 136–137

Ulysses, 159, 161

umuganda, 107

unconcealment, 19, 172

uniqueness, 137, 138

uprootedness, 32

urbanization, 30

utter loneliness, 133, 140

Varnhagen, Karl August, 43, 48

Varnhagen, Rahel, 28, 29, 39, 41–42, 49–50; action and, 141; assimilated Jews and, 67, 68; constructing narrative of, 154; early life of, 42; existentialism and, 47; experiential ontology and, 53; fundamental ontology and, 45; inauthenticity and, 156; Jewishness and, 50, 51; Prussian citizenship of, 48; self-disclosure and, 54; von Finckenstein and, 43

Veit, David, 46

verfallen, possible translations of, 7

Verwimp, Philip, 104, 107, 108

victim vulnerability, 109

vignettes, 39

Villa, Dana, 8, 64, 120

violent relatedness, 171

the visual, 148

Voegelin, Eric, 75, 109–110

Vogel, Lawrence, 155, 156, 188

volk, 23

von Brinckmann, Gustav, 47

von der Marwitz, Ludwig, 82

von Finckenstein (Count), 43, 47, 51

von Hannecken (General), 117

von Marwitz, Alexander, 48, 49

vorauspringen (leaping-ahead), 147, 149, 150, 155, 161, 187

vulnerability, 161, 162, 178, 180

Walzer, Michael, 77

Warsaw ghetto, 32

Weinstein, Harvey, 161, 167

"We Refugees" (Arendt), 137

"What is Existenz Philosophy?" (Arendt), 53

wide errancy, 155, 156, 178, 181

Wolin, Sheldon, 77

women, 137–138, 138, 143n36, 178

Woodhull, Victoria, 178

work, 134; authentic, 20; isolation and, 139, 141

workplace sexual harassment, 168

world, 133

worldliness, 133

Young-Bruehl, Elisabeth, 20, 21

Zionism, 32

About the Author

Kimberly Maslin is professor of politics at Hendrix College in Conway, Arkansas. She teaches courses in American politics, political philosophy, and gender studies. Recent publications include "The Paradox of Miss Marple: Agatha Christie's Epistemology," in *Clues: A Journal of Detection*. In her other life, she is an aspiring swing dancer and devoted baseball fan.

www.ingramcontent.com/pod-product-compliance
Lightning Source LLC
Chambersburg PA
CBHW050905300426
44111CB00010B/1384